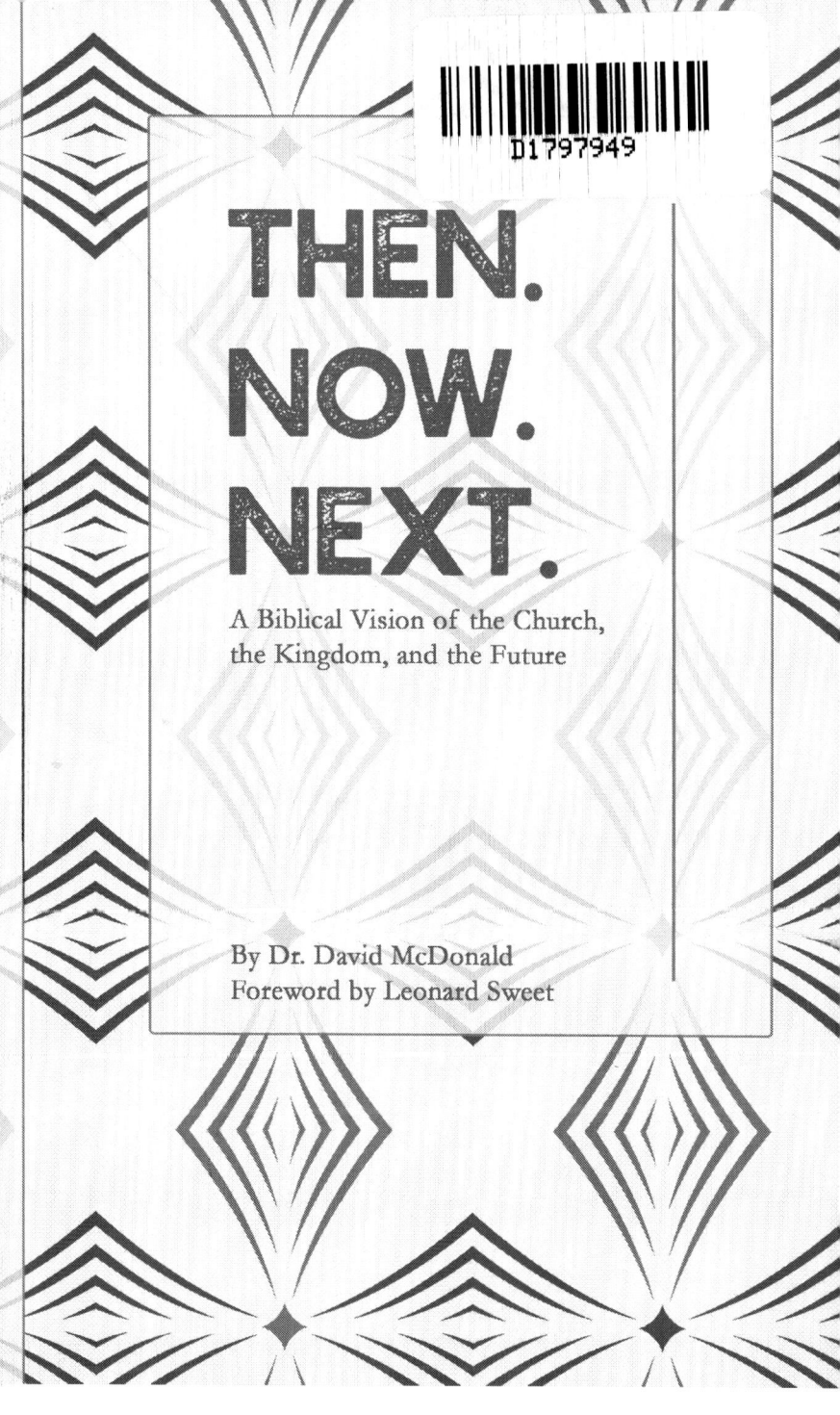

THEN.
NOW.
NEXT.

A Biblical Vision of the Church,
the Kingdom, and the Future

By Dr. David McDonald
Foreword by Leonard Sweet

To the people of Charis Christian Center, where it all began.

TABLE OF CONTENTS

amen

FULL OF FUTURITY

BY LEONARD SWEET

> We are not entering an era of change,
> but a change of era.
> -Pope Francis

Whatever way we turn, whichever direction we look, we see looming on the horizon wars on terror, nuclear war, climate change, Islamist jihadism, unraveling nation states, pestilence, and a Titanic-like tryst with an iceberg of time and technology unlike the world has ever seen. Mind-bending technological "progress" is moving far beyond moral comprehension with much less constraints. Fleas carrying the Black Death (bubonic plague) have been found in Arizona as recently as 2017. Welcome to the future, a future as bleak, some say, as Huxley's *Brave New World* or Orwell's *Nineteen Eighty-Four*.

One reason I enjoy science fiction is that novelistic imagination of the future gives us a tighter focus on and clearer mirror of the present. You might even say science fiction is less about the future than about what people see and fear in the present. In his academic study of *Apocalyptic Fiction* (2017), Andrew Tate shows how science fiction is now "haunted by dreams of a future that is a place of ruin." No wonder the *Left Behind* series sold 65 million copies, and counting. In a world where everything seems to be falling apart, paranoid delusion might be the very definition of sanity.

Every time I wonder why people are so fearful of the future, I remember that, even in the best circumstances, the future will wipe away our way of life, along with all those safety and security measures we've tried to cocoon ourselves in. It's easier simply to block it. Yet we stagger mindlessly into the future at a perilous price—the cost of deformation and death.

Set the alarm or not, morning comes. Ready or not, the future shows up. A default future arrives willy-nilly. A desirable future, not to mention a dream future, is birthed in blood, sweat, tears and a prophetic imagination. By discounting the future, the church never misses an opportunity to miss an opportunity.

The last prayer of the Bible points and pulls us to the future.

> He who has come is coming.
> The night will not be long.
> "Even so, come, Lord Jesus."[1]

Jesus comes to us from the future and pulls us forward. Jesus is the real inventor of futurology, even though the German political scientist Ossip K. Flechtheim (1909-1998) coined the term. Jesus is always ahead of his disciples. He pulls us towards him more than pushes us from the behind. To study Jesus is to study the future. Jesus was not in the business of making points but of making turning points, creating "turnings" that would turn-about (*metanoia*) our lives and the world to face God and the future. The gospel story is in the turnings, not the points. Biblical futurists re-turn the present toward the future. If a prophet is one who speaks for the future, we must all be prophets now.

When Jesus taught us to "live abundantly," he taught us to live OUT OF the past, to live IN the present, and to live FOR the future. You can't live in the past and go forward. Or in the words of Immanuel Kant (1724-1804), "Remembering occurs only with the intention of making it possible to foresee the future."

---

[1] Revelation 22.20.

In an echo of a departing Jesus' futuristic words to his disciples "I have much more to say to you, more than you can now bear,"[2] the artist/poet William Blake wrote to Thomas Butts (April 25, 1803), "I have a thousand and ten thousand things to say to you. My heart is full of futurity." How many of our hearts are "full of futurity?" In a world with hearts full of futility, we need hearts "full of futurity" for each other and for each other's future.

The academic discipline of futurology and futurist studies traditionally moves from present to future. In contrast, biblical futurology moves from future to present, from Revelation 21 and 22 to today, from the New Jerusalem to cities in peril and under siege. The phrase from the Gloria—*Qui sedes ad dexteram Patris,* or "Seated at the right hand of the Father"—is a prophetic promise of who owns the future, not a seating chart.

To live an inspired life is to live an in-spirited life or an in-the-Spirit life, a God-breathed life which enjoys the life of the future now. For the Spirit is the first fruits of the final harvest,[3] the earnest or down payment of what is to come,[4] the *arrabon* or "seal" of the future.[5] That's why to live inspired is to live dangerously. The Spirit does not sub-vent but subvert the status quo.

The renowned pianist Arthur Rubinstein was once asked to judge a piano competition in London. The scorecards were marked on a scale of one to 20, with the most outstanding performances rating a 20. During the competition Rubinstein listened carefully to the students' recitals and marked his cards as each finished.

---

[2] John 16.12.
[3] Romans 8.23.
[4] 2 Corinthians 1.22; 5.5; Ephesians 1.14.
[5] 1 Corinthians 1.21-22; Ephesians 1.13; 4.30.

At the end of the competition the sponsors looked at the scores and were shocked to see that most players had been given zeros. Only a few had rated scores of 20, and there were no scores in between. The sponsors hurried over to Rubinstein and asked him why he had judged the entrants in such an arbitrary manner. "It's simple," replied the great master. "Either they can play the piano or they can't."

Getting ready for the future is a lot like playing the piano. You can't be "ready" for the future. You just do your best to prepare and then play. Sometimes you're ready. Sometimes you're not. The first dice were used to tell the future. There always has been a bit of a gamble to futuring. Either you're ready for the future, or you're not.

David McDonald has written a stirring manifesto for the future that readies the church to play. "Nothing ages as fast as the future" writes Polish science fiction writer Stanislaw Lem (1921-2006). But Proverbs 31.25 assures us that the virtuous and valiant can "laugh at the future" and leave the church "full of futurity." You too will be "full of futurity" after reading McDonald's manifesto.

Leonard Sweet, best-selling author and futurist
Drew University, Tabor College, Portland Seminary

THE CHURCH WE SEE
AN INTRODUCTION

I once heard a famous pastor[6] make an offhand remark about a document entitled "The Church I See." I've never seen that document, but the title stuck with me. Whenever, I close my eyes, there's a Church I see, also—a perfected, glorified Bride for our King.

But this book isn't about "the church according to David McDonald." This book concerns the church WE see, and it encapsulates all we believe about the future of the church. And who are "we"? Well, now you are. Because with every conversation and concordant activity, you're helping the Kingdom Come.

I have discussed these ideas with PhDs and theologians, with chiropractors and stay-at-home moms, with Methocostals and wayward Catholics, such that this manuscript has more contributors than an Amish barn-raising. I've used examples of ministry at Westwinds Church[7] throughout, but this isn't to suggest that Westwinds has it all figured out. On the contrary, many of these beliefs are born of our failures. Yet we know what the future promises and have worked hard to cultivate that future now.

Then. Now. Next. isn't purely about what's coming, but about the future embodied in the present. The future is already here, albeit in embryonic form. This is the mystery of the Kingdom, which is already present but not yet fully manifest. "The

---

[6]   Brian Houston, Global Senior Pastor of Hillsong Church, https://hillsong.com/brian-bobbie/
[7]   www.westwinds.org

Kingdom of God is within you,"[8] Jesus said, but he also said the Kingdom is near[9] (implying it's not here just yet) and that we will enter the Kingdom in the future.[10]

The future is a surprisingly diverse topic in scripture, and was often employed by biblical writers as a means of proclaiming God's plans to heal the world.

Joshua told his elders to build a memorial near the Jordan River because he knew there would come a time when their descendants would ask what those stones signified.[11] Joshua knew **the future is never disconnected from the past.** Faith has a trajectory, and by looking at the best parts of our noble past and projecting them forward, we see a church that is increasingly refined.

The Psalmist takes up this theme, suggesting we ought to chronicle our efforts "for a future generation, that a people not yet created may praise the Lord."[12] Why? Because **the future is not wholly ours.** Our vision of the future may require we sacrifice present comforts because our preferences matter less than our calling; thus, we create the future with the wellbeing of others in mind.

The future promises to be sweet if we continue to apply our knowledge and imagination. "If you find [wisdom]," says Proverbs, "there is a future hope for you."[13] And who teaches us wisdom? Who has the insight required to guide us as we apply our knowledge to practical pursuits? The Spirit. The

[8] Luke 17.21, KJV.
[9] Matthew 4.17, NIV.
[10] Matthew 7.21, NIV.
[11] "In the future, your children will ask you …" Joshua 4.6, NLT.
[12] Psalm 102.18, NIV.
[13] Proverbs 24.14, NIV.

future may be uncertain, but there are as many joyful surprises as unexpected trials. The more we trust the Spirit, the more we can have confidence God will both guide and reward our cooperation in the "renewal of all things."[14]

Though the future may be far off, **those who know the Lord can anticipate the future.** The prophet Ezekiel, for example, spoke eloquently of the future.[15] But by speaking longingly about "the distant future," he courted those utopian qualities in the present, causing ordinary people to rise above their circumstances.

In all these examples, and many more besides, scripture clearly describes God's future Kingdom presently. We live in the time between times, amid the overlap of Later and Now. And I'm writing to help you foresee all God promises to perform.

My friend Kelly encouraged me to write this book. She and I have been working together for several years, and I was shocked to learn Kelly had little clue concerning my many ambitions for the Church at large. As we began to talk more, she became increasingly interested in what I was suggesting, until she finally concluded our conversation by saying simply, "You should tell people."

So I am, and I hope you respond with an equivalent enthusiasm as you consider the future of Christ's Church, also.

Dr. David McDonald,
The Priory at Westwinds Church :: Summer 2017

---

[14] Matthew 19.28, NIV.
[15] Ezekiel 12.27.

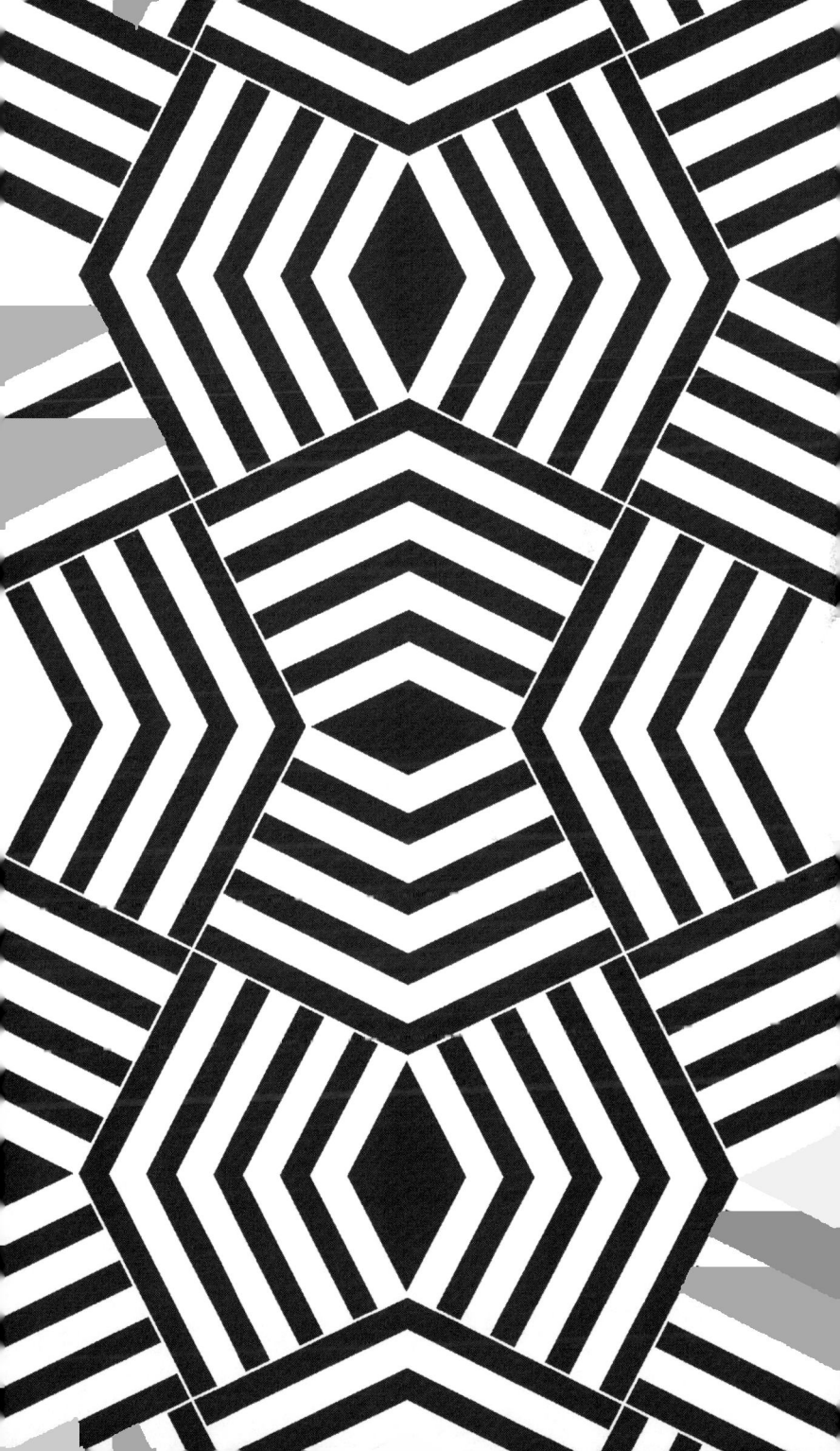

ONE | WE SEE A CHURCH

WIDE-EYED *with* PROMISE *for* THE FUTURE
RATHER THAN SAD-HEARTED *about* THE
FADING GLORIES *of* THE PAST;

a CHURCH *that* HAS BEEN HEALED *of* HER
CYNICISM
and MATURED *into* A SECOND
INNOCENCE;

that REFUSES *to* LET HER MINISTRY BE
DEFINED *by* HER WOUNDS,
but WILL LOVE RECKLESSLY *and*
GIVE EFFUSIVELY *of* HERSELF.

ONE.ONE

HURT

FINDING COURAGE TO GET BACK ON THE BIKE AND RIDE

When I was a child, I talked like a child, I thought like a child, I reasoned like a child. When I became a man, I put the ways of childhood behind me.
- 1 Corinthians 13.11, NIV

> *We must use our past pain to help others,*
> *rather than justify our antagonism.*

I began my tenure as a senior pastor ministering out of my wounds. Those early days were characterized by antagonism, both from me and toward me, until I learned to heal and to heal others.

So much of my ministry was a reaction to all of the things I had been told I wasn't allowed to do, or couldn't do, or shouldn't do if I was serious about leading a church. As a result, the novelties and innovations I first incubated were always tinged with an early expiration date. They didn't last and they didn't work.

Why?

Because I was like the kid who falls off his bike and gets a bloody gash on his arm. Proud of his survival, he sticks the half-healed wound in others' faces, demanding they look in awe and comment on his bravery.

I had scars from my adventures as a pastor's kid. I had survived growing up in church under the scrutiny of strangers and wanted everyone to acknowledge that my past pain had made me bold. But open wounds are gross, doubly so if they belong to another person; triply so if they belong to a child with no awareness of personal space.

That's what it's like when we set out to prove a point, or prove our efficacy, or prove our suitability for ministry. And the sad truth is that the longer we focus on proving ourselves, the less useful we are, both to God and to the others around us. It has been acceptable for us to remain "wound identified,"[16] instead of using our wounds to redeem the world according to the pattern of Christ.

---

[16] That is, using our victimhood as our identity, our ticket to sympathy, our excuse for not serving.

The church of the future will realize that we don't need to prove that life can be dangerous, or that we've survived past dangers; we just need to help others get on the bike and ride.

And there are *a lot* of other people who want to ride. But they're scared. And they have a million questions. So our commitment to showing them how it's done will require time and energy. And, from time to time, there will be people who want to tell us that playtime is over, or that we're too old, or that we never truly survived as well as we thought; but if we want to be useful, we cannot engage these people. We just have to set them off to the side and ignore them, helping more and more people enjoy the ride God has prepared.

Who would most benefit from hearing about your past experiences?

ONE.TWO

DISAPPOINTMENT

HOW TO BE MORE THAN A BUSH LEAGUER

Every good and perfect gift is from above, coming down from the Father of the heavenly lights.
- James 1.17a, NIV

> *You've got to do that which the Lord has placed within you to perform.*

When I first came to Westwinds there was a lot of talk about our church's national ministry. Our founding pastor was a main stage speaker at a well-regarded Christian leadership conference and had published several titles with major publishers. Others had long looked to Westwinds as a hotbed of innovation, creativity, and incarnational postmodern ministry. As a result, Westwinds had grown quickly and was on the radar of every Christian publication and media outlet in the country.

I didn't have anything to contribute.

When I arrived, there were some messes to clean up and some fires to put out. Mostly people waited until the church was clean (ish) and safe (ish) before they started prodding. "When are we going to return to the things that made us effective? When will we pay attention to our national platform?"

At first I didn't know what these questions implied. Having never enjoyed much success, I assumed it was ancillary to ordinary ministry. But over a very short time I learned that such a platform has responsibilities of its own, and like anything else, needs to be shepherded.

I was not up to the challenge.

I didn't have the opportunities to enhance our national platform because I wasn't as good as our founder. I wasn't as polished a preacher, or as intelligent a theologian, or as capable a leader. I didn't receive the same invitations, nor sustain contracts with any of the major publishers.

I was a bush leaguer.

Consequently, those that had been around during our good old days wondered if they had made a mistake. The expression of their disappointments was kind, if not subtle; but we all felt it: our church wasn't as good as it used to be, because our pastor wasn't as good as our founder.

In some ways, I'm still not good enough, though I have moved past the sting of it. No one bothers with the comparison any longer since there's thirteen years of water under the bridge, and I don't bristle when confronted with my lack of fame.

Why?

Time, mostly.

But the bigger reason is because I've stopped trying to get us back to where we were and instead put my energy into moving us into the future. I've stopped trying to live someone else's story, and begun doing that which the Lord has placed in me to perform.

I love what I do, and I love the church where I get to do it. Who else has this much freedom to write, preach, or create experiences? Who else gets to travel, train pastors, teach seminary students, and run conferences? And we had our own heyday, I suppose, when some of the ministry my co-pastor John Voelz and I crafted was featured in *Time* magazine, *The New York Times*, *The Wall Street Journal*, and on CNN. And I've had the privilege to write dozens of teaching atlases, earning some notoriety for both my thoughts and persistence. But I treat those experiences like the medals from high school sports. They're such cool memories, but they really don't mean as much as I'd hoped. Those interviews, those articles, and those publications are now all part of a past I can only idealize. The truth is that those were seasons when I was heavily invested

长东医疗器械集团有限公司
Everest Medical Products Group Co., Ltd

合格证
CERTIFICATION

产品名称 Produc Name	医用外科口罩 Disposable Sterile Surgical Mask
生产许可证号 Manufacturing License No.	豫食药监械生产许20150132号 Henan FDA Manufacturing License No. 20150132
注册证号 Registration No.	豫械注准20172640069 Henan FDA Registration No. 20172640069
材质成分 Material	无纺布:100%聚丙烯纤维70% 熔喷布:100%聚丙烯纤维30% Non woven Fabric(100%Polypropylene Fiber)70% Melt-blown Fabric(100%Polypropylene Fiber)30%
型号 Type	耳挂式/Ear Loop 17.5×17CM
包装 Package	25个/袋 25PCS/BAG
批号 LOT	200425
生产日期 MFG	2020-04-25
失效日期 EXP	2023-04-24
执行标准 Executive Standards	EN14683:2019 TYPE IIR
检验员 IQC	02

生产商地址：河南省长垣市佘家镇王庄村1号
Manufacturer Add: No.1 Wangzhuang Village, Shejia Town, Changyuan City, Henan
电话/TEL: 0086 373 8949888/777/666

产品说明书
PRODUCT INSTRUCTION

产品名称 Product Name	医用外科口罩 Disposable Sterile Surgical Mask
产品组成 Components	耳带、鼻梁条、无纺布、熔喷布。 Ear loop, nose clip, non-woven fabric, melt-blown fabric.
适用范围 Application	医用外科口罩有助于减少患者和医护人员的相互暴露在具有传染性空气传播颗粒物的危害。 Disposable sterile surgical mask helps reduce exposure of the patient and health care professional to potential infectious airborne particulate hazards.
使用前检查 Check before Use	使用前请检查包装状况。如果包装损坏或受污染，请勿使用。如果口罩耳带断裂或松弛，请立即更换口罩。 Please check the condition of the packaging before use. If the packaging is damaged or contaminated, do not use. If the facepiece belt is broken or not tightened, replace the facepiece immediately.
储存环境 Storage Condition	包装完好的口罩应存放在相对湿度不超过80%通风良好且无腐蚀性气体的清洁干燥处。 Packaged masks should be stored in a clean room with a relative humidity not exceeding 80%, good ventilation and no corrosive gases.

in people. I was working hard to love and serve others, to be a good pastor, to listen to the Spirit, and to remain faithful to my calling.

In the end, I created the kind of success I thought everybody famous had. And it didn't feel like success. It was just really, really fun.

So I've moved past my own glory days with much the same *joie de vivre* as I moved past Westwinds' glory days. Because you can't live in the past. Because memories, over-amplified, can spoil anticipations. Because if you are constantly challenged and embittered—whether through your own comparisons or those of another—you'll be joyless, frustrated, and small. But if you can move past all that and ask yourself what the Lord has put in you to do, there is a world of adventure just in front of you.

The church of the future will be driven by God's mission to heal the world and his long-term plan to bring heaven to earth. She will cooperate with God as he enculturates his Kingdom. She will work to bring together people of every tribe and tongue and nation. She will elevate Christ as the King of All, regardless of the fact that she will be ridiculed, opposed, and hurt for so doing. She will understand that God made the world in goodness and works to redeem every corner of Creation with us working alongside him.

And it is this vision of the future that will release the church from her grief over the past.

> All Christianity is eschatology.
> -Jurgen Moltmann

Are there any hurts or disappointments from your past that you need to release?

ONE.THREE

RENEWAL

LEARNING TO PRAISE YOUR HEALER NOT YOUR HURTS

From the sole of your foot to the top of your head there is no soundness—only wounds and welts and open sores, not cleansed or bandaged or soothed with olive oil.
- Isaiah 1.6, NIV

> *Wounds are meant to heal. They do not serve a purpose, but impede the healthy functions of a body. We live in a culture that fetishizes our wounds, but the church of the future will praise God for her health, not her brokenness.*

Our world is replete with hardships we are not well equipped to endure. We all suffer. The natural result of fragile creatures living in such a tempest is hurt, but that doesn't mean our injuries are the end of our story.

A wound, literally, refers to a breach of the skin through violence. Figuratively, a wound can be emotional, spiritual, or social. In any case, a wound occurs when someone takes action that tears open our protections, exposing us to enhanced sensitivity, and drawing our attention to the need for healing.

The problem with wounds, first, is that they were done *to us*. *They* hurt me. *They* did it. *They* said it. Someone is to blame, and that person has not yet made things right.

When someone hurts us, we often try and convince bystanders our transgressors should be punished. This is why we slander and gossip. We want others to hurt the villains like the villains hurt us. In the same way. With the same malice. Why? Because the offending party has left us exposed. They haven't yet undone the damage they caused. And so we seek recompense.

Wounds breach our skin, our outer layer of protection, and leave us vulnerable where we thought ourselves safe. They surprise us, providing evidence that we are exposed.

When others hurt us we're dazzled by how easy it seemed. It was just a few words, but they cut so deeply. It was just one exchange, but it left us struggling. In our shock, we shout out our pain, wanting others to acknowledge their surprise, also. We call for help. We want to be authenticated. We want to be seen. We want others to rush up and assist.

When we are wounded, we become increasingly sensitive— everything hurts. Nothing can be overlooked. Because there is no barrier between our most precious parts and the outside world. A light breeze stings. A jest is a slap. A laugh pounds on our flesh like a book on our toe.

When we are wounded, all we can think about is how soon someone else might make it better.

That's another problem, isn't it? We want "someone else" to fix what "someone else" has wrecked. We are infatuated with our hurts, and we want others to be, also. We think that only their attentions can heal, when in fact such healing can only be provided by God.

We live in a culture that festishizes our wounds. You've been hurt? Tell the world. Someone betrayed you? Brandish your victimization.

But we forget that wounds are ugly: "My friends and companions avoid me because of my wounds."[17] We forget that wounds are common, and commonly heal. We forget that an untreated wound will fester and new illness result, as again the Psalms are quick to point out: "My wounds fester and are loathsome because of my sinful folly. I am bowed down and brought very low …"[18] We reopen our wounds again and again and again to validate our suffering; but there's something off-putting about all this, particularly to starving people, malnourished people, or people who suffer from dehydration, lack of shelter, and insufficient family protection.

There is a difference between a wound and a scar. You can do nothing with a wound but nurse it or aggravate it. But a scar provides additional protection for a sensitive area; scar tissue becomes among the strongest on your body. Scars are proof

---

[17] Psalm 38.11, NIV.
[18] Psalm 38.5, NIV.

that we not only endured, but that we're healthy once more. We're not as soft as we were, nor as naïve; we're tougher now, and more convinced that our suffering is not meant to be celebrated, but redeemed.

The church of the future will no longer brandish her hurt, but her healing, offering hope to those still in recovery.

Is there anything in your life that you've held onto for too long?

ONE.FOUR

CYNICISM

BECOMING INNOCENTS

You can develop a healthy, robust community that
lives right with God and enjoy its results only if you
do the hard work of getting along with each other,
treating each other with dignity and honor.
- James 3.18, MSG

*The church of the future will enjoy a renewed innocence and will be
characterized by a new sense of belonging. Rather than feeling like they
belong to a church, these "Innocents" will feel a sense of participation in
the universal, eternal, glorified Church of Christ.*

It won't take long before someone hurts you. My friend Bob Hyatt says that "a church close enough to help is close enough to hurt."[19] That's a good caution. People are rarely capable of being careful with one another for long, and since the church is made of people, I'm surprised we aren't better prepared for the inevitable.

We're so stunned when church people hurt us, or disappoint us, or embarrass us. But if we remembered that the church is our family, we'd know just how awkward it will be to have others we do not like and with whom we do not identify speak on our behalf, and say something foolish.

Because of their hurts, some even leave Church altogether, not just whatever local congregation housed the offense. Those who have been "hurt by the Church" cannot easily be counted. Their wounds, however long ago they were received, are still open. These are bleeders, and if they ever return to our churches, they usually still require triage. Others, similarly wounded, have covered their hurts in additional outer layers of emotional and spiritual armor, and we are never likely to be welcomed into their lives again.

But those who stick around are left with a choice: confront and contend, or forgive and forget. The former involves causing a scene, disrupting a group, or endlessly prattling on about an unresolved issue. I think this is why most people who stay at church choose, instead, to forgive and forget. Because, let's be honest, most of our church-hurts are pretty small. Not all, but the great majority are things people said that we didn't like, or things people did that hurt our feelings. So, most of us just decide to pick up and move on, doing our best to overlook the offense and forgive the offender.

---

[19] Hyatt, Bob, *Ministry Mantras: Language for Cultivating Kingdom Culture*, 165.

But then we get hurt again. And again. At this point, the hurts aren't quite so hurtful, but our expectations have changed. We're no longer looking at the church as a safe haven or a new family. Now we're looking at the church like we're the only sober fans at NASCAR. We're surrounded by fools and enthusiasts, most of whom we'd prefer not to know and almost all of whom we'll politely ignore. This is church for a great number of Christians, especially those who have been born into the faith rather than experiencing conversion as an adult.

It's why we've become cynical.

Cynics were Greco-Roman philosophers who pursued the best quality of life independent of wealth, fame, power, or reputation. They were often upper class individuals who realized that money couldn't buy happiness, and so they eschewed their wealth and began to pursue their desires with an indifference to all the things others were chasing. Perhaps the simplest way to encapsulate their philosophy is to regard everything with the thought "It doesn't matter anyway."

The word "cynic" means "dog-like,"[20] and Aristotle suggested cynics made themselves into "a cult of indifference and, like dogs, eat and make love in public, go barefoot, and sleep in tubs and at crossroads." The famed philosopher further derided cynics because, like dogs, they were shameless "not as being beneath modesty, but as superior to it."[21]

Cynicism is a significant problem in our churches today. We're reluctant to participate wholly in worship, or to diligently pursue truth in scripture, or to lock arms with our fellows because "it won't matter anyway."

---

[20] "Cynicism (philosophy)," *Wikipedia,* https://en.wikipedia.org/wiki/Cynicism_(philosophy), accessed August 18, 2017.

[21] See Scholium on Aristotle's Rhetoric, quoted in Dudley 1937, 5.

No matter what, we'll still get hurt.

No matter what, we'll still get disappointed.

No matter what, we'll still get overlooked, left out, and under-appreciated.

But the church of the future will move past her cynicism into a second innocence. This is key. When I speak of virtue or happiness or God's plan to heal the world, there are always those who mistakenly believe I have never seriously considered the flaws of the church, the realities of our time, or the difficulties in getting a group of people to move together in faith.

But I am not naive.

I am as cynical as they come, when left to my own devices. But I have chosen not to live by my own devices. I have invited the Spirit to heal me, to heal my imagination, to heal my judgments, to heal my perceptions. I have asked the Spirit to restore my belief in others, knowing full well they will never satiate my desire for the good, the true, or the beautiful.

With the Spirit's help I can love crummy people and laugh at their lack of consideration. I can ignore their affronts and remain charmed by their flaws. When I walk in the Spirit, I can see Christ in each of them. And I must walk in the Spirit, for if I do not, then I hate everybody.

But with the Spirit, I can move past my hate. This is God's plan for the Church—not indifference, but impassioned engagement with the world. God's plan is for his people to love recklessly.

Reckless love buys the engagement ring even though she might say no; pays for rehab even though he might drink again; leaves a message even though they might not call back. Reckless love does not look for guaranteed returns on investment because that sort of return is too small.

The church of the future will be filled with people who believe the lost can be found and the first shall be last; who believe all we truly own is what we give away; who believe the blind can see and the darkness will blister in the sun. Because belief is a miracle all on its own, and "everything is possible for those that believe."[22]

What's the best opportunity for you to act with reckless love today?

---

[22] Mark 9.23, NIV.

TWO | WE SEE A CHURCH

COLORED *by* LOVE *and* FRIENDSHIP AT ALL
LEVELS;

a CHURCH *that* RECOGNIZES *our* TRUE BELONGINGS
ARE NOT OUR POSSESSIONS,
but OUR RELATIONSHIPS;

a CHURCH *that* DOESN'T MERELY PROMISE
but also EXPERIENCES
LAUGHTER,
JOY,
HOPE,
and STRENGTH.

TWO.ONE

FRIVOLITY

CHURCH OUGHT TO BE A PETTING ZOO FOR YOUR SOUL

So then you are no longer strangers and aliens, but you are fellow citizens with the saints, and are of God's household, having been built on the foundation of the apostles and prophets, Christ Jesus Himself being the corner stone, in whom the whole building, being fitted together, is growing into a holy temple in the Lord.
- Ephesians 2.19-22, ESV

> *Church ought to be a place where we try new things, sharing in one another's reactions and responding to one another's queries.*

My office is notoriously fun, on account of my strange collection of artifacts, objects, and works of art. I have turned my workspace into a curiosity cabinet, a laboratory almost like the *sancto sanctorum* of Dr. Strange or the Room of Requirement at Hogwarts. But nothing has been stranger, or more fun, than the year we had our pet hedgehog.

"Merton" lived on my desk amid the odd lamps, antique pipes, and discarded chess pieces. Whenever people came for counseling or prayer, they would inevitably be distracted by Merton. Despite his ornery personality and spiky tines, people loved to pick him up and rub his soft belly, and Merton provided a greater antidote for depression than any prayer or advice I was able to dispense.

My favorite moments were always when children would visit. I kept a pair of extra-small ski gloves in my desk so little ones could hold the strange rodent without being pricked. They would laugh as Merton balled himself up, barely looking out over his upturned-bum to sniff their noses.

This is a wonderful picture of how church should be. The older welcome the younger, introducing them to mysteries and curiosities only afforded by age and experience.

Church ought to be a petting zoo for your soul.

> Your standard-issue workplace—whether it's a cube or a corner office—should do more than just organize your stuff and be adequately comfortable. It should actually make you happy. And inspired. You should want to spend time in it.
> -Winnie Au[23]

---

[23] Au, Winnie, "Give your Office a Raise: a GQ Design Guide," May 2017, 70-76.

Earlier this summer I installed a barrel-stave swing in my office. I purchased it at a brewery and it hangs from a steel beam twelve feet above the floor, secured with iron chain.

Ever since I got the swing, meetings have been much more enjoyable. Our first elder meeting, for example, each member of our governing board took a turn going back and forth, back and forth, with their legs up and their smiles wide. We laughed, took photos, and tagged one another on Facebook.

Too often our churches are led through authority and control, where the paid staff and the trustees spend the majority of their time at one another's throats. We bicker. We argue. We clamor and defend and go home frustrated and discouraged.

But it doesn't have to be that way.

The church of the future will be governed by competent idealists, eager to discover solutions that embody the very gospel we're trying to cultivate. Love and laughter will be the norm, not the exception, and sound decision-making will occur alongside fellowship, community, and prayer.

My friend Rick jokes that he was often told, "Fun is for after the Rapture." His well-meaning superiors were certain that God's mission to save souls was so serious now there was no time to mess around with things like exercise, leisure, or silliness.

But this betrays a fundamental misunderstanding about both God's desires and God's intention.

God's plan is much bigger than simply getting people into heaven. He wants to get heaven into his people. He wants to get heaven into earth. He wants every moment, every relationship, every exchange, and every interruption to be bursting with heaven's life, heaven's joys, and heaven's pleasures.

That's what salvation means. *Soteria*,[24] the Greek word we translate as salvation, means health, wholeness, and happiness. *Happiness*! For us to be saved, in the true language of scripture, means we are to live now as though we were caught up in the best experience of life with God. Exercise is godly. Playtime is godly. A glass of wine with your wife is godly. So is laughter. Frivolity. Love making.

Everything the Lord made is good, and everything good is the Lord's.

> Love all God's creation, the whole of it and every grain of sand in it. Love every leaf, every ray of God's light. Love the animals, love the plants, love everything. If you love everything, you will perceive the divine mystery in things.
> - Fyodor Dostoyevsky

How is God leading and enabling you to enjoy life to the fullest?

---

[24] See Alcorn, Randy, *Happiness*; see also http://biblehub.com/greek/4991.htm.

TWO.TWO

HOSPITALITY

THE PROPER CARE AND FEEDING OF PEOPLE

For just as each of us has one body with many members, and these members do not all have the same function, so in Christ we, though many, form one body, and each member belongs to all the others.
- Romans 12.4-5, NIV

The church is meant to provide healthy community for all, inviting new people into the existing family of God.

In his letter to Titus, the apostle Paul reminds the older women of the church to take their younger counterparts beneath their wing and teach them to love their husbands and take care of their households.[25]

At first blush, many contemporary readers become sidetracked by Paul's controversial statement that women "should be happy working in their homes," but upon close inspection it becomes clear that Paul has something more expansive in mind than tea cozies and window coverings.

To fully understand Paul's intended meaning it might help to dissect the Greek word in question, *oikouros*. Literally, this word means "keeper of the home," but "home" (*oikos*) was a word that referred to your people—your family, friends, and closest neighbors and peers. If you were to celebrate a 50th wedding anniversary, your guest list would likely be your *oikos*. So a keeper of the *oikos* would be someone who managed your social network, bringing all your people together.

When I think about how to keep your *oikos*, I think about my mum's remarkable hospitality. Growing up, every Sunday Mum hosted lavish dinners for my brothers and their families, as well as any guests. In addition to enjoying great food and conversation, those were times when Christian values and behaviors were normalized, celebrated, and reinforced. Of course there are other ways to bring people together—single adults, for example, may host soirees or bonfires or get together for movies at the park—but the family table will always resonate strongest for me.

A good "keeper of the people" will stay up to date on everyone's needs, hurts, aspirations, and challenges. A keeper will pray, reach out, offer help, and provide assistance. A keeper

---

[25]   Titus 2.3-5.

shows unconditional love and hospitality—with their time and conversation as much as their home and possessions.

Again, the idea of *oikouros* wasn't limited to good housekeeping, but good us-making. A keeper shepherds their family with a strong emphasis on who we are as a community, a family, and a group.

The church of the future will cultivate more and more people-keepers so that those without family become adopted into the family of God; so that those who have no model of a healthy family are healed and taught to envision a safe future for their children; so that those who have already raised a family can help others do the same, avoiding the trap of spinsterism and loneliness so common among the aged.

Who are your people?

TWO.THREE

COMMUNITY

CONCERNING CHRIST AND CROSSFIT

I have been crucified with Christ. It is no longer I who
live, but Christ who lives in me. And the life I now
live in the flesh I live by faith in the Son of God, who
loved me and gave himself for me.
- Galatians 2.20, ESV

> *The church of the future knows her true identity isn't fully expressed
> by the events of the weekend, but finds its ultimate expression in the
> community of faith.*

Recently I attended an evening lecture by Bob Moesta, an organizational consultant who focuses on innovation in manufacturing. Bob is one of the key inspirations for the bestseller, *Competing Against Luck* (by Clay Christensen), and he had surprisingly insightful comments about religion in the 21st century.

"Do you know what the church's problem is?" Bob asked.

"Tell me," I replied, eager to see if he knew his stuff.

"The church no longer delivers. Church says 'I'll be there for you,' 'I'll be your family,' 'We can do things together.' But the Church is only open on Sundays."

I agreed, but was already formulating my rebuttal when he hit me right between the eyes. "The chief competitor to organized religion is CrossFit."

I laughed out loud. I've been an avid CrossFit competitor for years and love the sport. And, indeed, the crossover points between CrossFit and Christian spirituality have been well documented.

Bob continued, "CrossFit delivers what the church promises: community. And they do it so well people will pay two hundred dollars a month to attend class five times a week. What church even gets their people to come once a Sunday, for free?"

Bob is right, but he's missing some important elements, most notably that CrossFit involves a particular experience of strenuous activity, and it is that shared suffering (for lack of a better term) that provides the basis for the community. Sociologist Victor Turner referred to this as *'communitas'* and Zygmunt Bauman suggested that *communitas* is the community that happens as we do other things. It's accidental community. It's the bonds of friendship that form while we play sports, serve on a mission trip, or endure a trial like the Tough Mudder.

And healthy churches provide more opportunities for *communitas* than any other organization. Including CrossFit. In Nancy Ammerman's 1996 article "Bowling Together: Congregations and the American,"[26] she maintains values-driven communities afford unique opportunities in leisure, the arts, and community service. And these opportunities more than compensate for the American propensity to "bowl alone." Ammerman's research suggests that healthy churches make us feel safe, sane, and loved—and are more successful than any other organization on the planet.

But I don't want to suggest that the church of the future won't change. Or shouldn't. It must! And I think CrossFit is a wonderful example of a hands-on approach to spirituality, such that our design team at Westwinds often poses the question "How would CrossFit do it?" by which we mean, "How can we give our people a sense that this is something they can successfully achieve, despite the strong feeling they cannot?" We want our spiritual amateurs to become spiritual competitors. And, like CrossFit exposes housewives and fat dads to Olympic weightlifting and aerial gymnastics, we want to give our people the opportunity to experiment with Christian mysticism, contemplative prayer, and technologically enhanced worship.

Perhaps more important even than the community that results from shared achievement, the church of the future will also cultivate community resulting from affirmation,

---

26 Ammerman, Nancy T., Civic Order, Arizona State University Lecture in Religion, February 26, 1996.

64

encouragement, and praise. CrossFit does this well, but not as well as SoulCycle—the stationary cycling craze that's reinventing personal health and wellness, with the promise that their riders get "stronger mentally and physically."[27]

I attended my first SoulCycle class last year after my barista told me it was like "an orgasm, followed by the deepest religious experience of your life ... like you'd been to confession and then gone straight to heaven."

I was not disappointed. The class runs much like a routine spin class at any YMCA, but the instructor conducted himself like Tony Robbins—his cheerful, inspiring mantra of meme-like encouragement never faltered. He guided us through both our athletic and social challenges, reminding us constantly that the activity we had chosen to perform was making us stronger every second. It was empowering, revelatory, and kind—like the best altar call from the most loving evangelist you'd ever run a marathon to meet.

The church of the future will take this level of care with each participant, offering more opportunities for her people to grow together through shared experiences. She will authenticate their struggles and validate their efforts, reminding them over and over and over that they are in the process of becoming the best possible version of themselves for the glory of God.

> *How can you celebrate achievement, community, and success like SoulCycle and CrossFit?*

---

[27] Whelan, Melanie, "Bicycle Diaries," *Fast Company*, June 2017, 20.

TWO.FOUR

RELATIONSHIPS

EMBRACING OUR BLOOD, OUR TRIBE, AND THE WORLD

But our citizenship is in heaven. And we eagerly await
a Savior from there, the Lord Jesus Christ.
-Philippians 3.20, NIV

> *God is a being in community with himself, and we are meant to emulate*
> *the communal essence of our Creator.*

There are three major arenas of community within the Bible: the family (blood), the church (tribe), and the world (species).

The **community of our family** includes our immediate family,[28] our extended family,[29] and those we've welcomed into our family despite the absence of any biological connection.[30] Our responsibility to our family is to provide, protect, and prepare them for life in the world.

In Genesis 2.22, God helps man become part of a family by giving him a "helper like unto himself." Eve came to Adam because it was not good for "man to be alone." Our families have been given to us for our good, and that goodness is best reflected in mutual love and service. In Revelation 22.4, God marks man with his name upon the man's forehead, signifying God's adoption of humanity. We who "once were not a people, have now become the people of God."[31]

The **community of our church** concerns our identity as people allied with Christ. Though there are many things we might say about the nature of the church and our participation in it, we can never escape our responsibility to give financially,[32] serve one another in Christian charity,[33] and invite all people into the Kingdom of God's grace.[34]

In Genesis 2.16, God warns man not to eat from the Tree of Knowledge. To all outward appearances, there was nothing wrong with this Tree. However, God's instruction teaches us there are some things we may do (eat from any other tree) and

---

[28] Ephesians 5.23-31.

[29] Ephesians 6.1-4.

[30] Ecclesiastes 5.8-16.

[31] 1 Peter 2.10.

[32] 2 Corinthians 9.7.

[33] 1 Peter 4.10-11.

[34] Acts 8.26-39.

some things we must not do, regardless of our perspectives or opinions. Being part of God's church means accepting God's authority. In Revelation 21.2, God "marries" man in the form of the New Jerusalem, his bride, demonstrating that our allegiance to Christ has been rewarded with eternal love, fidelity, and unity.

The **community of our world** extends outward from us as individuals and envelops every person,[35] in every city,[36] on the entire planet.[37] We share a connection as people made in the image and likeness of our Creator, a fact that imbues us with dignity and humility, authority and responsibility.

In Revelation 22.5, the people of the world come to live in God's light, showing a permanent home that establishes a connection between those who walk in the light and the Light of the World.

We are social creatures. We need one another. We thrive on love and support. Whether introverts or extroverts, from large families or single-parent cabins in the woods, the truth is that we need friends to keep us healthy. So much so that lack of social support predicts all major causes of death.

In fact, my friend Becky recently passed me an article that suggests having insufficient friends is more dangerous than obesity and is the equivalent health risk of smoking 15 cigarettes a day!

> Julianne Holt-Lunstad, Ph.D., professor of psychology at Brigham Young University, did a meta-analysis of 148 studies and concluded that a lack of social support predicts all causes of death. People with a solid group

---

[35] Genesis 12.2-3.

[36] Revelation 21.2-5.

[37] Acts 1.8.

of friends are 50 percent more likely to survive at any given time than those without one. Holt-Lunstad calculated that having few social ties is an equivalent mortality risk to smoking fifteen cigarettes a day and even riskier than being obese or not exercising!
-"How To Make Friends Easily and Strengthen the Friendships You Have"[38]

Additional research suggests if you've got at least three good friends at work, you are 96% more likely to be happy with life overall.

Fowler and Christakis found that you are about 15 percent more likely to be happy if one of your friends is happy (overall, not in any particular moment). Even if a friend of your friend is happy, you're 10 percent more likely to be in a contented state. "We found that each happy friend a person has increases that person's probability of being happy by about 9 percent. Each unhappy friend decreases it by 7 percent," they write. Since these stats imply that happiness is more contagious than unhappiness, they conclude that "the more, the merrier" holds true, despite what is usually said about quality over quantity in friendships. They also found that an additional friend amounts to two fewer days of feeling lonely each year. "Since on average (in our data) people feel lonely forty-eight days per year, having a couple of extra friends makes you about 10 percent less lonely than other people. Interestingly, the number of family members has no effect at all.
-"How To Make Friends Easily and Strengthen the Friendships You Have"[39]

---

[38] "How to Make Friends Easily and Strengthen the Friendships You Have," *Barking Up the Wrong Tree*, http://www.bakadesuyo.com/2013/11/how-to-make-friends-easily/, accessed August 18, 2017.
[39] Ibid.

The church of the future will foster camaraderie, embodying Jesus' promise that we will no longer be servants, but friends.[40]

The church of the future will work together to fill the earth,[41] export Eden's culture to the world,[42] and bind ourselves to one another as people imitating the union and communion of our Creator.[43]

How is God calling you into greater community with the church?

---

[40] John 15.15.
[41] Genesis 1.28.
[42] Genesis 2.10-14.
[43] Genesis 2.24.

FRIENDSHIP

DISCOVERING THE EXAMPLE OF THE MORAVIANS

For by one Spirit we were all baptized into one body, whether Jews or Greeks, whether slaves or free, and we were all made to drink of one Spirit.
- 1 Corinthians 12.13, ESV

> *There can be no Christianity without community.*

Nikolas von Zinzendorf (May 26, 1700—May 9, 1760), a wealthy Saxon landowner, graciously hosted and received Moravian refugees during a season of Catholic persecution. Key to both their missiology and ecclesiology was the primacy of community, so much so that Zinzendorf boldly proclaimed "There can be no Christianity without community."[44]

> Like the Pietists, the Moravian Brethren believed that Christianity should be a "religion of the heart"—which went against the grain of the growing acceptance of Enlightenment beliefs. They emphasized experience of faith and love over doctrine, and thus were more accepting of varying denominational differences. In fact, Zinzendorf may have been the first churchman to use the word "ecumenism." The Moravians also placed special importance on community: families' allegiances were superseded by "choirs"—groups delineated by age, sex, and marital status.
> *-Christianity Today*[45]

The Moravians were effective missionaries, mainly due to their close knit communal atmosphere and their "love feasts," which feature entertaining music and culinary treats like sticky buns, milky tea, and good beer.

That sounds like a decent life to me, the kind Jesus described in John 10 as "life more abundant," or as I like to think of it, the best quality of life now and forever more.

---

[44] Zinzendorf, "Quotes by Count Zinzendorf," *SermonIndex.net,* http://www.sermonindex.net/modules/articles/index.php?view=article&aid=32366, accessed August 18, 2017.

[45] "Nikolaus von Zinzendorf," *Christianity Today,* http://www.christianityto-day.com/history/people/denominationalfounders/nikolaus-von-zinzendorf.html, accessed August 18, 2017.

But that kind of life can be elusive. Whether we're pastors, parents, or simply Christian people, we get caught up in ministering to others, overinvested in our projects and distractions, overextended through our networks and commitments, and the whole endeavor consumes us. We get burned up and spit out by our own ambition as we work harder and harder to make everyone and everything stronger or more clever or more effective.

None of those goals are bad, but neither should they be primary. God's ultimate plan is the renewal of Creation, which means his ultimate desire for us is to enjoy life as though we were back in Eden. There will always be work, but the work must be good, life-giving, rewarding, and satisfying. That means we'll need proper rest and recovery, and we'll need activities that rejuvenate us. We'll need friendship and community to supply color and relief to our adventures.

And we can't have any of that if we are so focused we are miserable, uptight, stressed out, or beaten down. Which, of course, makes me wonder what the Moravians might have said to someone like myself; someone who had the truth but couldn't enjoy sharing it?

> Every heart with Christ is a missionary, every heart
> without Christ is a mission field.
> - Zinzendorf[46]

I love the historical example of the Moravians, for it shows evangelism is as much about serving our guests as it is about saving their souls; the communion table was never meant to be a thimble-full of grace, but a second helping of friendship with God among his people.

---

[46]   Zinzendorf, "Quotes by Count Zinzendorf," *SermonIndex.net,* http://www. sermonindex.net/modules/articles/index.php?view=article&aid=32366, accessed August 18, 2017.

Are you experiencing the promise of abundant life in community, or just selling it to others?

THREE

WE SEE A CHURCH

FULL *of* NOBLE AMBITION *to* SHADOW GOD;

a **CHURCH** DEVELOPING NEW VOICES *to* REFINE *and* INVIGORATE OUR FAITH;

a **CHURCH** SO COMMITTED TO THE GOOD OF THE WORLD

that **WE** WILL TRAIN LEADERS *and* PREACHERS *and* INNOVATORS

for the **NEXT** 10,000 YEARS

to SING *the* LORD'S SONG IN TUNE WITH THE TIMES.

THREE.ONE

DELUSION

LEARNING NOT TO IDOLIZE, INFATUATE, OR EMBELLISH

Delight yourself in the Lord, and he will give you the desires of your heart.
-Psalm 37.4, ESV

> *Our passions can either direct us toward God or detour us away from faith altogether.*

Herod the Great idolized both himself and his accomplishments. Rather than using his political position to cooperate with God, Herod relentlessly pursued his desires at significant cost to his subjects. Famous for his ability to play Rome and Judea against one another, reviled by both yet bothered by none, Herod was constantly exploiting his people for political privilege and then manipulating the system of Roman government to gain relative autonomy within the Empire. His conniving allowed him to accomplish tremendous feats of architecture and engineering, but also cost him his health, his family, and his reputation.

In short, Herod sold out.

We do the same, sometimes, albeit in different ways. We sell our opinions, our popularity, and our worth in order to get the things we think we want. When confronted by a group of peers we want to impress, we change our opinions in order to create common ground. When presented with an exciting opportunity, we change our ideals in order to find permission when none is available. The Christian teen at the cool party finds it very difficult to be both young and holy; the Christian businessperson finds it difficult to be both ethical and efficient; the Christian athlete, needing an edge, finds it difficult to be both competitive and above reproach.

When we idolize our ambitions or our possessions or our heroes, we sacrifice everything else to please them. Why? Because idols demand sacrifice. So we must constrain our ambitions, forcing them to serve God rather than enslaving us.

The church of the future will help her people understand that the things we want are hidden within the things we love. She will caution us not to forfeit that which we love for that which we want, and help us to mature beyond self-gratification to do good work.

How will you keep from selling out the next time your convictions are put to the test?

THREE.TWO

PURPOSE

FINDING DEEPER MEANING IN EVERYTHING

The Lord God took the man and put him in the
Garden of Eden to work it and take care of it.
- Genesis 2.15, NIV

All work is good when we do it unto the Lord.

I have been a scuba diver for many years and have gone on hundreds of dives across North America. Three have been environmental rescue dives. I visited sites in crisis and worked with teams of volunteers to ensure the local ecology remains protected. I have no doubt God was pleased with my work in service to his Creation. Yet I am equally certain God is pleased by my work as an artist creating robot-themed lamps out of electrical conduits. I experience God's pleasure while creating weird housewares, just as I do while scraping mollusks off underwater rock formations.

How can this be? How can two totally different pursuits—one selfless and one frivolous—both serve as portals to God's pleasure?

There is no actual boundary between godly work and good work. The fact that we see ourselves in cooperation with God, regardless of what, specifically, we're doing, helps us understand that God's project of ongoing Creation is as varied as it is large.

Our fulfillment depends on good work that not only improves the world, but us also. That's one of the biggest takeaways I discovered while researching *The Adventure of Happiness*[47]—that we have the power to ascribe worth to our actions, behaviors, and relationships regardless of what they are. The trick, simply, is to connect what we do to a larger purpose. And for me, that larger purpose is always God's plan to heal the world both with and through his people. This cooperative work can be industrious or playful, the work of a professional or a hobbyist; the only determining factor is whether we perceive God's involvement, pleasure, and oversight as we do it.

---

[47] McDonald, David, *The Adventure of Happiness*, Westwinds: Jackson, MI, 2016.

> Our job in this life is not to shape ourselves into some ideal we imagine we ought to be, but to find out who we already are and become it.
> - Steven Pressfield[48]

I understand why this is tricky for some to understand, which is why I maintain you've just got to do the things in front of you, trusting that God will reveal himself if we are open to the involvement of his Spirit. The church of the future will be filled with people who figure it out as they go, knowing "the hands will [often] solve a mystery that the intellect has struggled with in vain."[49]

What work are you most proud of?

---

[48] Pressfield, Steven, *The War of Art: Break Through the Blocks and Win Your Inner Creative Battles.*

[49] Jung, Carl, "Carl Jung Quotes," *BrainyQuote,* https://www.brainyquote.com/quotes/quotes/c/carljung108090.html, accessed August 18, 2017.

THREE.THREE

PASSION

HOW TO REMAIN ENERGETIC AND COMMITTED

Commit yourself to God completely ...
- Job 11.13, NIRV

> *In order to last, our passions require fuel.*

Our closest translation of the Greek word *eros* is "passion." In the broadest sense, passion is the invigorating energy that fuels our pursuits, desires, and ambitions. Of course passion can be sexual, but sexuality is only one of *eros'* many manifestations. We can be passionate about our families, about our work, about our hobbies, about causes such as racial reconciliation or ecology—we can even be passionate about grammar or the Dewey Decimal System.

Philosophers have often compared *eros* to fire. Like fire, passion can focus us, it can draw us together, it can provide protection and safety.

- Every fire needs two kinds of fuel: kindling and firewood. Kindling burns easily, but is quickly consumed. Our passions have kindling—ideas, insights, role models, or materials that cause our imaginations to flare up and kick us into high gear.
- Firewood is the fuel that keeps the fire burning longest and hottest. The firewood of our passion usually requires much effort for a more sustainable yield, depending on things like research, practice, and personal investment.

Often, we rely too much on our kindling to keep our passion burning, but there are only so many times you can fall in love with that cute smile or experience the joy of jumping around just for fun. Eventually, that first spark ceases to flash and we become bored. When that happens, we must deliberately feed our passions with the long-burning fuel of intense discipline and intentionality.

The church of the future will both ignite and sustain passionate people. She will provide excitements that spark new enthusiasm and equip her people to burn brightly for a long, long time.

What's your passion?

THREE.FOUR

INVESTMENT

MAKING A DIFFERENCE WHERE WE LIVE

For [we are] looking forward to the city with
foundations, whose architect and builder is God.
- Hebrews 11.10, NIV

> *The church of the future must take great pains to ensure she does not
> slide into irrelevance or irresponsibility. She must refocus herself routinely
> on the mission of Christ to heal the world.*

One of the greatest gifts to the Midwest has been the contributions of the Illitch family in Detroit.[50] Wealthy business owners with a longstanding love for their city, the Illitchs have invested massive amounts of their resources into revitalizing the city. When others believed Detroit was long-dead and would never resurrect, the Illitch clan put their money where their heart was and have almost single-handedly brought one of America's historic cities into a wrought iron renaissance.

The church of the future will be increasingly motivated by God's love for God's people. She will see the world and perceive the Lord. She will recognize that the investments she makes are eternal investments in the City of God amidst the cities of man.

Zygmunt Bauman was one of the greatest sociologists of the 20th century. One of his favorite means of talking about the ways we interact was to distinguish between "tourists" and "vagabonds." I've always felt this distinction needs to be further developed to include "vagrants" and "resident-aliens" in order to better understand God's calling for his people to be a city of light within the world of darkness.

Here's how I've come to apply Bauman's categories to the church.

A vagrant is a hostile person living downtown. Vagrants are often listless and purposeless, but if provoked will quickly turn violent. Many Christians live as vagrants. They have no noble purpose, but seem to be everywhere, drawing attention to themselves. If approached, Christians can lash out and do great harm to those around them, yet never seem willing to accept responsibility for their actions. Some Christians seem convinced their violence is necessary.

[50] http://biography.yourdictionary.com/mike-ilitch.

Vagabonds, by contrast, sleep under park benches and keep their libations in brown sacks. They are rootless and without family. Christians can also be vagabonds, pitiful creatures, always trying to solicit sympathy for their suffering. They wonder why the world doesn't help them, growing frustrated and despondent that their plight isn't addressed.

Tourists are people who visit downtown but take no responsibility for its wellbeing. They look and laugh, spend a little money and go shopping, but the only legacy they leave behind is their spare change. Some Christians play tourist in the world. They taste its goods and enjoy their stay, but never leave their mark. They're players, not producers.

It's clear God never intended us to be tourists, vagabonds, or vagrants. We are citizens of heaven, but we live on earth. We are not native to our earthly city, and it has been so long since we lived "at home" that we hardly feel like immigrants, either. The best way to describe us is as resident aliens. We're from *there*, but we live *here*. We still do heaven things quite naturally, but we also commit ourselves to the good of the earth; we live by earthly rules, we obey earthly government, and we participate in earthly community.

> Christianity is the story of how the rightful king has landed, you might say landed in disguise, and is calling us all to take part in a great campaign of sabotage.
> - C.S. Lewis

The church of the future will be filled with resident aliens, contributing to the good of the world, but governed by heaven's values, customs, and relationships.

Which of these terms best describes you up until this point—vagabond, tourist, vagrant, or resident-alien?

THREE.FIVE

CLERGY

CULTIVATING INNOVATORS IN MINISTRY

Now the Lord God had planted a garden in the east,
in Eden; and there he put the man he had formed.
– Genesis 2.8, NIV

The church of the future will remind her preachers, leaders, and innovators that they are not merely heralds of God's grace, but recipients.

There is no larger gap than that between the training for and actual requirements of, Christian ministry. Biblical Studies, theological certifications, and ministry degrees (especially the coveted Masters of Divinity) simply do not prepare pastors for the daily challenges of church leadership. Ministerial students receive little (if any) instruction on recruiting volunteers, managing teams, launching missional initiatives, or understanding cultural trends; yet those are basic requirements for any pastor, from youth ministry to women's league. As a result, pastors feel discouraged, ill-equipped, criticized, and betrayed, all of which contribute to their early departure.

Though we are seeing significant increase in both the number of megachurches and the attendance within those congregations, many churches are closing their doors and many Christian organizations are imploding. The sad truth is that too many churches are copying a model of sameness and safeness, with the bland leading the bland. For some, these churches provide comfortable containers for family programming and convenient services. But longitudinally the church must change, or die.

We need to cultivate innovators as they grow, giving them support so they can pursue the dreams and passions God has given them for the future, rather than forcing them into a mold that will soon expire.

> Leadership is best thought of as a behavior, not a role.
> - Margaret Wheatley[51]

Earlier this year I secured charitable status for a 501c3 with the intention of opening a research and development center for pastors. This was the impetus for Francis Schaeffer's *L'Abri* retreat centers, though I intend to create space where

[51] Wheatley, Margaret, *Leadership and the New Science: Discovering Order in a Chaotic World*, 24.

preachers, leaders, and innovators from all over the world come, not only for solace and development, but also to incubate the future of the church.

The church of the future will cultivate preachers, leaders, and innovators for professional ministry. The church of the future will celebrate the role of clergy while maintaining her commitment to the priesthood of all believers. She will harmonize both the passion and the development of apostles, prophets, pastors, teachers, and evangelists whether as paid staff or committed volunteers.

> *What do you think a research and development center for pastors would look like?*

FOUR | WE
SEE
A
CHURCH

that **RAISES** TECHNOLOGISTS *the* WAY
AMERICAN CHURCHES ONCE RAISED GOSPEL
SINGERS;

a **CHURCH** *that* DEVELOPS *and* IMPLEMENTS NEW
STRATEGIES
>*for the* **HOLISTIC** INTEGRATION *of* SCIENCE,
>TECHNOLOGY, *and* FAITH;

a **CHURCH** *that* MELDS METAPHYSICS WITH
QUANTUM PHYSICS,
>*that* **BELIEVES** OUR HUMANITY *is*
>REVEALED *through* OUR TREATMENT *of*
>OTHERS.

FOUR.ONE

TRAINING

RAISING THE NEXT GENERATION OF AUTEURS

Don't let anyone look down on you because you are young, but set an example for the believers in speech, in conduct, in love, in faith and in purity.
-1 Timothy 4.12, NIV

> *The church must become an incubator for technological talent.*

Aretha Franklin. Elvis Presley. Whitney Houston. Little Richard. Usher. Avril Lavigne. Jessica Simpson. Justin Timberlake. Katy Perry. Britney Spears.[52]

The list goes on.

In the twentieth century, there were dozens of singers, musicians, and celebrities who emerged from the local church to take the secular entertainment industry by storm. Why? Because the church provided a platform for performance. These artists could sing in front of a crowd that was more appreciative, more diverse, and more sizeable than anything else available. Sure, some kids could perform in school concerts and pageants, but those events were heavily scripted and only occurred three or four times a year. Church was weekly and allowed for more spontaneity and freedom of expression, especially in African American and Charismatic settings.

The church gave artists instant mentoring. Whereas in schools or performing classes, critique came from a few, in the church, "everyone's a critic." The older church ladies had heard a lot of hotshot singers in their day, and they knew who's really got it and who needs to work on it. Likewise, these older woman knew how to work a crowd and could give instruction to their younger stars as they progressed through the ranks. The older women knew ego when they saw it, and were quick to dress down those whose arrogance surpassed their talent. They kept young people humble and teachable, and the best young people responded enthusiastically to their coaching.

[52] See http://madamenoire.com/436918/singers-who-started-in-the-church; http://www.deseretnews.com/article/865610585/10-celebrities-who-get-their-start-in-church.html; http://www.ranker.com/list/celebrities-who-sang-in-the-church-choir/celebrity-lists?utm_expid=16418821-310. smDnXTH_QT6V93qtvQFoXw.0&utm_referrer=https%3A%2F%2Fwww. google.com%2F.

The church has always connected the abilities of artists to worship. Right out of the gate, special giftedness was celebrated as being from God, designed for the glory of God. Consequently, deep meaning became attached to performance and those that were raised in church understood their abilities had power to change lives, heal wounds, reconcile broken families, and transcend ordinary life.

There are now almost as many opportunities for musicians and actors outside of the church as within it. Perhaps even more so. Between school programs, private lessons, community theater, and new tools affording the pursuit of personal ambition (Garage Band, YouTube, etc.), artists no longer benefit from the special privilege of growing up in a church.

But they could.

Because the church still offers one category of opportunities the world hasn't yet provided: hands-on experience with technology.

> Technologies are exploding and conjoining like never before, and our brains can't easily anticipate such rapid transformation … historically, value has never been created this quickly."
> - Peter Diamandis and Steven Kotler[53]

Whether using a lighting rig, running a soundboard, controlling a six-camera shoot, or learning the Adobe Suite, there are dozens of opportunities at contemporary churches for twidget-fingered teens to run the world. Every week. And kids are fast learners. A 12-year-old can learn to run Media Shout or

---

[53] Diamandis, Peter H. and Steven Kotler, *Abundance: The Future is Better Than You Think,* 35.

ProPresenter in about two weeks, but it takes most 30-year-olds closer to six.

Yet many are reluctant to trust teens with tech because young people are not always careful. Their attention spans are short. They miss cues. They panic or flame out. But these are solvable problems and, in light of how we could be equipping our youth for such superior innovation and service, easily reconciled.

We need to invest more heavily in creating opportunities for hands-on technical expertise. Most churches wait until the kids are at least out of high school, if not college, before entrusting them with something significant. But by that time, we've lost most of our kids and they won't soon return. If at all. The church of the future will invest in our youth while they are *young*, capitalizing on the similarities between church and gaming, church and programming, church and mobile devices, instead of throwing our hands up in the air wondering why kids don't read any more.

Who do you know that would love to learn technology at church?

FOUR.TWO

MEDIA

PRESSING THE BOUNDARIES OF DIGITAL ENGAGEMENT

I have become all things to all people so that by all
possible means I might save some. I do all this for the
sake of the gospel, that I may share in its blessings.
- 1 Corinthians 9.22b-23, ESV

> *Our use of screens must evolve beyond fear or fascination, into thoughtful,*
> *responsible engagement.*

The new frontiers of liturgical media exist in the intersection between Marshal McLuhan, multi-screening, and gamefication. The church of the future will be neither cowed nor dazzled by screens, information, and accessibility, but will prove such tools are always sanctified when constrained toward godly purpose. She will explore new pedagogies, experiences, and insights born from her simultaneous consumption and production of visual and auditory content.

Marshal McLuhan was a well-known media theorist whose famous maxim, "the medium is the message,"[54] taught us that *how* we consume information matters just as much as the fact *that* we do; furthermore, that the medium alters not only the content of the message but our interpretation of it, and dictates the parameters within which we respond.

But McLuhan's media-driven insight[55] also contends that every new technological innovation must inevitably endure the moral questioning of its audience. Simply, we're always going to want to know if this new thing is "good." But McLuhan suggests we ask four concurrent questions instead, each representing opportunities and threats (rather than the inherently moral questions of goodness or badness):

> A. "What recurrence or RETRIEVAL of earlier actions and services is brought into play simultaneously by the new form? What older, previously obsolesced ground is brought back and inheres in the new form?"

> B. "When pushed to the limits of its potential, the new form will tend to reverse what had been its original

---

[54] McLuhan, Marshall, *The Gutenburg Galaxy.*

[55] McLuhan, *Laws of Media: The New Science.*

characteristics. What is the REVERSAL potential of the new form?"

C. "If some aspect of a situation is enlarged or enhanced, simultaneously the old condition or un-enhanced situation is displaced thereby. What is pushed aside or OBSOLESCED by the new 'organ'?"

D. "What does the artifact ENHANCE or intensify or make possible or accelerate? This can be asked concerning a wastebasket, a painting, a steamroller, or a zipper, as well as about a proposition in Euclid or a law of physics. It can be asked about any word or phrase in any language."[56]

If, for example, we were to apply this tetrad to church online, we might surmise that church online **retrieves** the flat hierarchy of the earliest Christian communities, on account of the fact that the internet is always a level playing field. The sage on the stage is no longer the ultimate authority, since participants in online discussion forums are free to express their disagreements, skepticism, and provocations without fear of being "shushed" like they would in a physical environment.

And yet church online also **reverses** some components of corporate worship, leading us far back into spectatorship among congregants. It is all too common for people to attend "church in the sheets" and only tacitly concern themselves with the liturgy while they fold laundry, doze, or continue watching the NFL with lowered volume.

Church online makes **obsolete** the community aspect of church—like greeting strangers sitting next to you, being

---

[56] https://social-epistemology.com/2012/11/11/gregory-sand-strom-laws-of-media-the-four-effects-a-mcluhan-contribution-to-social-epis-temology/.

forced to make eye contact, and having a face-to-face conversation. It also makes obsolete the notion of dressing up in your Sunday best, as well as Sunday School being an integral component of Church Day, where families do something together, often followed by group meals and a whole set of activities related to physical church attendance.

Perhaps the greatest opportunity for church online is that it **enhances** the speed of response. If you post a prayer request, you're much more likely to receive prayer from the Internet prayer team than you would if you filled out a card and placed it in a box at the back of the auditorium. Also, any requests you might make for more information or additional resources can easily be supplied with hyperlinks and one-click purchases. This immediacy could never be achieved in a physical space. Additionally, church online affords new levels of engagement with the teaching, as we can now pause, go back, and replay key points. We can have teaching discussions in our satellites while actually watching the teaching at the same time, rather than having to recall what we heard last Sunday, which could have been 5 or 6 days ago.

All these examples demonstrate that media is an ever-evolving, constantly complexifying phenomenon. Consider, for example, **multi-screen use**—a now common practice that would once have been unthinkable.[57] Currently, 90% of all media interactions are screen-based, and we spend over four hours of leisure time every day in front of our screens.[58]

The two main modes of multi-screening are sequential usage (moving from one device to another to "pick up where we left off") and simultaneous usage (either multi-tasking on unrelated

---

[57]   https://www.thinkwithgoogle.com/advertising-channels/mobile/the-new-multi-screen-world-study/.

[58]   Not at work, and not working on special projects for our home or personal development. Leisure time is "play time."

activities or complementary use for related activities). In their report on multi-screen use, Google determined that the varying devices largely dictate which content users consume:

* Smart phones keep us connected
* Tablets keep us entertained
* Computers keep us informed
* TVs keep us searching for inspiration

This research has led us to believe that the church of the future will need to reconsider how she uses screens during worship. Currently screens function as magnifying glasses, helping audience members see the stage more easily; but we've been experimenting with multi-screen use in the auditorium at Westwinds to great effect, adapting Google's research to fit in-room liturgical needs. This hasn't progressed flawlessly, but our current scenario employs vertical televisions like smartphones, suggesting next steps, connection points, and saturating our people in scripture; our side-fill screens are like televisions, showing us content we might otherwise miss (the "old" way of magnifying what's on stage), as well as giving us the main points of the teaching; and our main, central screen is used laptop-style as the vehicle for in-depth information.

One major reason we're so immersed in technology is, of course, video games. The fast-reward mechanism of games supplies both dopamine and adrenaline, making them intensely desirable regardless of age, gender, or race. These benefits have fostered the new trend of gamefying absolutely everything in order to make ordinary life more fun.

Gamefication is a strategy now being employed by nonprofits—the Ice Bucket Challenge,[59] for instance— insurance companies—safe driving rewards and cash back

---

[59] http://www.alsa.org/about-us/ice-bucket-challenge-faq.html?.

incentives have actually been around for a long time—and the collision of companies like Starbucks and Foursquare.

Coupled with the sharp increase in actual physical board games (even popular video games like XCom, Bioshock, and Warcraft now have "hard" manifestations), I think we'll continue to see our culture exploit physical games in increasingly creative and Facebook-share-worthy ways.

The backbone of gamefication is game theory, which has four main components: the players, their actions, the payoffs, and the necessary information.

The **players** are the people who make decisions and are actually playing the game. But they're not the only people involved. There are also characters who don't decide anything. These passive characters are part of the environment (like a damsel in distress or a potential victim of the Zombie Apocalypse) and have to wait for the actual players to do something before they are affected in any way. There is a third category of characters called pseudo-players who have very limited decision-making ability. A pseudo-player might be something like Nature or another "triggered" character that only gets the chance to play once in a while and usually follows strict rules (i.e. roll the dice to determine if Nature has a lightning storm, an ice storm, or does nothing).

The **actions** are the different things the players can do when it's their turn. There are usually only two or three actions available, but every player gets to do something.

The **payoffs** are the big mechanic in game theory. They're the reason some games are super fun and others are terribly dull. Payoffs are, of course, the reward the players receive for choosing smart actions that benefit their characters. In

Monopoly, you receive $200 every time you pass "GO." You get buckets of cash if someone lands on Park Place and you've erected a hotel.

Finally, the **information** in a game is the basic stuff you need to know in order to advance the storyline or win the overall contest.

Here's why I think this matters: if we apply game theory as a rubric to evaluate church, our services (and programs and missional endeavors) are the worst games ever. And, in a culture that's currently gamefying everything, that's going to be a bigger and bigger problem as time goes on.

Who are the **players** in church? You might think the members of the congregation, but you'd be wrong. At best, the congregation consists of pseudo-players who get to choose whether to sing, pay attention, or give money. But if we're honest, we'd have to acknowledge that most people at church are passive characters. They wait for the pastor to say something that affects them. They watch while the people on stage worship, in hopes they can benefit from a little spill-over. In order for church to matter, we have to figure out how to get our people in the game. They have to be given opportunities to make choices, to take risks, and to have some control over what happens to their spirits and how.

This leads us to consider the **actions** our people are permitted in their spiritual pursuits. I'd guess most people still think about behavior modification when they think about Christian spirituality—they're still trying to figure out how to sin less and pray more. To be clear, there's nothing wrong with either of those things. However, when we limit our spirituality to a series of DOs and DON'Ts, we're on a track to boredom, frustration, and lifelessness. Our actions must increasingly include things like initiative—trying significant, passion-driven,

risk-intense, forays into personal ministry—experimentation—
going against the norm, changing our routines, and delving
into unfamiliar-though-orthodox means of knowing God—
and investment—giving sacrificially of ourselves, our expertise,
our finances, and our attention to people and projects that may
only interest us.

Initiative, experimentation, and investment come with inherent
payoffs. However, most Christians seem comically limited
in their ability to think about spiritual rewards. We tend to
think of either "going to heaven when you die" or "getting a
bigger mansion in heaven so when you die you can enjoy the
view." Again, these aren't sinful ways to think about spiritual
rewards, but they're not helpful, either. Scripture promises a
host of rewards in the here-and-now: happiness, love, meaning,
a sense of contribution, intimacy with God, the fulfillment
of cherished hopes and dreams, meaningful relationships,
and provocative personal experience. By focusing on narrow
actions—DOs and DON'Ts—we limit our available rewards
to things that only happen later on, provided we don't screw
up in the meantime. When we expand what we're allowed to
do, we also expand what we receive. The only way we'll get
to experience even the possibility of fulfilling our cherished
hopes and dreams is by taking initiative. Experimenting with
new ways to pray or new ways to read Scripture is the only
way we'll stay fresh in our spirit, and it's a great way to ensure
our personal experiences with God are both more frequent
and more intimate. The only way our relationships deepen is
if we invest in others—otherwise, we all sit around waiting for
someone else to make the investment, and the long-term result
is a culture of entitlement, victimization, and malaise.

We, as churches, haven't given our people the opportunity to
make decisions that pay off in the here-and-now, and as a

result Christianity in the Western world often deteriorates into doctrine, dogma, and behavior modification.

Which brings me to the final game component, **information**. In a game, the information you're given moves the story along and teaches you how to win. But in church, the information we most often receive is only given so we "do it right," "say it right," or "get it right." We're taught the creeds, the core doctrines, and the most pertinent scriptures that will ensure we become nicer. But the information we need—the information we really crave—is the stuff about how we draw closer to God, how we hear the Spirit more clearly, how we're wired spiritually, and how to best govern our habits and peculiarities and inoculate ourselves against our own personal temptations, how we show and express love, how we enter into and enjoy community, etc.

In short, we need information about us and our relationships with God, other people, and the world. Most Christian teaching expounds facts about God. But we need less facts and more "marriage counseling" so we can get along with our heavenly spouse.

The church of the future will recognize that this, after all, is the game we're meant to play: finding meaningful ways to ensure our people are active in ministry, given the opportunity to interact with the world and to experience the benefits of knowing God through any medium, device, or engagement.

Play. On.

> *In what healthy ways has new media enhanced your relationship with Christ?*

FOUR. THREE

SCIENCE

HEALING THE RIFT BETWEEN THINKING AND BELIEVING

When I consider your heavens, the work of your
fingers, the moon and the stars which you have set in
place, what is mankind that you are mindful of them,
human beings that you care for them?
- Psalm 8.3-4, NIV

> *Science is God's prophet, not his competition.*

The church of the future will press aggressively into the overlap between science and technology, recognizing that every new discovery and every new advancement is a manifestation of our obedience to the cultural mandate.[60]

The perceived gap between science and faith has shrunk to almost nothing. This may not be true in the public consciousness, but it's absolutely true for the two biggest groups of people that matter: theologians and scientists.

Galileo was famously convicted of heresy by the Roman Catholic Church in 1633AD for his support of heliocentrism. It's an embarrassment to all people of faith, and the church has since worked hard to atone for the foolhardiness of our forebears. Whether through the writings of people like John Polkinghorne, twin PhD in theology and astrophysics, or Francis Collins, leader of the Human Genome Project, or Dennis Venema, expert geneticist, scientific Christians now know and have confidence that their work matters to God. They don't shy away from difficult questions and they won't be ostracized, illegitimized, or martyred like they were in the past.

Some of our greatest theologians have also been remarkable scientists, like Pierre Teilhard de Chardin[61]—a Jesuit priest who lived in the early 20th century and helped discover the Peking Man, an important fossil that demonstrates the process of evolution as it especially concerns Chinese ancestry.

> Science alone cannot discover Christ. But Christ satisfies the yearnings that are born in our hearts in the school of science ... Science will, in all probability, be

---

[60] Genesis 1.28 NIV "Be fruitful and increase in number; fill the earth and subdue it. Rule over the fish in the sea and the birds in the sky and over every living creature that moves on the ground."

[61] "Pierre Teilhard de Chardin," *Wikipedia,* https://en.wikipedia.org/wiki/Pierre_Teilhard_de_Chardin, accessed August 18, 2017.

> increasingly impregnated by mysticism.
> - Pierre Teilhard de Chardin[62]

Chardin was an outspoken and opinionated rogue, a philosopher, geologist and paleontologist. He developed extensively the concept of the noosphere, commonly referred to as "the life of the mind." Chardin believed that human history was rushing forward to a final climatic consummation with Christ, in which the Cosmic Christ would finally be all and be in all things.

> Christ has a cosmic body that extends throughout the universe.
> - *Cosmic Life*, 1916

Chardin believed every living thing had some essential spark, some élan *vital*, that made it worthy of respect and also that it had a key role to play in the eschatological reconciliation of Creation with Creator. He was also an evolutionary theologian, one of the first among Church leaders to not only embrace the theory of evolution but also use that theory to speak about the natural processes through which God was working to heal the world.

> By virtue of creation, and still more the incarnation, nothing here is profane for those who know how to see.
> - *The Divinisation of Our Activities*

You don't have to agree with Chardin in order to appreciate the way he blended his scientific beliefs with his biblical understanding. I certainly don't, though I am often awed by his ability to hold two seemingly opposite perspectives in perfect

---

[62]   Teilhard de Chardin, Pierre, *My Universe*, 1924, IX, 83.

tension, and to use that tension as a catapult into an entirely new way of thinking.

> Love is the only force which can make things one without destroying them. ... Some day, after mastering the winds, the waves, the tides and gravity, we shall harness for God the energies of love, and then, for the second time in the history of the world, man will have discovered fire.
> -Chardin[63]

The church of the future will perceive "all truth as God's truth, regardless of where it is found,"[64] encouraging her people to investigate, innovate, and discover more about God's Creation without feeling threatened by what she might learn.

Who do you know that needs to be encouraged in their scientific pursuits?

---

[63] Chardin, as quoted in *Seed Sown: Theme and Reflections on the Sunday Lectionary Reading* by Jay Cormier (1996), 33.

[64] Guinness, Os, *Fit Bodies Fat Minds: Why Evangelicals Don't Think and What to Do About It.*

FOUR.FOUR

SPACE

BECOMING MISSIONARIES TO MARS

Behold, I am doing a new thing; now it springs
forth, do you not perceive it? I will make a way in the
wilderness and rivers in the desert.
- Isaiah 43.19, ESV

New discoveries will both require and inspire new theological reflections.

One significant technology the church has failed to explore theologically is space travel. Consider that we have had the technology to live on Mars for decades, and with the advent of privatized exploration endeavors like SpaceX and Mars One, it is increasingly certain that human beings will live on Mars in our lifetime.[65]

> If everyone isn't talking about our journey to Mars at the dinner table, I want to change that ... [that means] leading the agency's 18,000 employees and 40,000 contractors toward a successful crewed mission to Mars by the 2030s.
> - Heather Hansman[66]

The Sparrow and *Children of God* are a pair of novels by Mary Doria Russell that tell of a Jesuit astronaut and his troubled missionary endeavors in space. I was reluctant to read the stories at first, imagining them to be too try-hard to be interesting, but found them riveting. Among the many merits of these books stands the characterization of Emilio Sandoz, whose work as a linguist uniquely qualifies him for making first contact with a new species. He does not seek to convert, only to befriend. Sandoz is a child of a single mother, put up for adoption, and yet has complex dialogues with other churchmen about issues like abortion and stem cell research. He is a man of learning, enraptured in belief, and a healthy model for curious, scientific, Christians.

Of course we should not be surprised at the reconciliation between faith and science. After all, the Bible is not a scientific book. And the reason some perceive a conflict between science and faith isn't because they don't know enough about science,

---

[65] Venton, Danielle, "A Timeline of US Missions to Mars," *Wired Magazine*, October 2015, 64.

[66] Hansman, Heather, "Dava Newman on getting people to Mars in one piece," *Popular Science*, September 2015, 32.

but because they don't know enough about the Bible. The more intensely we study the scriptures, the more we'll come to know and understand that scripture is our starting place, not the repository of all final answers. The Bible is our root soil, our fertilizer[67], not our decoder ring. The Bible fills us with nutrients and energy, providing intellectual and moral and relational fuel for our healthy wellbeing and development. But there will be an increasing number of issues upon which the Bible is silent and for which we must craft our own responses. Our Christian responses must be formed *with* the Bible, rather than *from* the Bible, since—again—the Bible simply will not tell us what to do about galactic exploration, cloning, or colonizing other planets.

We must decide for ourselves.

This, I think, may be part of what is commonly overlooked in Jesus' instruction that "whatever [we] bind on earth will be bound in heaven, and whatever [we] loose on earth will be loosed in heaven."[68] The expressions "bind" and "loose" were Jewish legal phraseology determining something forbidden or allowed. This is not just the authority to determine if we have sinned, but to determine what practical things are permitted or prevented. We're not changing God's Law (do not commit adultery) but we are telling people how to apply it (be cautious with your relationships lest you develop unhealthy romantic attachments). Like the Jerusalem council in Acts 15, believers can bind and loose the application of Law. We bind it tighter (women must cover their head) when the people need tighter guardrails and we loose it (drink a beer) when Christian freedom can be expressed.[69]

---

[67] See Brueggeman, Walter. *Texts Under Negotiation.*

[68] Matthew 18.18.

[69] See also https://www.gotquestions.org/binding-loosing.html.

The church of the future will perceive scripture as our constant conversation partner. Her people will be reading the Bible, studying the Bible, talking over the Bible, considering the Bible, inferring new conclusions and implications based on the stories and characters of the Bible. We will consider the Bible our intellectual and moral spouse, our "better half" without whom we can make no healthy determinations, but who is unable to offer a clear position on some issues. And during those times when the scripture offers no clear guidance for, say, how to colonize space, we will hold the Bible firmly in one hand and extend an open grasp to the future.

Can you think of other contemporary concerns where the Bible is silent and we must use our best judgment about how to proceed?

FOUR.FIVE

ANDROIDS

WRITING A CATECHISM FOR ROBOTS

Once you were not a people, but now you are the people of God; once you had not received mercy, but now you have received mercy.
-1 Peter 2.10, NIV

> *Technology will increasingly affect sociology and anthropology, and the Church is better primed to help the world answer these new questions than anyone else.*

It doesn't take a great imagination to realize there will be entirely new kinds of life on earth in the next hundred years. Some new life will be entirely artificial, and we will always wonder if they are "truly" alive. Some new life will relocate the old into the new, and we will always wonder if that's "still them."[70] Some new life will be hybridizations; like, perhaps, the offspring of two androids, or the descendants of an artificially inseminated clone.[71]

My point is that **there are people currently making people**. For example, investors put almost $170 million into robotics startups in 2014, and an unprecedented 25 robots competed in the $3.5 million Darpa Robotics Challenge Finals in 2015."[72] Given that this is a reality, we ought to consider what the robot-world means for us and whether our faith has any bearing on the spiritual wellbeing and cultivation of new people.

I think, clearly, it does.

Historically, the Church has most often interacted with new people in exploitative and hostile ways (the indigenous people of North America, for example, or the Australian aborigines and nationals of India). But, where other human peoples had moral and relational paradigms to guide them, technologically new people ('teleosapiens') would be cognitively and historically un-storied. They would have no gods or laws to curb their baser impulses. They will come into the world having been created by men, and men are corrupt. Consider, then, what might happen if the first generation of new people only ever experience hatred and fear from the Christian

---

[70] Vlahos, James, "A Son's Quest to save his Dying Father through Artificial Immortality." *Wired*, August 2017, 56.
[71] See Diamandis, Peter H. and Steven Kotler, *Abundance: The Future is Better Than You Think*, 159, for a quick overview.
[72] Patel, Neel V. "The Guide: Robot vs. Robot", *Wired*, June 2015, 43.

Church. What would happen if they are forced to rely solely on the wisdom and virtue of those who wrote their programming? By and large, such programmers are "antisocial people"[73] who "can reimagine the world in code, but lack the soft skills and everyday experience to relate to people they're serving," which means they will not possess the ability to offer appropriate ethics, virtue, or moral reasoning.

The church of the future must be willing to acknowledge the possibility that new people are alive, that they have souls, and that they must be treated with dignity, respect, and honor. Not necessarily because teleosapiens are human, but because we are.

> The future is more beautiful than all the pasts.
> - Pierre Teilhard de Chardin[74]

The issue of where our soul comes from has been on the table with differing kinds of new people for much longer than we might assume. Monozygotic (identical) twins, for example, occur when a single fertilized ovum splits during the early stages of embryonic development and forms two separate fetuses. One of the reasons cloning has become so controversial[75] in the last several decades is because the same biological process occurs in many cloning procedures, except that the zygote is intentionally split in a controlled laboratory environment rather than naturally in utero.[76] But in both the case of monozygotic twins and laboratory cloning, the two

---

[73] Thurston, Baratunde, "Tech Needs a Hug," *Fast Company*, December 2014/January 2015, 148.
[74] de Chardin, Pierre Teilhard, Letter (5 September 1919), in *The Making of a Mind: Letters from a Soldier-Priest 1914–1919*.
[75] See https://scholarblogs.emory.edu/philosophy316/2014/01/27/twinning-versus-cloning/.
[76] See http://www.differencebetween.net/science/difference-between-twins-and-clones/.

resulting human beings carry the same phenotype (observable characteristics of a living being) and genotype (genetic makeup). No one has ever questioned whether twins have a soul, so it is reasonable to assert that clones might also have souls, given that the biological process is the same.

And what "is" a soul? In Genesis we're told God breathed his breath into Adam, thereby imbuing him with a soul. The soul wasn't innate to Adam, but implanted. Yet Adam's soul was mysteriously passed onto Eve, who then birthed new people with souls already intact. Doesn't this, at least, leave room for the possibility that the souls of new people could likewise be implanted, perhaps through a process like zygote-splitting? New people, once simply robots, would be like idols that come to life.

This, incidentally, is the literal meaning of *imago dei*: we are idols of God's.

Genesis tells us God made humanity in God's image and likeness. That word "image" (*tselem*) can also be translated "idol."[77] The many prohibitions in scripture against idolatry are concerned with those who reduce God to a little wooden statue. But God intends to enhance his imagery, rather than allow people to reduce his divinity; consequently, God wants idols that move and think and can act independently. And it is that independence with which God first marks human distinctiveness. With consciousness comes agency, and with agency comes responsibility; and God works in his people through conscious, responsible action.

---

[77] Hebrew, *tselem*: a phantom, i.e. (figuratively) illusion, resemblance; hence, a representative figure, especially an idol -- image, vain show. *tselem, Strong's Concordance* 6754, http://biblehub.com/hebrew/6754.htm, accessed August 18, 2017.

Could God also do this with other new people? Is there a better word than "soul" for the self-aware, morally-conscionable, aesthetically-driven choices of teleosapiens?

If we engage the possibility that clones have souls, then we must also acknowledge that human beings can make other human beings through means distinct from "the natural path." And if humans can create souls, we must also wonder if humans have the ability to create souls in non-human things as well.

Can we meld quantum physics and metaphysics? Can we put a soul into a robot? A vehicle? A mechanical pet?

I first had this conversation with a close friend more than a decade ago, and she was deeply disturbed by what she perceived to be impish arrogance on my part. I was hypothesizing then that new people will exist within my lifetime and that they ought to be welcomed into our churches and into our faith. I made the assertion that they will have souls and be made *imago dei*, on the basis that anything we make as image-bearers of God has God's fingerprints upon it, since we work to perpetuate God's original Creation.

My friend disputed my logic, claiming that by this line of reasoning a nuclear warhead must have God's fingerprint, also; but here I agree with futurist Kevin Kelly. Our creations are blemished, but our creative capacity, overall, is "a positive force, a positive charge of good. And that good is primarily measured in terms of the possibilities and choices it presents us with."[78]

---

[78] Katelyn Beaty, "Geek Theologian," *Christianity Today* Interview, July 15, 2011, http://www.christianitytoday.com/ct/2011/julyweb-only/geektheologian.html, accessed August 18, 2017.

I maintain our cooperative work with God entails perpetuating what God began in the garden, which was unfinished at the end of the seven-day Creation cycle.[79] By design, the garden was a starting point, and human beings are meant to keep the earth growing in wonder and complexity, innovation and change.

This has startling implications. Many ethical debates have centered around "when human life begins" *in utero*, but the church of the future will also wrestle with when "human life begins" *ex technium* (through science and technology), just as she must engage when human life might cease to retain its humanity.[80]

Our humanity is revealed in the way we treat others. As Bishop Desmond Tutu famously stated, "A person is a person through

---

[79] Otherwise why would we need to "tend it and till ?" To "fill it and subdue it'?" To "be fruitful and multiply?"

[80] Is it possible, for example, that new people will have the *imago dei* by proxy? "[I am working on a catechism for robots because] We are made in the image of God; God is a creator, and God created free-will beings. So, I believe we will create free-will beings in the form of robots. And I believe they will have increasing degrees of autonomy. We will need to educate them about the difference between good and evil, about who made them (and who made us), what to do when they do something wrong. And at some point, one of them will come to us and say, "I am a child of God." When [that happens], how will we respond? Does Jesus' salvation cover them? This is a question I've been asking theologians. They shrug their shoulders. When we begin to make robots, I think the secular scientific world will appreciate what Christians have been talking about for a long time. If you make something with its own purpose, you need to give it moral guidance. If you give it moral guidance, what values are you going to give it? Teaching technology is like teaching children. At the point we make autonomous robots, Christians can step forward and say, "We know about this.". . . It will take every possible type of invented mind to even begin to appreciate the greatness and mystery of God. Our human minds alone are so limited. We need others who "think different." See Geek Theologian, *Christianity Today* Interview by Katelyn Beaty | posted 7/15/2011 09:52AM.

other persons." And the evolution of teleosapienism will require us to rethink the boundaries of goodness and morality.

The first ethical issue we'll need to resolve is slavery. Why? Because people are making sex-robots, and the edge of innovation in teleosapienism is the desire for a better orgasm.[81] But what happens when those new people gain self-awareness? What happens when they learn their only use is abuse at the hands of those who cannot function healthily with others?

What will happen when new people learn their creators are perverts?

This begins, but does not exhaust, the new arena of consideration for the Church. The renewal of all things has suddenly become far more complex!

Human beings, generally, are dysfunctional. We take pleasure in ridicule and celebrate the exploitation of others. We're greedy. We're sick. But God won't give up on his vision for humanity, so neither can we. Christ is the Prototype who has shown us how great humanity can be, and the church of the future will recognize her people have been made by God to be like God,

---

[81] In 2007's 'Love and Sex with Robots', artificial intelligence expert David Levy predicted that by 2050 'love with robots will be as normal as love with other humans.' He even predicts that Massachusetts will be the first state to legalize marriage to robots. Stowe Boyd, M.S., a futurist and analyst of emerging technologies, went even further, claiming in a 2014 Pew Research Center report that by 2025 'robotic sex partners will be commonplace, although the source of scorn and derision, the way critics today bemoan selfies as an indicator of all that's wrong with the world.'…Doug Hines, the founder and president of True Companion, expects that even before the end of this year, we could have commercially available robot partners that don't just submit to sexual fantasies but also offer 'unconditional love and support.'… The sex robots of today aren't especially tempting. But the sex robots of tomorrow might just embody everything you want from a woman." See Eric Spitznagel, "The Sex Robots Are Coming," *Men's Health*, June 2016, 147.

which entails that we treat new people like those who "were once not a people, but are now the people of God."[82]

> *How do you imagine you would react to teleosapiens in the church?*

---

[82] 1 Peter 2.10.

FIVE

WE SEE A CHURCH

that **CELEBRATES** TALENT, PASSION, *and* SKILL;

that **PERCEIVES** PERFORMANCE *as a* CONDUIT OF FAITH,
not a **COUNTERFEIT MANIFESTATION** *of* WORSHIP;

a church **COMMITTED** *to* CONTENT CREATION *and* RESOURCE DISTRIBUTION, *where* **ARTIFACTS, EVENTS,** *and* **INITIATIVES** EMBODY THE GOSPEL.

FIVE.ONE

CREATIVITY

ACKNOWLEDGING THE LIMITS OF OUR CAPACITY (AND CELEBRATING THEM, TOO)

All the nations you have made will come and worship before you, Lord; they will bring glory to your name.
- Psalm 86.9, NIV

All creativity is derivative.

Aesthetics has to do with the experience and perception of reality that we associate with imagination, including: metaphor and symbolism, games and playfulness, design and interface. Aesthetics is about more than "art." It is about perceiving reality through ways other than rational enquiry or moral endeavor. Theological aesthetics is about faith seeking to understand reality from the perspective of God's beauty as revealed in both Creation and redemption.

Creativity is what we do with what we've been given after we've digested, processed, and absorbed all the good we can for our souls. That's why I think the best biblical image to shape our understanding of creativity is dung.

Consider that dung is what's leftover after the body uses everything it can. It is messy, fetid, and undesirable. The prophets made exceptional use of dung. Ezekiel, for example, was commanded to cook with dung[83] as a sign that God considered Israel's worship unworthy. The flesh, skin, and dung of a sacrificial animal were discarded outside the camp as a sin offering meant to signify purification.[84] There were occasions where dung was used as currency,[85] much like art is traded today. Several of the most provocative stories in scripture involve God destroying his enemies, making them into dung, which then becomes fertilizer from which new beauty grew.[86]

This image of "divine fertilizer" is especially rich, telling us that God destroys old and lifeless things, so new things might spring from their expiration.

Is there application for us here? Is it possible some old things in our churches have been destroyed precisely so new things

---

[83] Ezekiel 4.12-14.
[84] Exodus 29.14; Leviticus 4.11.
[85] 2 Kings 6.25.
[86] Jeremiah 8.2, 9.22, 16.4, 25.33; Nahum 3.6.

could grow? And by "old" I don't only mean traditional—though there are certainly some traditions that qualify—but un-sanctified, un-refined, un-consecrated acts of half-hearted worship?

In Luke 13.6-9, Jesus curses a fig tree for being fruitless, but after the farmer begs for one more year, promising to fertilize, Jesus relents, with the caveat that the tree had better produce. Maybe that's the current situation with the Western Church. Producing no fruit, but begging God to give us a chance with the fertilizer of our best creativity. So God says "sure, but it's gotta grow, for if there's no fruit *even with fertilizer,* then the tree has to come down."

What if this is our last chance before we sunset Christianity in the West?

> Why do flowers grow in manure?
> - Robert LePage[87]

It is, of course, crass to refer to the noble work of creating with God as "dung," but I find it's a useful reminder not to become too enamored with our own genius. Because all creativity is derivative. Whenever we create, we are bringing forth new things out of already-existing materials after we have absorbed them, digested them, worked them over, and then spun them out.

One word of caution: creativity, though godly, can be robbed of its inherent holiness if we become infatuated with it. Consider the story in 2 Kings 18.27 about men eating their own dung and drinking their own urine. It poisons them. Similarly, we can be poisoned if we become infatuated with our own originality.

---

[87]   LePage, Robert, *Connecting Flights*, 85.

Nevertheless, our "dung" can be beautiful, good, and true…so long as we don't swallow it.

This is why Thomist philosophers developed the Three Transcendentals of Being as an adjudication of beauty, truth, and goodness.

- How do you know if something is true? If it's beautiful and good.
- How do you know if something is beautiful? If it's good and true.
- How do you know if something is good? If it's beautiful and true.

The Church in the West has been woefully disinterested in goodness (other than personal piety) and beauty (other than songs about heaven and paintings of warm cottages), and truth (other than theological propositions).

We've forgotten that beauty has a revelatory component. Gone are the days when the Church was both patron and purchaser of the Arts. We no longer want great art for fear that it may distract people from the Truth—but I contend that there is Truth in Art, deep Truths that reveal who we are, both alone and together as children of God.

We claim to be the purveyors of deep mystery and spiritual wholeness, yet we never seem to talk about mystery or mysticism or the invisible world. We talk instead about a kind of bland behaviorism, reinforced with archaic, convoluted dogma and stern faces. We have been choking on the truth rather than imagining the image of our invisible God and dreaming about his designs for redemption.

Louis Markos, an English scholar dedicated to studying the works of C.S. Lewis, outlines the real purpose of an artist.

Markos maintains that our chief aim is to connect our world to another, invisible world that better highlights true aesthetics. But this "beautiful" world isn't perfect. Like Narnia or Middle-Earth, the beauty is imperiled and protagonists are summoned to defend it. As they do, we are invited to "rejoice with and suffer with those creatures in an act of sympathetic imagination."[88]

The church of the future will press into her creative capacity, knowing that the most powerful forces in the universe are invisible—will, intention, imagination, love, spirit, and ambition.

> It's not the trees that move the wind, it's the wind that moves the trees.
> - GK Chesterton[89]

In what ways do you resonate with the idea of creativity as "dung"?

---

[88] Markos, Louis, *Lewis Agonistes: How C.S. Lewis Can Train Us to Wrestle with the Modern and Postmodern World.*

[89] Chesterton, G.K., "The Wind and the Trees," http://www.online-literature.com/chesterton/tremendous-trifles/12/, accessed August 22, 2017.

FIVE.TWO

EXCELLENCE

OFFERING GOD OUR BEST

Moreover, there are many workmen with you,
stonecutters and masons of stone and carpenters, and
all men who are skillful in every kind of work. Of the
gold, the silver and the bronze and the iron there is no
limit. Arise and work, and may the Lord be with you.
- 1 Chronicles 22.15-16, NASB

> *Performance can be worship when we attune our hearts to God.*

The old adage "practice makes perfect" is better rendered "practice makes permanent" because we practice the way we perform. If we practice half-heartedly, with little focus and energy, then we have lesser reserves and greater nervousness for the real thing, as though our work only becomes "real" when there exists the possibility of applause. But worship is designed for an audience of One, so God must enjoy our preparation-as-worship equal to our performance-as-worship, since God is present in both venues.

I know why people are skeptical of "performance." I've been to church services and Christian events where the leaders and organizers enjoyed the limelight too much, where they spoke of God but the audience got the feeling the ones on stage were the ones eager for praise. It's nauseating.

But it's also uncommon.

We think it's more prevalent than it is precisely because it's so off-putting, but when I think critically about the thousands of gatherings I've attended, I can only find about a dozen examples where someone let their ego get in the way. That's a pretty good ratio.

On the flip side, nearly every time I've attended an event with Christians, my companions have expressed concern about "performance" either beforehand, during, or afterwards. That means we're going into these events with the expectation that someone will probably let their ego run rampant, even though our experiences should be sufficient proof they will not.

Doesn't that say something about us? About our desire to judge? About our proclivity for damning those with the courage to lead?

Isn't it possible that our willingness to sit in judgment is demonstrative of an even more insidious pride than the showboat worship leader or self-satisfied preacher?

Many of us understand the importance of excellence. We know that great music, for example, will attract a crowd and that environment will allow people to experience healthy celebration. And while there are undoubtedly those who push this to the extreme—who judge and shame poor performances, who put such pressure on artists and technicians that they are robbed of their joy—in the great majority of instances this balance is well-kept and, more importantly, the orientation of our ambition is well-placed.

When we do anything, and we do it with everything we have, that's worship. Whenever I empty the tank, squeeze out the rag, and leave myself a quivering smear on the floor, that's worship. So I exhaust myself in readiness, not only so I'm prepared but also to increase my work capacity. I know if I push myself to the limit now, my limits will continue to expand. This expansion is worship. It's how God "enlarges my territory."[90]

Great performance is great worship. God enjoys music we have rehearsed, prepared, written, agonized over, and meticulously arranged more than music we just play. Did you catch that? If not, let me repeat it: God likes it better when we try.

> It's troubling how homogenized, uniform, similar, stream-lined, and packaged our corporate worship has become in the church world. It's an assembly line. It's Costco. It's IKEA. It's clip art.
> - John Voelz[91]

---

[90] 1 Chronicles 4.10.
[91] Voelz, John, *Quirky Leadership*, 124.

The prophet Malachi adamantly contended for the purest, most exceptional offerings. He reprimanded God's people for offering diseased animals as sacrifices, demonstrating that anytime we give God something less than our absolute best we dishonor God and ourselves.[92]

> Great design implies a level of care, and care comes with some overtones of safety and security. In many ways, it resembles love.
> - Tom Barlow[93]

Westwinds brings old and new together, merging technology and sacrament. We measure success based on the level of participation, not the quality of our performance; we never repeat an experience; and we help people encounter God, playfully. This is neither flawless nor effortless. We have had more misfires, mishaps and liturgical disasters than could easily be catalogued, but the adventures are worth it.

Our philosophy of ministry rises from our core convictions about what it means to be human beings made in the image of our Creator; about what worship is, and who is invited into it, and how that invitation manifests across the spectrum; about work and industry and generativity; about love and faithfulness, community and pedagogy.

The church of the future will worship with the conviction that failure to invest is an insult to both God and ourselves, for when we half-ass it, we demean God's image.

Do you always offer God your best?

---

[92] Micah 1.8.
[93] Barlow, Tom, "Why Design Matters," *How Design*, May 2014, 60.

FIVE.THREE

HEART

DEVOTING OURSELVES ENTIRELY TO WORSHIP

It is God who reveals the profound and hidden things;
He knows what is in the darkness, and the light dwells
with Him.
- Daniel 2.22, NASB

God honors our hearts, and monitors them.

One of our most foolish conceits is the belief that God prefers campfire worship to the lights and lasers of a Sunday morning. This may, sometimes, be true; but not because the campfire is unprepared and unrehearsed. God appreciates the spontaneity and simple purity of campfire worship. It may even be possible that God is the one who sponsors the impulse to pick up the guitar and begin singing. It's unrefined and honest, and therein lies its true worth.

But we cannot take the campfire to a Sunday morning and expect the same experience at scale.

Why not?

Because all the variables have changed. At the campfire, you were surprised to find yourself slung into grace, wooed into God's presence. But on a Sunday, you've had all week to prepare (and you didn't), days and days to pray and study the Word in order to purify your motives (which you avoided), and now you show up and hope God honors your simplicity? Because, all of a sudden, you're earnest?

No. A far more accurate scenario of "what God enjoys" would involve team members who begin every week, every day, with honest engagement of the Word and their hearts; who weave worship into every activity; who practice gratitude in all things; who invite the Spirit to change them and rejuvenate them daily; who wrestle their thoughts and desires toward their Father; who practice until their fingers bleed and their wrists get sore; who innovate and tinker and play and tease; who show up early and stay late; who laugh and pray and listen to one another; who ready their gear as well as their hearts; who arrive with charts despite the fact that they had them memorized days in advance; who offer to help the sound techs with their final free moments; who clean up coffee cups and old sheet music because they perceive the auditorium to be holy ground.

That's worship.

The church of the future will be filled with people who praise God before anyone else shows up, and then perform at their optimum once the liturgy begins.

How can you weave worship into every activity, honoring God?

FIVE.FOUR

MEDIOCRITY

A CALL TO RISE ABOVE WHAT'S ACCEPTABLE

Everyone who competes in the games goes into strict
training. They do it to get a crown that will not last,
but we do it to get a crown that will last forever.
- 1 Corinthians 9.25, NIV

We do everything with excellence and care.

We must work hard for our best to become better. Because even if the things we create are not as professional or as mainstream or as polished as those of the pros, they're ours. They represent what God is doing in our community. They are localized to our people. And when we offer all we have and all we are, regardless of how good our best efforts are in comparison to someone else's, God accepts our gifts as our best.

The creative process is one of the ways God refines us. We are discipled as we iterate and refine our craft. God shows us how we get better, and we draw closer to God through that process, also.

Consider the story of Cain and Abel. Without instruction or provocation, Abel offered the best of what he had. Cain simply brought an offering in order to fulfill an obligation. God was pleased with Abel. Cain, on the other hand, was derided. Could there be anything worse than bringing an expensive, time-consuming, gift of devotion and having God scoff because deep down, you didn't put your heart in it?

And that's why, whenever we do whatever we do, we ought to do it with pride. Pride is such a dirty word in church. We think it means "ego." It does. It can. But it can also refer to dignity, excellence, and care.

I've been in church long enough to know there are people who do things for God because they love God and eagerly desire to worship with the fullness of their being. And there are people who think they're doing God a favor and want to fulfill an obligation.

Is it any wonder who does better work?

149

One of the saddest things to witness is someone who will not bother brushing their teeth or changing out of their pajamas when they go to the store for groceries. I had never seen this until I was in my thirties, when I was confronted by a severely overweight woman in her middle-years shuffling through the grocery store wearing only one slipper. Her hair was like a birds' nest and her teeth like cobs of corn. You may think I'm trying to be funny, but I remember feeling an overwhelming sadness because it was apparent she had lost the base-level dignity of being made in the image of God.

Is this the "pride" of which we're all so afraid?

I remember a guitar player at our church who had shown up late on a Sunday unprepared. He didn't know his music. He had to borrow some cables and batteries so his gear would work. During worship, he played several wrong notes and was noticeably out of sync with the rest of the team. At the end, somewhat abashed, he told me, "Oh well. It's just church."

Is he any different than the sad-looking lady at the grocery store? Or is his pride the sin we should be warned against—the arrogance of assuming the church ought to put up with laziness, failure, and distraction because you're doing God a favor?

Is this why so many churches struggle with low-quality music and the arts? Because we have lowered the bar? Because we have cultured mediocrity? Because we have deceived ourselves into thinking that accepting compliments for exceptional effort and preparation is tantamount to Satan's jealous rebellion? Because we are begging for volunteers and so must accept anyone eager to step on any stage for any reason, forcing the amateur alongside the professional, who now feels as though their time and talent are being disdained?

But the church of the future will not settle for giving God her unfinished, unkempt, un-stewarded offerings. She will enjoy the process of preparation as much as the experience of giving an offering, and recognize God's pleasure in both directions.

Is there an area in your life where you feel like you're "doing God favors?"

FIVE.FIVE

AUDIENCE

LEARNING WHY PEOPLE DON'T LIKE WHAT WE MAKE

When I consider your heavens, the work of your
fingers, the moon and the stars which you have set in
place, what is mankind that you are mindful of them,
human beings that you care for them?
-Psalm 8.3-4, NIV

Art must always consider its audience.

I am regularly asked to evaluate other churches' creative ideas. I enjoy this work, and do my best to encourage others, but there are some common missteps worth elucidating.

So, why don't people better appreciate your work?

1. **It's folksy.** Most of our art is the work of amateurs, and we get into trouble when we demand our congregations appreciate them as masterpieces. We tell our people "a great artist made this" and when they fail to be impressed, we lose credibility.

2. **It's too obscure.** No one understands what the work is supposed to mean or why it's supposed to matter. And, because artists are often very sensitive about their work, we're not prepared to deal with the knee-jerk reactions of a popular audience. As a result, we tend to become angry when audiences don't "get it" and immediately categorize them as cretinous children of an empty-headed culture whose only aesthetic sensibilities come from Target. But the truth is, our churches aren't made up of artists, and people need help understanding why art has value, how it should be appreciated, and what place it holds in the life of a congregation. If we don't help them think through these things, we can't very well expect them to arrive at substantive conclusions all on their own. We must prepare our artists for the possibility of misunderstanding, and prepare our congregations for their need to interpret the work critically. We also ought to set expectations that ensure artists don't give themselves permission to disconnect their commission from their congregation. All our work is both of, and for, the people as much as it is the Lord.

3. **It doesn't connect with scripture, Jesus, or the gospel.** You'll enjoy life more if you can remove confusion from the majority of your audience. That doesn't mean you need to explain every detail of your work, but give them something

to go on, perhaps in the title or with a short dedication. And not all art needs to either clarify scripture or focus on the biography of Jesus; but when a Christians creates, there will be some manifestation of the fullest gospel—of the creation and redemption, the prophetic reimagining of the world—not to prove to an audience they are godly, but because the godliness of Christians cannot be hidden.

4. **It's self-indulgent.** Most art is therapy. There's nothing wrong with that, but if it's just a whimsical expression of your inner struggles, then don't put it on display. Nobody cares about an eight-minute piano lamentation, and we should not burden our congregations with a demand to appreciate what they cannot access. Few plumbers attend the ballet. Few football coaches settle in for a good poetry sesh. When we take a congregation and constrain them to appreciate art that has not been designed for their enjoyment, but ours, we create a "captive" audience, and they will increasingly chafe under our authority.

5. **It's got a short tail**. Art doesn't have to have a point, nor does it have to give direction for actionable progress. But we often get our feelings hurt when people like our art but not as much as we do or as much as we think they should. To protect ourselves against such disappointments, it's good to ask: *What am I hoping for with this display/experience/exhibit?* And then: *Are these actually the kind of people who might respond accordingly?* Chances are, they're not, so you have to accept their reaction and begin cultivating art appreciation over time so more people can better experience what you're offering.

We are God's apprentices. Like a Master Chef, God wants us to get hands-on with his ongoing Creation. Sadly, we are like children who tear the ingredients away, sullenly muttering "Let me do it." And God will let us. He will sit back and watch as we ruin the recipe, burning the bread and pouting at the smoldering mess we insisted on making alone. Until, eventually, God steps back in, reminding us we are not making things for ourselves but for God, and for the good of the world.

And so our teacher teaches us again. And again. Cautioning us against too much seasoning, chiding us for taking our eyes off the stove for too long.

This is as true with art as with life and all things in between.

The church of the future will encourage a robust theology of the arts and be able to explain why the things we love are also dear to God. She will acknowledge art is important, but it isn't obvious.

How is God teaching you to love and serve others through your creativity?

FIVE.SIX

CRAFTSMANSHIP

WORKING LIKE WE CARE

Let every skillful man among you come, and make all
that the Lord has commanded.
- Exodus 35.10, NASB

Abandon the pursuit of fame in favor of pursuing your craft.

Fame is a toxic pursuit. Fame itself may be neutral, but the pursuit of fame makes us anxious, furious, and insufferable. We're scared we won't make it, angry that someone else has, and too eager to explain the complexities to anyone foolish enough to ask about our career.

It's no secret that Christian art and music have become commercialized. The sad truth is there's only a market for the broad middle—in worship music, in literature, in teaching, etc. But rather than bemoan the broad middle, it's healthier to us if we abandon fame and pursue, instead, craftsmanship.

> I asked [my father] what craftsmanship was. He replied, "It's working like you care."
> - John Maeda[94]

After all, if you limit your exposure to what's available through the big outlets, you're only going to experience the generic, the bland, and the safe. But on the outskirts, there will always be risk-takers and innovators who are pursuing their interests, passions, and sanctified fantasies. Not only do we learn from these one-of-a-kind artifacts a much more expansive understanding of the gospel, but we see a model of what you can do with drive and ingenuity. This gives us permission to pursue our own passion-projects, in service to our own people, broadening the bandwidth for what's acceptable, useful, and meaningful. And just as others have provided these resources for us, we want to provide our resources for the wider world.

Print magazine ran a story about a group whose passion has driven them to self-publish, but they aren't writers. They're designers. They make image-rich coffee table books, fueled by their own creative conviction, simply because graphics and story matter that much to them.

---

[94] Maeda, John with Becky Bermont, *Redesigning Leadership*, 7.

> All our books are highly designed artifacts (but never
> at the expense of the content) and come with high
> production values.
> - Steven Heller[95]

I love the spirit of this work! I love the boldness and self-sufficiency of true artisans. Their work reminds me that some of my favorite books have also been the product of peripheral voices. Casey Treat's little book *Renewing the Mind*, for example, gave me a helpful framework for learning to govern my thoughts well in advance of ever visiting a therapist. Derek Webster's *The Abbot and the Dwarf* is a masterpiece of academic creativity. Rather than adding to the heap of inaccessible material on the Desert Fathers[96], Webster crafted bite-sized narratives about a fictional monk and his erstwhile companion that present timeless truth in clever puzzles. Rock and Roll Worship Circus released a bootleg recording of "See the Lord" that I listened to for hours and hours on a borrowed cassette. I still remember raising my hands at the kitchen table, alone, as God renewed my spirit.

There are many, many other amateur projects that have shaped and formed me, from *Habakkuk before Breakfast* (by Brian J. Walsh) to *Building a Discipleship Culture* (by Mike Breen); from "What Wondrous Love" (as covered by Ex Niliho on the Rain City Hymnal), to *A Thousand Churches in Abbotsford* (by Johnny Hughes); from *Confessions of an Ex-Cross Maker* (by E.K. Bailey) to *Leadership and Self-Deception* (by the Arbinger Institute).

None of these will ever be featured on the *New York Times* bestseller list. Most of these are available used for $0.01 on

---

[95]   Heller, Steven, "Building a book business", *Print*, October 2014, 27.
[96]   The Desert Fathers were early Christian hermits, ascetics, and monks who lived mainly in the Egyptian desert beginning around the third century AD.

Amazon, or via outlets like Noisetrade.com, but they are clever and inspiring and I have enjoyed them repeatedly.

What if that's what we're all meant to do? Not be famous or successful, but allow our creativity to bless and inspire others.

What if we're only a footnote, a spark, or a catalyst for our coworkers and congregants? What if God has tasked us to change the life of one person in the chairs or online?

What if that one person is you?

What if you were primed, such that no matter what I said, you heard it through the mouth of God and knew today was the day you were being called up from the ranks to make a difference?

What's stopping you?

SIX

WE SEE A CHURCH

that **ELEVATES** WOMEN *to the* HIGHEST OFFICES
as **EQUAL PARTNERS** *with* MEN,
SHADOWING GOD;

      that **PAIRS** SURROGATE PARENTS *and*
      GRANDPARENTS,
            MENTORS *and* REVERSE-MENTORS,
               so **EVERYONE** EXPERIENCES
               HEALTHY FAMILY AMONG *the*
               PEOPLE *of* GOD.

SIX.ONE

EGALITARIANISM

CREATING SPACE FOR FEMALE PASTORS

Jesus said to them, "Why are you bothering this woman? She has done a beautiful thing to me."
- Matthew 26.10, NIV

> *The biblical perspective on women was way ahead of its time, and in many ways is still ahead of ours.*

After an 8-month candidacy, I was finally invited to my first face-to-face at Westwinds. When I arrived, I drove straight to my first meeting, then slept for a few hours in a dirty motel before my second interview the following morning. I was in town for three days, had 11 appointments, and preached 5 times for a variety of audiences. Somewhere in there I met our Elders. Sometime during that meeting I learned Westwinds was complementarian and, concordantly, did not allow women to be pastors. I'd never heard the term before, and when they explained it to me, I laughed. "We'll need to change that right away," I said.

In my job interview.

Little did I know, there were godly people who felt as strongly about complementarianism as I did about equality. I forced the issue onto our monthly agenda for four years. At first, the conversation was confrontational. Over time, I learned not to push so hard and we resorted to studying the Bible slowly, asking honest questions—many of which I was unprepared to answer. I learned a great deal about leadership, exegesis, and faithfulness during that process. We kept notes on our dialogue and soon had a binder over 2 inches thick with arguments and explanations, counterpoints and scholarly references. After 46 months, we unanimously decided to change our position and allow women to the highest offices in our church.

In the middle of our journey, I remember several bloggers attacking us for our complementarian stance. There were six or seven blogs that mentioned myself and my co-pastors by name, calling us misogynists and citing our church constitution as an example of sexism in ministry. Most of our accusers were women. Several had applied for the job I was awarded and were embittered because they were not seriously considered.[97]

Those were strange days. I spent much of my time trying to graciously defend the reputation of our church concerning an issue with which I strongly disagreed. But you've gotta dance with the boy who brought you; and, for better or for worse, I was with Westwinds and fought hard to ensure my church wouldn't suffer unnecessarily.

The turning point occurred when Randy, one of my co-pastors, made a public appeal to the bloggers to be gracious with us because this was "an issue under consideration." That was the most we ever said. We never betrayed the fact that we disagreed with our own stance. We never joined in the cause of our accusers. We let ourselves be tarred and feathered along with everybody else because we were a team. Our accusers relented after several weeks of persistent complaint. Only one responded to Randy. She said, "It must be nice to have that luxury."

She was right. We did have that luxury. But her comment, made publicly, was seen by many and hurt our cause with the Elders as we worked to change our policy. One read it and said, "That's why women can't be pastors. They're petty."

I wish I could have been something other than an enemy for those bloggers. I wish I could have helped them. Maybe I'm not the right person. Maybe that's not the kind of relationship men can have with women. Maybe everything I would have offered would've deteriorated into mansplaining. I don't know. But if it were any other group hurting so badly with so much potential, I would offer to help just as quickly. I'd probably

---

[97] Side note: if you don't get a job you want, please avoid attacking your would-be employer on the Internet.

screw that one up, too. But maybe not, and maybe I could find a way to help them see that you can catch more flies with honey, even if it feels like they've been calling you honey for years.

I have written extensively about the Bible's elevation of women, their full inclusion in ministry, and their unique contributions to faith, family, and friendship. I have been called a feminist (and an idiot), a champion (and a cheat), and been thanked (and reviled) dozens upon dozens of times for my contributions in this regard. But I've never written anything other than what I think the scriptures advocate.

Of course, there are unique leadership challenges for women, but the church of the future will see women pastors who are more concerned about their calling than their gender. She will create an environment and an expectation where egalitarianism is the norm rather than the exception, where woman lead in either stilettos or Chuck Taylors, according to their personalities rather than their desire to avoid distraction.

What do you think would be the hardest part about being a female pastor?

SIX.TWO

WOMEN

ACKNOWLEDGING UNIQUELY FEMALE CONTRIBUTIONS TO MINISTRY

Many women were there, watching from a distance. They had followed Jesus from Galilee to care for his needs. Among them were Mary Magdalene, Mary the mother of James and Joseph, and the mother of Zebedee's sons.
- Matthew 27.55-56, NIV

Jesus had many female disciples who occupy a significant portion of the gospel narratives.

The business world is struggling to close the gender gap, both in compensation and promotion. The issue is routinely featured in *Forbes*, *Fast Company*, and the *Harvard Business Review*, and one common thread that emerges reveals many assume the chief obstacle to a woman's success is herself.

> At a certain point the belief that a woman's primary career obstacle is herself became conventional wisdom, for both women and men. From "opting out" to "ratcheting back", the ways we talk about women's careers often emphasize their willingness to scale down or forgo opportunities, projects, and jobs. The very premise seems to be that women value career less than men do, or that mothers don't want high-profile, challenging work. Yet framing the conversation like this doesn't reflect reality."
> - Robin J. Ely, Pamela Stone, and Colleen Ammerman[98]

The church of the future will recognize she needs to create more space for women, normalizing and encouraging egalitarian partnerships in the boardroom, staff room, and pulpit.

In order to encourage these partnerships, it may help to have some biblical models, and there can be none better than that of Jesus' female disciples.

Much has been made about the female followers of Jesus. In Matthew 27, we read about Mary Magdalene, Mary the mother of James and Joseph, and the unnamed mother of James and John. Luke 8 adds Joanna and Susanna to this list. Mark 15

---

[98] Robin J. Ely, Pamela Stone, and Colleen Ammerman, "Rethink what you 'know' about high-achieving Women," *Harvard Business Review*, December 2014, 108.

mentions another female disciple, Salome, and also tells us many other women followed Jesus even to his crucifixion.[99]

I think we would learn a great deal about Christ if we turned the camera lens to an over-the-shoulder perspective of the Marys, Martha, and Joanna. Then, by adjusting the prose from third-person limited omniscient to first-person plural[100], we would see how often women were in right in the thick of Jesus' ministry, funding his travels and making arrangements for both his public teaching and social appearances. We would also earn a greater appreciation for the pace of Jesus' life, how exhausted he must have been, how hard he must have driven himself, and how his male disciples were too enamored with his genius to care for him properly. As a result, our awareness would increase concerning the cost associated with ministry, the requirements for community and family, and the high status Jesus afforded women in Second Temple Judaism. And we would only be privy to this perspective because we decided to see Christ from the unique vantage of women. A female perspective on Jesus wouldn't simply demonize men or elevate women; a truly female telling of Christ's life would supply new insights concerning Christ himself.

Because women have more to offer than their gender.

The church of the future will see men and women leading, both separately and together, in emulation of Jesus' first followers.

Who are the female leaders in your church?

---

[99]   Mark 16.1.
[100]   i.e. "We saw Jesus taken to Golgotha" instead of "Then Jesus was taken to Golgotha"

RELENTLESSNESS

REALIZING OUR HEARTBREAKS ARE BEST OVERCOME WITH THE CHURCH

But God has put the body together, giving greater honor to the parts that lacked it, so that there should be no division in the body, but that its parts should have equal concern for each other. If one part suffers, every part suffers with it; if one part is honored, every part rejoices with it. Now you are the body of Christ, and each one of you is a part of it.
- 1 Corinthians 12.24-27, NIV

Church provides tremendous opportunity for community, solidarity, and growth as we navigate life together.

The Church is the bride of Christ, and she is an amazing beauty. Her teeth may be crooked, but her smile is sexier than Hell. Her eyes are so bright you never notice her crow's feet; and, though she wears too much perfume it's still nice when you get close.

On Sunday morning, the church gathers for worship, prays for people to be healed, educates her family in the way of Jesus, studies the scriptures, and sings. Sometimes the church takes a special offering—for a pizza delivery person, for instance, so we can knock their socks off; or a ministry rescuing victims of sex trafficking, so we can pay for their rehab. We welcome former enemies with open arms. We rejoice with penitent prostitutes. When a little boy with a terminal genetic condition comes in a wheelchair, all hands are on deck to bless him, pray for him, and usher him into the Kingdom of heaven. We broadcast God's love to the world.

Church is where we hear about cancer and heart attacks, counsel rape victims and their families, walk through recovery with the mentally ill, and provide solace to those involved with failed adoptions. It's church that helps us with family—both coping with our existing families and providing new families when we have none.

Church is incredible. When we're part of the church we go from the most wretched experiences of human life into the lightness of games, back and forth, 10,000 times in a week. It's all the gravity of social work with all the hilarity of kindergarten.

Where else does this happen?

The church of the future will continue to bear one another's burdens, celebrating our triumphs and consoling one another amid our tragedies. She will laugh with those who laugh and weep with those who weep, aware that God's Kingdom is already here and yet not fully realized.

What is your best and worst memory of church?

SIX.FOUR

DISCOMFORT

GROWING THROUGH ALL THINGS UNDESIRABLE, UNCOMFORTABLE, AND UNCOOL

> But in fact God has placed the parts in the body, every one of them, just as he wanted them to be. If they were all one part, where would the body be? As it is, there are many parts, but one body.
> - 1 Corinthians 12.18-20, NIV

God grows your character through endurance and engagement.

When we come to church we're surrounded by people we don't know and might not like. Some over-share. Some are touchy. Some are fidgety and harrumph during the sermon. Some sing off key. There's always a few weirdos. There's always a few zealots. There's always some lady trying to sign you up for a pyramid scheme or some guy trying to get you to vote.

But we come to church with an understanding that we are all part of the family of God. Consequently, there's a sense in church in which you cannot escape. Or maybe even should not. Unlike a football game or the shopping center, at church you feel like you have to be nice. Which means you're in situations you would otherwise ignore. And those situations, accompanied by your sense of responsibility, transform you.

This doesn't mean you should ignore common sense and walk off into the dark parking lot with a stranger; but it does mean we're compelled to extend common courtesy at church in ways it has long since evaporated outside it. Church provides space for us to engage those most unlike us, with mental or physical impairments, from differing socioeconomic backgrounds, across genders and ages. Church is the last place where civility reigns between those of different political convictions, tribal allegiances, or educational awareness.

The church of the future will be characterized by diversity across all spectrums. She will be more of a salad than a melting pot, celebrating every ingredient for their unique contribution.

What is the most uncomfortable experience you've endured at church?

MENTORING

LEARNING FROM, AND WITH, OTHER BELIEVERS

They devoted themselves to the apostles' teaching and to fellowship, to the breaking of bread and to prayer.
- Acts 2.42, NIV

God will grow you continuously, mainly through your interactions with other people.

The church of the future will be committed to helping people become the best possible version of themselves in Christ. This will require significant effort, most notably in the arena of mentoring.

One of my favorite mentoring initiatives was the Westwinds Windternships designed and administrated by Del Belcher, our former campus pastor at the Hub, and Terri McGarry, our children's pastor. This program was designed for youth ages 10-12 and gave the kids opportunities for hands-on experience with our espresso bar, media, Christian Education, and worship. Participants completed a six-week internship that fostered 21st Century job and ministry skills through mentor-based learning.

Windterns gained competency, solved problems, and interacted in team settings. They developed inter-generational relationships and fostered community, gaining awareness about their own talents and interests. Additionally, these Windternships offered participants community service and credit hours often required from their schools.

The results have been wonderful—friendship, laughter, camaraderie. Sometimes even sports. Sometimes dates. Sometimes babysitting and movies.

Another pair of staff members, Ben Redmond and Lori Gordon, have been connecting our Owners to those people who get baptized. That's also been amazing. Our Owners have been adopting new believers, bringing them gifts and writing them encouraging letters, signing prayer journals and giving spontaneous hugs.

It's starting to feel like we're a church.

This, clearly, is what scripture intends through use of "shepherd" imagery. A shepherd[101] tends herds or flocks, not merely feeds them. **Shepherds are skillful, committed, and loving.** So, too, are good mentors. They know in advance that this endeavor will be costly and require increased study and diligence on their part. But that's what they've signed up for, and they enter into the relationship joyfully.

A shepherd will protect their sheep, like David protecting his sheep against the lion and the bear. A shepherd will also watch over their sheep at night. A good mentor is concerned about the safety and wellbeing of their charge. Not just their physical safety, but also their intellectual, emotional, and spiritual safety. This is why mentors often caution against certain relationships, associations, or peers—they perceive danger where the charge perceives none.

A shepherd will search after sheep who wander off. In my experience, mentoring relationships usually trail off as the charge becomes more and more distant. Sometimes this demonstrates maturity and self-sufficiency; others, this is due to increased rebellion or malaise. Regardless, having made a significant investment in their charge, the mentor will often pursue them.

Shepherds are tender with their flocks, showing compassion to the weak and endeavoring to heal and strengthen the diseased. Here is possibly the greatest difference between a mentor and a pastor. A pastor is compelled to care for the whole of the congregation. That means, when there are those with special needs, the pastor is drawn to give them special attention. But a mentor works differently. Typically, *mentors are investing in the strengths of their charge.* Those high-level capacities

---

[101]   4166 *poimén, Strong's Concordance,* http://biblehub.com/greek/4166.htm, accessed August 22, 2017.

are what attracted the mentor in the first place. The weaknesses are there, but the mentor is helping to eliminate them or work around them, not to carry their charge as they struggle. Consequently, mentors can be quite hard on their charges; but, again, I'm not sure this is unhelpful. In many cases, especially with young men, the unwillingness to coddle is a long-term nutrient for healthy development.

The church of the future will ensure mentoring relationships like these will be the norm, not the exception. She will continue to pair the older and the younger together, so that our young people can enjoy surrogate family with big brothers, big sisters, and additional sets of grandparents upon whom they can rely.

With whom are you involved in a mentoring relationship?

181

SEVEN

WE SEE A CHURCH

that **UNDERSTANDS** WHAT YOU DO *flows* FROM WHO YOU ARE,

because **IDENTITY** *and* **VOCATION** *are* **ENTWINED.**

GENIUS

UNDERSTANDING JESUS CHRIST WAS MORE THAN THE SUM OF HIS SKILL SET, AND SO ARE YOU

God has chosen to make known among the Gentiles the glorious riches of this mystery, which is Christ in you, the hope of glory.
- Colossians 1.27, NIV

To become the best possible version of ourselves, we must first pursue Christ.

Leaders and creatives both miss the point when they try to develop their "leadership" and "creativity." There is something deeper than management or artistry, something more primal than strategies or wordsmithing.

Consider that there has never been a more revolutionary leader, nor a more provocative artist, than Jesus Christ. With twelve miscreants and fifty-odd stories, Christ reshaped morality, ethics, and relationships for all time. Yet no honest disciple ever studies "the leadership secrets of Jesus Christ" without some embarrassment, nor mines the scriptures for the "inspiration behind Jesus' greatest tales."

Why? Because Jesus is more than the sum of his skill set.

And so are we.

Jesus spent less time honing his skills than he did connecting with the Father, less time learning how to be "creative" and more time alone in the scriptures. When people study the life of Jesus looking for tips and techniques, they make a categorical error. During his tenure as a Nazarene, Jesus' leadership left something to be desired. He only had a few fistfuls of followers, and they struggled to understand his teaching. His first clear objective was confronting the often-violent political and religious structures of his time, which meant even the few followers he had soon abandoned him.

Jesus' only clear gameplan was obedience. That's what made him brilliant. When people saw him, they saw God.

One of Jesus' favorite comparisons was that of a tree and its fruit. In short, he claimed we'd be able to ascertain the quality of an individual by that which they produced. A lover loves, like an apple tree grows apples. A faithful wife practices fidelity, like figs ripen early in the summer.

If you want to become a better leader or a more creative person, the secret is not to focus on either quality. Focus, instead, on your connection to Christ, the True Vine. Because everything you do flows from who you are, and who you are cannot be separated from the person God is calling you to become. All your efforts to increase your competencies will be uneven and ineffectual unless you're meaningfully connected to Jesus Christ.

One man illustrates this beautifully: Charles Williams, author of *The Greater Trumps* and *The Place of the Lion*. Williams was a mystic who wrote to uncover the fabulous world hiding behind the seemingly mundane. He tackled tarot with angelology[102] and mysticism with a theology of romantic love.[103] A member of the Inklings,[104] Williams' vocal admirers included T.S. Eliot, W.H. Auden, and Dorothy Sayers. He was a hero of heroes.

How did Charles Williams become such a literary and theological genius? What makes him stand the test of time, attaining the high esteem of such mighty company?

Williams devoted himself to the indwelling presence of Christ. His theology wasn't an abstraction, but the record of his descent into the otherness of God.

---

[102] *The Greater Trumps* hypothesizes a connection between the occult and the supernatural, where occult activity is a counterfeit means of controlling the invisible world.

[103] *The Place of the Lion* suggests that angels are corporeal manifestations of Plato's types, and that the strongest type of Love was Christ.

[104] The brilliant group of English novelists that included C.S. Lewis and J.R.R. Tolkien.

In order for you to become the best possible version of yourself, Christ needs to be revealed. He lives in you, but has been covered up by ego, confusion, and neglect. Your old habits have to be discarded. Your destructive behaviors have to be lasered off. Your sin has to be cut away, bit by bit, so Christ is seen more clearly.

You are like diamond, and your true brilliance is hidden. Diamonds are among the most precious materials on earth. We do not possess the skill to improve upon a diamond; rather, diamonds have their less-appealing qualities stripped away to reveal their innate worth. The process is difficult and can only be accomplished by a highly specialized diamantaire. Diamonds don't have to be constructed, only revealed.

The church of the future will realize that the most beautiful things are often deeply hidden. She will invest in her people, watching their diamonds glow, knowing the light of our lives isn't really ours at all. It's his; or, more accurately, it's him.

How would you describe the best possible version of yourself?

DESTINY

REALIZING YOU ARE THE ONLY PERSON GOD CAN USE

Dear children, let us not love with words or speech but with actions and in truth.
-1 John 3.18, NIV

> *God has place you here, now, in these circumstances and among these people, to heal the world.*

My daughter's favorite story in the Bible is Esther, but I'm not sure that's a good thing. Anna is eleven, just at the end of her princess-and-pony innocence, so I don't want her to be exposed too quickly to the horrors of our world, and Esther definitely highlights the uglier side of human nature.

On the one hand, Esther is a thrilling story of a courageous beauty who defies convention and risks her life to save God's people. On the other hand, Esther is about a harem concubine; her demanding uncle who exploits her beauty; and a genocidal maniac manipulating a weak king.

This is not precisely the story I want to form my daughter's perception of the world.

Nevertheless, it is (thankfully) possible to share Esther's story by focusing on the protagonist's moral development. It is a story about a young woman whose foremost merit was physical attractiveness. There are many young women who could relate, in every culture. Maybe that's not fair, but it's as near a universal truth as I've ever encountered. Maltese women and African women, Philippine women and Haitian women, Brits, Germans, Swedes and the Dutch … women want to be beautiful.

By the same token, women understand there has to be a deeper, interior beauty for the exterior loveliness not to feel like a ruse. The empty-headed vapites adorning the Internet, for example, are hardly anyone's first choice for a life-long partner, just as the socialite elitism favored by reality TV producers makes more of us groan in frustration than longing.

True beauty is a dialectic between appearance and character. Esther, then, is a story about a pretty girl who becomes beautiful. She finds her courage with her family. It is her family that will not allow her to play house and eat cake. It is her family that reminds her she must rise above her station. It is her family that presses her to accept her calling and save her people.

True beauty is never grown in isolation. Beauty is cultivated in love as our responsibilities are embraced and faithfully discharged.

Esther is a great example of why identity and vocation are entwined. No one but Esther could have accomplished what she did, because no one else was in her place. The opportunity was hers on account of who she was and who she became. Only a great beauty could become Queen. Only the Queen had access to the King. Only a courageous and intelligent Queen could defy her King and live. Only Esther could convince her husband he was blind to his enemies and in error concerning his policies.

The legendary line in the story occurs when Esther's uncle, pleading with her to become something more than just a lovely face, reminds her God may have placed her in the King 's court "for such a time as this."[105]

Maybe we have all been placed in our jobs, in our families, and in the circumstances of our lives for such a time as this. Maybe the only person who could raise your children is you. Maybe the only person who could provide unconditional love for your spouse is you. Maybe you are the answer to the prayers of your people.

---

[105] Esther 4.14.

The church of the future will both model and embody an unbroken wholeness available to those in Christ Jesus. She will unify our passions and our purpose, our desires and our fantasies, our ambitions and our efforts, so that her people glorify God equally at work, at home, and in isolation.

> *How would you describe the opportunities*
> *God has placed in front of you?*

SEVEN.THREE

CIRCUMSTANCE

EMBRACING OUR LIVES, RATHER THAN SEEKING TO ESCAPE THEM

> Therefore, holy brethren, partakers of the heavenly calling, consider the Apostle and High Priest of our confession, Christ Jesus …
> - Hebrews 3.1, NKJV

The best place for you to begin proclaiming Christ is amid your ordinary life, regardless of how unpleasant your life may be.

In one puzzling episode, Jesus saw a Samaritan woman standing near a well and sent his disciples away so the two of them could be alone. Because we know the story, and we know how it ends, we often miss the implied scandal.

Jesus was not supposed to be alone with women. That was culturally inappropriate.[106] This woman, we later learn, is cohabiting with a man and has been married five times. Her position in society is exceedingly compromised. This is why she is at the well in the middle of the day, the worst time to draw water on account of the heat. She gathers water at noon to avoid the other village women, to escape their scorn.

Sometimes when we read this story we imagine this woman has had five divorces because she was promiscuous, but that fails to take seriously the historical context. Then, a woman could be divorced for almost any reason, so long as it was the man putting her away. She had almost no legal rights. He had almost no legal responsibilities. He could divorce her for disobeying him, for failing to please him, or for failing to provide an heir.[107]

In all likelihood, it was the latter that cost this woman her marriages.

But if the men of the village knew she was infertile, why would four subsequent men marry her?

Why would any man, ever, make a hasty and ill-advised union with a scorned woman?

---

[106] "Jesus' interactions with women," *Wikipedia,* https://en.wikipedia.org/wiki/Jesus%27_interactions_with_women#The_woman_at_the_well_in_Samaria, accessed August 24, 2017.

[107] Greenburg, Blu, "Divorce in the Bible," *My Jewish Learning,* http://www.myjewishlearning.com/article/divorce-in-the-bible/, accessed August 24, 2017.

It's simple, isn't it? She was beautiful.

In a male-dominated society where women are treated as little more than property and given little say in their future, why wouldn't shallow men rent a wife for a few years just to "be sure" she was the problem and not her former husband?

Back to the story...
Jesus sees this beautiful woman by herself and decides he wants to speak with her. Alone. The disciples, understandably, were upset.[108]

Are you sure? This seems out of character ...

Maybe. By all accounts Jesus craved the company of women. Mary. Martha. Joanna. Mary Magdalene. I think Jesus was lonely.

Consider that Jesus could have married, but a marriage to the Messiah would have been absolute hell. His wife would always be deprioritized over his mission. She would always be scrutinized for her behavior. Given that Jesus never answered questions directly, their relationship would likely have been very tense. And everything would have been "her fault" on account of his "sinless perfection." She may have come to resent him, and he may have had to challenge her resentment publicly in order to avoid disruption among his followers. If they had children, Jesus' sons (especially) would wrestle first with privilege and then with bitterness. Or maybe they would have been hunted. Or enthroned. And what of the possibility they might be God's grandchildren? Could there be a line of Messiahs? What would the relationship have been like between Jesus' wife and mother? At best they would have aligned together to rescue Jesus from his mission, as Mary often sent

---

[108]   John 4.27.

Jesus' brothers to talk sense into him. But at worst, they could have been at odds, both frustrating Jesus' attempts to obey the Father and both entrenched in the pigheadedness of love.

Of course, when God gets involved, who can say what will happen? Perhaps Jesus could have made it work far better than our earthly marriages, and perhaps the reason he didn't get married wasn't because it would have been unconscionable, but because he was already devoted to the Church, his bride to be.

Christ took the Church for his bride, and when we emulate him we pursue the path of self-sacrificial love. That makes for better families, better husbands, and better men than the model Jesus likely would have provided as a "normal" husband.

Back to the story …
In their conversation, the woman at the well seems unimpressed with Jesus. She is not afraid, but neither is she hospitable. Instead, it is easy to read her portion of the conversation in the tired cadence of one used to attention, already rolling her eyes as she waits for the inevitable pickup line.

Perhaps Jesus knows all of this and enjoys it. Perhaps he has this entire conversation with a goofy grin, eagerly anticipating her reaction when she discovers he's different.

And Jesus *is* different. Their conversation ranges from sexuality to spirituality, from disputed doctrine to marvelous metaphysic, and in the end this jaded woman is overcome with wide-eyed energy. She races through town, proclaiming that Jesus is better than the rest, truer than religion, and more loving than any other man.

Then. Now. Next.

This is another strong biblical example of why vocation and identity are entwined. Who else could make these claims, other than the Samaritan woman at the well? Who else could testify that Jesus was the first man to truly know a woman, the first to forgo knowing her in the biblical sense so he could know her wholly?

> Come and see a man...who knows me inside and out.
> -John 4.29, MSG

The church of the future will, like Jesus, engage society's outcasts with genuine love and friendship. She will also, like the Samaritan woman, proclaim boldly that Jesus is better than any religion, romance, or relationship on earth.

In what ways was the woman at the well an ideal evangelist?

198

AUTHENTICITY

DISCOVERING WHO GOD IS CALLING US TO BECOME

For we are God's handiwork, created in Christ Jesus to do good works, which God prepared in advance for us to do.
- Ephesians 2.10, NIV

God is summoning us to become the best possible version of ourselves for his glory.

If we want to be our authentic selves, we need to focus on the people God is calling us to become. This is what Tom Wright refers to as "eschatological authenticity," or Voltaire called "the best possible version of ourselves." Because the underlying truth of our identity is that we are still becoming, and the posture with which we continuously engage this development will determine the shape of our relationships, our intellect, and our vocation.

This kind of development requires that we think less about our qualifications and more about our character. Are you, for example, helpful? Energetic? Curious? These are essential character traits among any who have ambition for advancement. A willing and passionate life-long learner is an asset to everyone, whereas an educated know-it-all is perhaps the least desirable coworker imaginable.

> A simplistic understanding of what it means can hinder your growth and limit your impact…When we view authenticity as an unwavering sense of self, we struggle to take on new challenges and bigger roles. The reality is that people learn—and change—who they are through experience. By trying out different leadership styles and behaviors, we grow more than we would through introspection alone. Experimenting with our identities allows us to find the right approach for ourselves and our organizations. This adaptive approach to authenticity can make us feel like impostors, because it involves doing things that may not come naturally. But it's outside our comfort zones that we learn to the most about leading effectively.
> -"Spotlight: Soft skills you can't neglect"[109]

---

[109] "Spotlight: Soft skills you can't neglect," *Harvard Business Review*, January-February 2015, 54-59.

The central issue here isn't our character *now*, but the promise of who we will continue to become as we tenaciously pursue our development. I don't think of myself as a biblical scholar or pastor or professor, because if I did there are a host of tasks I would never perform. Instead, I think of myself as David, and David is someone who helps clean up and holds open doors, who smiles and laughs and is industrious and passionate.

I've made a hobby out of self-discovery, such that during my tenure as a pastor, I have explored dozens of personality tests, profiles, and strategic insight initiatives in order to best understand who I am and how I'm wired.

- The DISC test helped me understand the dynamics between myself and my coworkers.
- Ian Cron's book *The Road Back to You* made sense of the Enneagram, which I consider a spiritual weakness inventory.
- Howard Gardner's groundbreaking *Frames of Mind* introduced me to his multiple intelligence theory, which revolutionized my understanding of giftedness.
- *The Hidden Spirituality of Men* by Matthew Fox outlines ten metaphors that gave me the language of masculine maturity.
- Owen Weston's book *Spiritual Gifts: Your Job Description from God* remains my preferred text on the topic of charismata.
- Gary Chapman's *Sacred Pathways* discusses the many ways in which we connect with God.

Eventually I began to develop my own tools for uncovering spiritual identity. Not personality per se, but a mix of your spiritual gifts, your spiritual pathway, your learning style, and your style of intelligence. I called my first attempt the

Pneumalabe, after the astrolabe used by early sailors to navigate the stars. It was a terrible name, and an unusable tool, despite my sense of satisfaction with the idea of spiritual navigation. Eventually, I published my work in *Archetypes: Uncovering Your Spiritual Identity*, and continue to be amazed at how many people find it liberating, insightful, and true to their experience.

I must admit it feels good to create an artifact that helps others understand their spiritual composition. It is a healthy example of how I'm practicing what I preach and allowing my passion projects to flow out of my identity and giftedness.

Perhaps because of this core belief, I have always been puzzled to see those who enter the workforce and decide they should not be doing low-level jobs. The newly-employed often have a strong sense of self and cannot reconcile who they think they are with what they're tasked to perform. If, for example, they perceive themselves as leaders, then they are confused when instructed to follow. If they consider themselves strategists, it is uncomfortable to be excluded from important planning.

But in the ultimate determination, only we have the power to love our work or despise it, to invest in our vocation or shirk our development. For better or for worse, work is who we are in the world. Work is how we reveal our character to everyone outside our home. Work is our testimony. We will be judged for our work. By God? Maybe. But before God ever gets the chance, everyone else will pass judgment on God because of our work.

> Entitlement is the furthest path away from enlightenment.
> - John Maeda[110]

---

[110] Maeda, John with Becky Bermont, *Redesigning Leadership*, 61.

There is more to authenticity than revulsion for seeming fake. And that's why this developmental piece is so critical.

The church of the future will be filled with those focused on becoming the people God has fantasized about since the Beginning.

> *Who is God calling you to become?*

SEVEN.FIVE

OPPORTUNITY

SEIZING NEW LIFE WITH GOD

This day I call the heavens and the earth as witnesses against you that I have set before you life and death, blessings and curses. Now choose life …
- Deuteronomy 30.19, NIV

> *God provides everyone opportunity to leave their past behind and choose that which is right, however difficult it may be.*

Scripture is filled with stories of foolish people still loved and employed by the Lord. For example, when Israel's spies surveyed the Promised Land (see Joshua 2), they spent the night at an inn. That seems normal, except that the inn housed prostitutes. Perhaps that was a common feature of city inns, but the oddness of it has always struck me: God's servants spent the night in a whorehouse.

It's difficult to imagine any of us feeling like that was a sound decision in today's context.

In addition to spending the night there, it's clear the spies became well acquainted with Rahab, the prostitute. Again, there seems altogether too much room for speculation as to how they knew her and knew her so well, but the purpose of the story isn't to focus on their sin but on God's use of Rahab.

I just can't get there quite so quickly.

It's weird that God's servants went to a brothel and befriended a hooker. In her bedroom.

(At this point it feels appropriate to acknowledge my own Christian upbringing was considerably more conservative than this ...)

Rahab helped the spies evade capture and in turn they spared her family when they invaded her town, the home of their ancient enemies. She seized an opportunity to change her life in an instant, cooperating with God and God's servants to deliver God's people.

God uses us all, regardless of who we are and where we are. Do not disparage either yourself or your past. Instead, pay attention—God is calling you out, summoning you beyond your circumstances.

The church of the future will be filled with people who refused to miss their moment. She will be pock-marked in grace and unified by a love she knows she does not deserve.

> *What would it look like for you to leave your past behind entirely?*

EIGHT

WE SEE A CHURCH

that **INTERRUPTS** EVIL *and* SETS CROOKED PATHS STRAIGHT;

that **INVESTS** *in* MAKING *and* KEEPING THINGS RIGHT;

that **OPPOSES** *the* SOUR *and* CULTIVATES THE SWEET *in* **ANTICIPATION** *of the* RIGHTFUL KING RESUMING HIS THRONE.

EIGHT.ONE

RESCUE

COMMITTING OURSELVES TO THE WELLBEING OF OTHERS

> ... Let us throw off everything that hinders and the
> sin that so easily entangles.
> -Hebrews 12.1, NIV

---

*Justice is both demanding and elusive, but the church of the future will
pursue all that is right with strength and focus.*

Sergeant David Mascarenas, supervisor of the Underwater Dive Unit of the LAPD showed tremendous courage and resilience by descending into the La Brea Tar Pits to find evidence of a homicide.[111] These tar pits are "bubbling cesspools of primordial ooze," and experts said it would be impossible to dive them "because of the chemicals, contamination, [and] gasses … which are toxic and flammable."

I cannot imagine what it would have been like to travel into something the consistency of molasses, but Mascarenas took his commission seriously. "His planned seven-minute dive became a 77-minute dive and he descended to more than double the 8-foot maximum depth; his depth gauge failed at 17 feet." Eventually, however, he found what he was looking for. The LAPD has kept his discovery classified, but the evidence was sufficient to push for a conviction.

That's the kind of dedication we ought to have in our pursuit of what's right. Sin is a tar pit, and we've got to penetrate it with Christ. We must take seriously Christ's commands to preach the gospel to the ends of the earth—not only the gospel message of eternal life, but the more holistic gospel of life "on earth as it is in heaven." That life—the one we now live—requires us to cooperate with God and heal the world.

The church of the future will invest in making and keeping things right—right as God defines them; right as Christ, right with Christ, right like Christ. And that means we cannot simply talk about justice, but must uphold it, celebrate it, work for it, and model it ourselves. We must be the ones who dive into the tar pits of quagmired families, systems, and hurts. We must be divine divers, searching and rescuing the lost of God.

Which "tar pits" is God directing you to enter in pursuit of justice?

---

[111] "Dark Waters: police divers descend to new depths for justice," *Alert Diver*, Summer 2015, 46-49.

CHRISTOLOGY

UNDERSTANDING THE INCARNATION DEFINES GOD AS CHRIST-LIKE

He has shown you, O mortal, what is good. And what does the Lord require of you? To act justly and to love mercy and to walk humbly with your God.
- Micah 6.8, NIV

Jesus' self-sacrificial death was more significant than either his remarkable teachings or his courageous behaviors.

Since the Bible is such a vast and complicated book, complete with variances in genre and intent, authors and cultures, it's vital to acknowledge that the ultimate test of God's intent is found in the example, teaching, and ontology of Christ.

God is Christ-like, so we must always ask ourselves questions concerning Jesus' behaviors, Jesus' teachings, and especially the significance behind Jesus' arrival into our world as one of us. What does it mean that the final manifestation of God's justice was to conquer death through dying?

Jesus never taught anything other than the best of Judaism, which means Christ is more than the sum of his teachings. Consequently, when we defer only to Jesus' prophetic action and rabbinic wisdom, we miss out on the true significance of God-made-flesh.

God isn't just someone who watches from a distance and gives instruction; no, God gets his hands dirty. And God isn't just someone who, in disgust, tosses those hands in the air and walks away; no, God always provides a way back, at great personal cost. And God isn't just someone who leaves us to suffer interminably for our sins; no, God promises to make all things new.

The church of the future will, likewise, extend the hand of friendship to those who have spurned faith again and again. She will draw deeply on the justice and authority of God in order to supply mercy. The church of the future will tirelessly offer a new beginning to everyone—everyone!—who feels used up, exhausted, worn out, or abused.

There can never be a separation of Christ and his people, so there can never be a separation of the Church and the world.

Remember that God made the world,[112] and loves it,[113] and any biblical cautions against the "love of the world"[114] refer to being contaminated by the world's corrupted values, not the Christ-infused design of Creation.[115] Nothing will impede God's people from loving, and living, in every corner of God's Creation cooperating with their Creator to welcome the King as he makes the world his home.

The church of the future will allow the Spirit of Christ to govern and penetrate all she does in every arena she enters, acting justly as we lay claim to this earth alongside the Lord.

How is the Spirit driving you to love and serve the world?

---

[112] Genesis 1-2.
[113] John 3.16.
[114] 1 John 2.15-17.
[115] Romans 12.2.

JUSTICE

ACKNOWLEDGING THE DIFFERENCE BETWEEN RETRIBUTION AND RESTORATION

Love the Lord your God with all your heart and with all your soul and with all your strength.
– Deuteronomy 6.5, NIV

We must work for peace in ourselves and in our world simultaneously.

There are two kinds of justice: restorative and retributive. Retributive justice involves punishing offenders to both dissuade others from following their example and to satisfy the hurts caused against the victims. It is the basis for our approach to law in the West, though concerns have frequently been raised about it effectiveness due to the steady increase in violent crime.[116]

Why isn't our justice system functioning better? That's a complex problem, and frankly one I'm not qualified to evaluate; however, as a spiritual advisor I can attest to the effects retribution has on a personal level, having counseled hundreds of people as they work through their grievances, offenses, and resolutions. This isn't to suggest there should never be a time for punishment, only that we ought to be wary of how often and how harshly we mete it out.

Countless societies have overfed the monster of retributive justice, as evidenced by death penalties for seemingly minor infractions, canings for disobedience, stoning for adultery, honor killings, acid attacks, and unlimited prison sentences. These are still realities and they are the product of a well-fed monster. The monster needs to be kept on a leash, subdued, and at bay. If we feed it too much, it will break loose and destroy us.

Restorative justice, on the other hand, takes into consideration the personhood of both the victim and the offender. Solutions are creative, specific, and singular—designed to make things right on the part of the victim, which often requires something unique from the offender in recompense. But this doesn't mean the offender gets off easy, or with an apology, or at all. It means the powers in charge must take seriously the crimes and

---

[116] Sanburn, Josh and David Johnson, "Violent Crime Is On the Rise in U.S. Cities," *Time*, January 20, 2017, http://time.com/4651122/homicides-increase-cities-2016/, accessed August 24, 2017.

work toward a healthy solution, asking "How would we make this right?"

The Truth and Reconciliation Committee in South Africa, after Apartheid, is a good example of how complex and diverse this process is. And how exhausting. I remember hearing the story of one police officer, whose denials and blindness were broken down during trial until he was forced to acknowledge his racial prejudice and past crimes. He then spent the last twenty years of his life serving the community he had once persecuted. He voluntarily rebuilt homes. He took his children to clean up the yards of people he had once abused. He made things right. He chose to do this on his own, and provided a beautiful example. He died embraced by the people who once hated him as he had hated them.

He atoned.[117]

That's justice, however elusive it may be, and is what the scripture refers to as *shalom*. Commonly defined as "peace," *shalom* is more holistically understood as well-ordered flourishing between Creation, Creator, and Created. It is the unbroken wholeness keeping the world sane, safe, and loved.

But even restorative justice is not a magic bullet solution for the sins and crimes of this world. Our commitment to wade into the tar pits of sin and injustice doesn't guarantee we will come out having successfully rescued our charges, or come out clean, or come out at all. To find real solutions to real problems requires more than just the commitment of rescuers. Such solutions require contrition on the part of the offender and grace on the part of the victim, and not all offenders are like this policeman. Some glory in their wickedness, and we must oppose their continued actions without unnecessarily feeding the monster inside ourselves.

[117] See Krog, Antjie, *Country of My Skull.*

How are we to do this? How can we ever hope to navigate the complexities of the human heart?

Only the power of Christ, alive in his Church, can combat the secret evils of our interiority. Only Christ gives us the wisdom and discernment we need. Only Christ convicts us of our own complicity in the affairs of sin. Only Christ can warn us when the monster is overfed. Only Christ can make us care.

To make and keep things right, we have to invest in holiness, in godliness, in saintliness for ourselves and for our families, in our homes and in our neighborhoods. "Finally, brothers and sisters, whatever is true, whatever is noble, whatever is right, whatever is pure, whatever is lovely, whatever is admirable—if anything is excellent or praiseworthy—think about such things."[118] We cannot wait until something goes wrong before we make it right, springing into action to judge or punish or creatively solve some problem.

The church of the future will uphold the priority of making and keeping things right in ourselves. Heart. Mind. Soul. And strength.

> *How are you keeping your monster of retribution on a leash, starved, and at bay?*

---

[118] Philippians 4.8.

PEACE

DISCERNING WHETHER WE WORK FOR PEACE OR AGAINST THOSE WHO DISTURB IT

God will bring into judgment both the righteous and the wicked, for there will be a time for every activity, a time to judge every deed.
- Ecclesiastes 3.17, NIV

The purpose of justice is peace, not punishment.

A plowshare is used to cut through the soil in preparation for agricultural development. The image of beating "swords into plowshares" is meant to convey that we must stop fighting and begin rebuilding sustainable community amid a peaceful society.[119]

This idea has been widely popularized in many cultures, as evidenced by the statue in the United Nations art gallery by Yevgeny Vuchetich of a bronze man beating his sword; and the idea has taken on local color among musicians, such as Peter Tosh and Wyclef Jean, who have appeared on stage playing guitars made from assault rifles. The point is that there is something for us to aspire toward other than murder, conquest, violence, and war. Those may be common components of life on earth, but are ultimately unacceptable in God's New Creation.

Scripture intends for us to be caretakers, tending and tilling God's Creation. Again, that's what the prophets meant when they told us to "turn our swords into plowshares." But there is a third tool implied in this imagery, the hammer that beats the sword upon the anvil.

Could there be a better image for retributive justice than the hammer, smashing the sword over and over and over again, until the blade of the sword has been dulled and the weapon loses its shape forever? Never mind that the hammer must also continue beating the now-shapeless metal into something else—for those who love to smash swords, it is enough that they have the blacksmith's blessing to beat.

Is it possible we are more excited to live as the hammer than the plowshare? Have we have forsaken the fields because we enjoy the anvil?

---

[119] Isaiah 2.4; Joel 3.10; Micah 4.3.

The more we focus on beating, beating, beating—with the accompanying identification of swords-as-people who must be hammered until they lose their identity—the more we set ourselves up for destructive behaviors and sanctify them with biblical rhetoric.

The church of the future will realize that healing is more important than punishment. She will renew her commitment to cooperative work with God, bringing New Creation to bear rather than becoming enamored with an endless assault upon the unjust.

Can you think of a time when you acted as the sword, the hammer, and the plowshare, respectively?

GRACE

HOW TO NEITHER CHEAPEN NOR OVERLOOK THE MERCY OF GOD

Flesh gives birth to flesh, but the Spirit gives birth
to spirit. You should not be surprised at my saying,
"You must be born again." The wind blows wherever
it pleases. You hear its sound, but you cannot tell
where it comes from or where it is going. So it is with
everyone born of the Spirit.
-John 3.6-8, NIV

> *Over time, we tend to lose sight of why we believe as we do and deteriorate*
> *into either legalism or liberalism.*

When we become followers of Jesus, our new lives are characterized by change. We used to be governed by alcohol or lust or whatever, and when Christ makes us new we turn our back on those old gods. And when we have children, we teach them that Christ is the source of our new life and that those old things are only destructive. Over time, those destructive things become outlawed in our homes, and our children's children come to think of those prohibitions as absolutes. The reason vanishes, and yet the requirement remains.

We now have rules for no reason.

The problem, of course, is that when our children's children's children return to the scripture, they see no honest evidence for why we've eschewed these supposed vices. Drinking is not a sin in itself. The prophets were experts in profanity. The saints went to war.

And so the next generation abandons our Phariseeism and begins to experiment with following Jesus and enjoying these pleasures. It doesn't take long before they overindulge, and the pockmarks of destruction appear. At this point, they are not yet aware of their need for grace, only that grace is a term they've heard bandied around and seems here appropriate. They ask for grace. They demand forgiveness. Reluctantly, they might receive absolution for a time.

But Grace only shows up when everyone else has left the building. Grace is always late, it seems. She arrives when we're stumbling home drunk after the show and none of our friends—even our Christian friends—want puke in their car. So Grace lets us in the front seat and gives us bottled water. She chides, but for once we're willing to acknowledge that we're lucky to have her. She's amazing, and she gets us home safe.

When we come in the door, our Father is waiting and Grace explains it's all been sorted. We're done with such foolishness.

Cheap grace is when we receive mercy and fling it away, returning to our old habits and patterns as though forgiveness was not worth keeping. But when we act upon the grace we have received, demonstrating our acceptance of the fact that we needed it, then the full measure of our reconciliation is revealed. We experience the complexity of grace as our relationships heal and our past misdeeds are slowly unraveled. It is this commitment to proceed in the grace we've received that ensures grace is extravagant.

The church of the future will find the balance between moral guidelines and the guidance of the Holy Spirit. We won't insist on a new Phariseeism—rules built around rules to keep us from accidentally violating the original rules—but will teach our children, our communities, and re-teach ourselves to attend to the Spirit through meditation, contemplation, and prayer.

The Spirit will guide us away from sin and toward paths of righteousness. The Spirit will tell us how much, or how little, we should drink or cuss or talk or dance or hold or cling or buy or weep. Because the truth is we don't know, clearly. And we're different from one another, and so the boundaries must be different—to a point. We're even different from ourselves from time to time. Sometimes we are strong, and sometimes we like to wallow. Who can tell when it's time for us to be more vulnerable and empathetic, and who can tell when it's time to gut up and quit whining? Is there always a right answer? The Spirit knows. The Spirit will teach us what, and when, and how much.

The church of the future will neither legislate morality, nor avoid morality altogether. She will teach that our lives are meant to be conversations and that there is no cruise control for the life of the Spirit or multiple choice answer for holy living. Always, it's dialogue. And anything that gets in the way of that conversation—any pleasure, any rule, any relationship, any circumstance—needs to be excised if we are to live as God intends.

How is God's Spirit guiding you to live a more godly life?

EIGHT.SIX

ACTIVISM

BECOMING SPIRITUAL TRAILBLAZERS

"Make level paths for your feet," so that the lame may
not be disabled, but rather healed.
-Hebrews 12.13, NIV

> *Our commitment to straighten out the world must not make us crooked*
> *along the way.*

History tells us trailblazers would strike out in advance of an army, leveling roads and straightening paths so the marching forces wouldn't need to slow down or be in danger of ambush due to bottlenecks on their journey. Hebrews alludes to spiritual trailblazers, people who make crooked paths straight in order to help others progress along their journey with Christ. We must be like that—finding new ways forward as we straighten environments, prejudices, and futures.

We need people to straighten and level—not others, for we can never truly straighten out another person—but people who can blaze trails so those that follow see clearly.

For the last several years I've been working with a large multi-national denomination that perceives justice to be at the heart of their mission. At first I was excited. I am also passionate about justice, and the thought that some people are maligned and mistreated based on the boxes they check on a census survey infuriates me. But over time I've come to realize that the louder we clamor for justice, the more prone we are to condemnation. We get angrier and angrier at injustice, never stopping to consider what toll constant fury takes upon our souls.

> At times, I have found myself performing activism more than doing activism. I'm exhausted, and I'm not even doing the real work I am committed to do.
> -Frances Lee[120]

To be fair, we might also ask about the continued toll on our souls of injustice—how much does it cost us to ignore the plight of the oppressed because we're so worried about playing

---

[120] Lee, Frances, "Kin Aesthetics: Excommunicate Me from the Church of Social Justice," *Catalyst Wedding Co.*, July 10, 2017, http://www.catalystwedco.com/blog/2017/7/10/kin-aesthetics-excommunicate-me-from-the-church-of-social-justice, accessed August 24, 2017.

nice? But consider the longitudinal effects of telling ourselves that we must expose evil *at all costs*, and the reign of our oppressors *no matter what*, and sacrifice anything—*everything!*—for what's right. Consider how long it might take before someone decides another person—their boss, their father, their school teacher, their rival—is such an oppressor. What then controls their reactions? What limits their response?

If the local news is any indication, then the correct answer is nothing. Absolutely nothing stands in the way of our misguided attempts to destroy those we perceive to be destroyers. Even if they're not—even if we're wrong—we will kill the monster with an even greater monster of our own.

This is an issue, of which our culture is so aware, that we see it regularly in film, television, and literature. It occurs in *Game of Thrones*, *The Man in the High Castle*, and most notably as the driving arc behind Kassian's character in *Rogue One: A Star Wars Story*.

How can we know that those who oppose injustice can, themselves, become unjust; that despite our cause being so righteous, and our adversaries so evil, our actions are not always justified? How can we know this, and yet remain so blind when it occurs within our hearts?

These are complicated issues, and I don't intend for us to solve them in a paragraph, only to suggest that for every evil outside ourselves we expose, another evil inside us struggles to conceive.

So what will the church of the future be like?

We will be a church that gets our hands dirty, that provides a way back, and that makes all things new. We will be the church of the Incarnation—showing the world what Christ would do if he were here, acting as his hands and feet. We will be the church of the Atonement—inviting others back into relationship with God, with one another, with Creation, and with their true selves as image-bearers of the divine. We will be the church of the Resurrection—working tirelessly to take what has been broken and mend it, so that it is better than ever before.

With God working inside of us, we have his power on loan to change who we are and how we are. Forever. For good.

> *How can you ensure God's work* in you *is not compromised by God's work* through you?

GOODNESS

INVESTING IN OUR PRIMARY SPHERES OF INFLUENCE

For we are God's handiwork, created in Christ Jesus to do good works, which God prepared in advance for us to do.
-Ephesians 2.10, NIV

We do good works because good works.

JK Rowling, author of *Harry Potter*, once told a group of graduates, "We do not need magic to transform our world; we carry all the power we need inside ourselves already; we have the power to imagine better."[121] I applaud Rowling, both for her ability to phrase this concept so succinctly and for her willingness to communicate it in person.

We've tried to do likewise.

Several years ago, Westwinds decided to get very specific about where we wanted to "imagine better." Convicted by our need to incarnate the gospel, and yet aware of how massive a task that is, even in a small Midwestern town, we corralled our people to perform "good works because good works." We decided on five primary venues in which we would aim our efforts—at home, at work, at school, in their neighborhoods, and in our city—because these were the places we felt not only needed the greatest investment but also afforded the greatest opportunities.

We want good works to begin at **home**, since that's the primary training ground for the next generation of Christians and the incubation chamber for the future of the Church. As much as we can teach and grow people at church, nothing compares to the investment of parents in their children. You cannot outsource spirituality. However you live is whatever you'll teach, and children are exceptional learners. So we want parents to be intentional about filling their homes with kindness, love, scripture, prayer, adventure, fun, and love. These good works generate and create healthy families.

We want good works to happen at **work** since, for most adults, that's the group of people who will know them best and see them in the least flattering light. We spend most of our lives

---

[121] Rowling, JK, *Very Good Lives*, 67.

at work. We have opportunities for the greatest satisfaction, happiness, and frustration at work. We develop entirely new spheres of relationships and ambitions at work. So we want to bring our faith to work and watch the transforming power of God's Spirit in the lives of our coworkers as they rediscover not only joy at work, but the joy of cooperative work with God.

We want to do good works at **school** because that is where we're most frequently confronted with the breakdown of families. Especially elementary school. And school is where it's easiest and least weird for us to provide surrogate families to those kids who've suffered massive disruption. By the time those kids are in high school, many may have already hardened or chosen a path of self-destruction. It is more difficult to bring them into our homes and they are more resistant to our overtures. By doing good works in schools we're able to model and to offer and to welcome kids into a better paradigm for the family home.

We want to do good works in our **neighborhoods** because they provide countless opportunities for spontaneous social interaction. We bump into our neighbors. We hear our neighbors. We see our neighbors. And in all these happenstances, we are available to our neighbors to listen, to help, to see, to laugh and to love.

Finally, we want to do good works in our **city** because the city is the collective term for us all. When we think about our city, we're thinking about people we don't know but with whom we identify. We might not be like them. We might not like them. But we cannot escape that what affects us, affects them. What happens to us, in us, and through us, happens to them also. We are interconnected in a way that people from other cities aren't. Because we're here. And because we're here, we want to make a positive impact working for societal transformation. We want to gather resources for the good of the world, putting them to intelligent use for mutually beneficial ends.

The church of the future will realize that good work ultimately results in the kaleidoscopic beauty of truth and goodness, bringing glory to God and joy to God's people.

> *How is God leading you to perform good works at home, at work, at school, and in your neighborhood and your city?*

NINE

WE SEE A CHURCH

that **UNDERSTANDS** IMAGINATION *is* GODLY; *that* **TRIES** NEW THINGS *and* AVOIDS SACRALIZING CURRENT METHODOLOGIES.

WE SEE THE CHURCH *as a* PALACE OF ENDLESS IMAGINATION, **DRAWING** *the* WORLD IN WONDER *to the* MIND OF GOD.

EDEN

GOD INTENDS US TO COLLABORATE

Be fruitful and multiply and fill the earth and subdue
it and have dominion over the fish of the sea and over
the birds of the heavens and over every living thing
that moves on the earth.
- Genesis 1.28, ESV

> *God intends our relationships to be marked with creativity and love.*

Eden was God's paradigmatic happiness, and I've always been fascinated by it. The garden was God's first project, and the first moment God exclaimed, "Like this!" It was all opportunity, adventure and exploration, Creation and co-Creation. Like a parent creating a toy room for their children, God placed us in Eden and stood at the threshold watching us play.

Can you imagine God's delight when Adam and Eve would taste a new fruit? Find a new species of plant? Encounter a new animal?

That Adam and Eve were mean to subdue[122] the earth entailed something they had to overcome. Hostile wilderness? Untamed animals? Who knows? But there was something over which they had to exercise dominion.[123]

And how did the first people pass their time? I have ideas, some from the biblical witness and some from our understanding of ancient Mesopotamia. Eastern gardens, for example, had buildings, which means it's likely Adam and Eve would have constructed pergolas, trellises, arbors; great, multi-tiered canals; even follies—tall stone towers with no purpose save perspective.

Think of it this way: Adam and Eve didn't need money, food, or shelter. What occupies healthy, noble people when our basic needs are met and our base desires satiated?

Creativity.

---

[122] H3533 *kabash:* "to conquer, to subjugate, to bring into bondage," *Strong's Concordance,* http://biblehub.com/hebrew/3533.htm, accessed August 25, 2017.

[123] H7287 *radah:* "to prevail against, to reign, to rule," *Strong's Concordance,* http://biblehub.com/hebrew/7287.htm, accessed August 25, 2017.

> Imagination is more important than knowledge.
> - Albert Einstein

When we have nothing else to do, we do what we want.

But ... weren't they bored?

This is the reason I qualified my statement above by asking what "healthy, noble" people do when their needs are met—because boredom is the fertilizing principle of unloveliness. Boredom is a lack of creativity, industry, and imagination. Boredom is spiritual laziness, and like my mother-in-law used to say, "Smart people are never bored. They make their own fun." When you are the best possible version of yourself, downtime becomes playtime.

The church of the future will faithfully execute her responsibilities, enjoying her work with God and applying her creativity to noble purpose.

What is your favorite creative work?

NINE.TWO

CURIOSITY

LEARNING TO SEE GOD AT WORK EVERYWHERE, AND JOINING IN

> Ye are gods; and all of you are children of the most High.
> -Psalm 82.6, KJV

Our curiosity, as much as our fidelity, guides our relationship with God.

In 2002, Mark Millar, Grant Morrison, Tom Peyer and Mark Waid[124] pitched a never-published reimagining of Superman, painting the Man of Steel as a stronger, more alien superbeing. In the pitch, Superman's pure spirit and remarkable intellect have given him an almost Eden-like perspective on earth, and he devotes himself to creative pursuits.

> Superman becomes the hobbyist par excellence, the polymath who's interested in EVERYTHING. The Fortress becomes trophy room, laboratory, gymnasium, observatory—the perfect hangout for the ultimate being. Let's see the Fortress stuffed with incredible artifacts from all space and time. The Titanic hangs from the ceiling (Supes and Lois dine in the great staterooms, overlooking the wonders of the Fortress).

What I love most about this version of Superman is how inherently Christ-like he becomes. For, if Christ is indeed the Second Adam come to inaugurate the New Creation, then he must be guided by many of Adam's impulses like vision, creativity, and ingenuity. Perhaps this explains why Jesus never performed a miracle the same way twice, or why there are variations in his parables, or why he refused to answer questions directly, or why he repurposed the scriptures of the First Testament to suit his needs in the present. Maybe Christ did all of this because he wanted to, because it satisfied him to apply his mind, and because he, too, was looking to explore the wonders of this world as both an inhabitant and creator in the same way Adam and Eve explored Eden.

> We also see Superman as the ultimate communicator—invulnerable to pain, he needs none

[124] See https://sites.google.com/site/deepspacetransmissions/Resources/superman-2000-proposal.

of the physical defensive postures we take for granted and so would be incredibly relaxed and open—the big smile, the instant handshake, the conviction that everyone he meets is to be regarded as a friend until he proves otherwise. Superman should be indefatigable and trustworthy.

If Eden was a place of never-ending creative work—naming animals, subduing Creation, exercising dominion, tending and tilling the garden, cultivating habitats for the ultimate provision and sustenance of families, drawing resources together for transportation and expansion—**and if Christ came to *inaugurate* New Creation**—the moment when everything is made New, when Christ will be all in all, when the City of God descends to the world of men, where all the kings of the earth pay homage to their King, the Lord of All, when every tribe and tongue and nation are gathered at the river and receive healing from the trees in the Orchard of Life—**then we should also ask, what will that New Creation be like when it is complete?**

What will we do once we're supermen?

In Eden, Adam and Eve cooperated with God to perpetuate God's Creation. But the Bible clearly indicates God intended to work with people forever, which is why heaven, like Eden, is presented as a place where God and God's people continue joint endeavors for eternity.

The church of the future will help her people cooperate with God in whatever endeavors we choose, because what we will want is good as a result of the Lord "[giving] us the desires of our heart."[125]

---

[125] Psalm 37.4, ESV.

If you had limitless power, how would you use it?

NINE.THREE

IMAGINATION

COOPERATING WITH GOD TO PERPETUATE CREATION

> Do you see a man skillful in his work? He will stand before kings; he will not stand before obscure men.
> - Proverbs 22.29, ESV

> *God's ideal relationship with humanity involves cooperation on creative tasks that manifest and complexify the beauty of Creation.*

Some have imagined heaven as a place of constant worship, typified by the angels and elders bowing before the throne and calling "holy, holy, holy." But worship is not exhausted in song or obeisance. Worship means "to ascribe worth," and the Hebrew word for work is the same as that for worship.[126] That means every activity in which we participate can be repurposed as worship, which is undoubtedly what Brother Lawrence meant when he famously declared we have been made to "practice the Presence of God."[127] Sewing can be worship as much as singing, and calculating spreadsheets can be exhortation as much as casting crowns.

What Adam and Eve did in Eden, we will do in heaven, because we were designed for imagination, creativity, and cooperative work with God. Yet the church of the future won't wait for heaven to exercise her capacity for ongoing creative endeavors. She will, instead, embody the reality of Jesus' prayer that God's will would be done, that God's Kingdom would come, that God's name would be hallowed now on earth as it is in heaven.

> There is another world, but it is in this one.
> - Paul Eluard

God is first revealed to us as a Creator, and we are made in his image. When we create, we are like God. Regardless of the fact that our creations are always derivative, we are never more like God than when we are making things and making things up.

Take, for example, the trash-to-treasure movement. In France, they call it *Bricolage*. Now, we run HGTV shows about

---

[126] H5647 *abad, Strong's Concordance,* http://biblehub.com/hebrew/5647. htm, accessed August 25, 2017. Also, Huber, Dave, "Avodah Word Study," https://www.efcatoday.org/story/avodah-word-study, accessed August 25, 2017.

[127] Brother Lawrence, *The Practice of the Presence of God.*

repurposing old antiques. Or steampunk. These design threads all celebrate the same basic motif: take something of no value, add imagination, and imbue that which was worthless with new worth. *Voila.* A $2 chandelier from the thrift store is now a $500 *objet d'art.* Isn't that what God does with us? We were adopted. Inherited. Gifted. Named. Anointed. We had no people, we had no name, but we became the people of God. And now we're valuable.

What God does *for* us, God also does *with* us. He makes us new. He empowers us to make new things. What else does this new-making energy require than imagination?

> Fantasy is a natural human activity. It certainly does not destroy or even insult Reason; and it does not either blunt the appetite for, nor obscure the perception of, scientific verity. On the contrary, the keener and clearer is the reason the better fantasy will make it.
> - J.R.R. Tolkien[128]

To imagine is to see something that only exists in your mind, and the ultimate manifestation of that image is to fashion it in the material world. To bring it forth. To create it.

How might you consider your creative work as worship?

---

[128]   Tolkien, J.R.R., *on Fairy Stories*, 65.

BEAUTY

PERCEIVING GOD AESTHETICALLY

The Lord God made all kinds of trees grow out of the ground—trees that were pleasing to the eye and good for food.
- Genesis 2.9, NIV

God speaks through beauty.

All beauty comes from God, reflects God, and reveals God to the extent that we can have conversations about God every time we see something truly wonderful. Even more significantly, independent of any conversations about beauty, God can use beauty to reveal himself directly to people.

Why? Because beauty is how God penetrates the armor of our indifference.

We grow deaf so quickly to teaching and sermonizing and authority—blind to example and skill in living. Sometimes the only thing God has to work with in our stubborn idiocrasy is the beauty around us. If he can get us simply to recognize something beautiful, then he has a portal through which he can speak.

We see beauty in acts of charity, justice, and creativity. We see that there is more to being beautiful than simply having certain physical proportions, certain hair and clothes, or a certain frame. We also see through the fake and vain beauty that much of our world has embraced, calling into question what others have decided is beautiful by asking questions about whether true beauty can be purchased (through surgery, for example), prostituted (through excessive social media sharing, for example) or Photoshopped (through post-production fixes, for example). And, in all this, we realize that God is teaching us, through our aesthetic sensibilities, about himself.

The fact that God became a man brings truth and reality crashing together in a new way. The Incarnation gave us the definitive example of how life was meant to be enjoyed by those who love and honor God. That life was one of real beauty—the beauty of a person wholly committed to selflessness and love.

Our creativity cultures a holy beauty. It calls us to God through wonder, causing us to open up to the promise of ongoing metamorphosis.

Many would claim that art, beauty, and aesthetics are a waste of time given the broken state of our world, and that we should forgo all such nonsense in favor of simply doing more good works. We see this sentiment in denominations that argue about musical preferences, adornments and decorations, expenses related to grounds keeping and marketing—all because these issues seem like distractions from "true worship" rather than manifestations of it. We also see this sentiment in some sectors of government and education, as evidenced by the widespread defunding of arts and music programs in elementary schools. And we see this sentiment among activist groups and justice-seekers, who perceive artistic endeavors as a waste, wondering how anyone can care about beauty when people are homeless or hurting or alone. But it's a mistake to think that stopping our creative efforts and instead putting more effort in acts of justice will yield greater effect than what we're doing now. On the contrary, art and beauty enliven us to continue the work of redemption. If you took away all our inspiration, what would ever make us want to help others, since obligation quickly turns to resentment?

> O worship the Lord in the beauty of holiness: fear before him, all the earth.
> - Psalm 96.9, KJV

The church of the future will recognize the refinement of her aesthetic sensibilities represents a deeper longing for God.

What's the most beautiful sight you have ever witnessed?

ARTISTRY

EXPLORING THE RELATIONSHIP
BETWEEN ART AND FAITH

Ascribe to the Lord the glory due his name; bring an offering and come before him. Worship the Lord in the splendor of his holiness.
- 1 Chronicles 16.29, NIV

Christian art should save, not sanitize, teasing out the abundant graces of exhilarating life in Christ.

There is a strong relationship between art and faith: art reveals the spiritual world; art invites interpretation; art raises questions about ourselves, our world, and our God.

But not everyone sees it this way. In fact, many Christians and many churches struggle with the relationship between faith and art. It's like we've met some couple at a dinner party and the husband, Art, is quirky and witty, while the wife, Faith, is prim and dour. Occasionally Faith squeezes Art's hand to let him know he's gone too far, perhaps even scoffing at his outlandish remarks and crude stories; other times Art rolls his eyes at Faith's monochromatic voiceovers and teases her for being such a stick in the mud. It's too bad, because we like Art, but Faith seems like she's no fun; or maybe we like it that Faith is so intuitive, but it bothers us that Art is dismissive of sensitive social situations.

We want to challenge this split between Art and Faith. They're a lovely couple, and we want to continue helping them work out their issues in godly community.

Now, there may be some of you who think I'm going too far in my portrayal of Faith and Art. You may be thinking that many churches have wonderful artists and that there are some lovely songs sung by Christians for Christians.

This may all be true.

Yet, it is also true that much of what we consider art within Christendom is saccharine: family films about togetherness, skippy songs and happy endings. But these works do not portray the world as it is, nor do they honestly portray the world as God once created it to be and intends for it to be again. They create art without the Fall—so there is nothing broken (unless it is a charming old barn), nothing hurting (except for a marriage between a stubborn man and a flighty woman), and nothing with any sense of longing (unless it is a high school senior preparing for the big game). Yet the Fall is irrevocably a part of our world. We have to take notice of our brokenness and acknowledge it. We have to monitor our perceptions, because we know that they are distorted by sin—even the sin of ignoring evil in hopes that good will win out by default.

> My own feeling is that writers who see by the light of their Christian faith will have, in these times, the sharpest eyes for the grotesque, for the perverse, and for the unacceptable … redemption is meaningless unless there is a cause for it in the actual life we live, and for the last few centuries there has been operating in our culture the secular belief that there is no such cause.
> - Flannery O'Connor

If you need an example of art that deals seriously with the Fall, consider Rodion Raskolnikov in *Crime and Punishment* (by Fyodor Dostoevsky). Raskolnikov is a student, poor and without many resources, who decides to murder a pawnbroker and steal her money. Raskolnikov convinces himself his actions are actually motivated by a greater good, since the pawnbroker is an unjust and immoral person. Raskolnikov also convinces himself he will perform good deeds with the stolen money, thereby more than compensating for the murder (since the villainous pawnbroker should die anyway).

Dostoevsky's complex portrait of human depravity is an excellent example of art in conversation with faith. Throughout the book, readers get a strong sense of the author's judgment against his own protagonist—not simply for the obvious crime of murder, but also for the more insidious sin of a murderer convincing himself of his moral superiority.

How much more honest would "Christian" art become if we understood self-righteousness as something that blinds us instead of a quality only belonging to our adversaries? If we were as wary of our justifications as our temptations?

Another concern regarding Christian art is defining salvation by sin's absence instead of God's Presence. Thus, Christians often portray redemptive themes as bland and sexless pictures of serene carelessness. But God is certainly Present where sin exists, calling us out of our messes and into something more true, something more beautiful, something good. We're supposed to be living in God's Presence in each moment, truly alive with ecstasy and experience, exhilaration and exuberance.

We think God wants us to be sedate, when he wants us to be consumed with Holy Fire. We think God wants us to be monks, when he has called us to be stewards. We think God wants us to be friendly, when what he really wants is for us to explore.

The church of the future will delve more deeply into scripture and into the work of God in our own souls so we can forge a truthful, imaginative, and compelling vision of the world that reflects the Presence and the Splendor of our God.

What is the greatest work of redemptive art?

NINE.SIX

ICONOCLASM

OVERCOMING OUR FEAR OF THE UGLY TRUTH

> If it is possible, as far as it depends on you, live at peace with everyone.
> - Romans 12.18, NIV

Iconoclasm is no more godly than idolatry.

One of the great tragedies of our time is the destruction of ancient arts and artifacts by ISIS. Motivated by religious zealotry, these men have broken into countless temples and smashed statues, idols, and decorative walls. ISIS has destroyed entire ancient churches, mosques, and even cities all in the name of establishing tawhid-monotheism.[129] It's brutal, thuggish, and nd unimaginably shortsighted given that one group, during one thoughtless season of zeal, has removed several historical landmarks forever. They have obliterated the past and stolen from the future.

Of course many of our most well-regarded Christians did the same thing during the Protestant Reformation. John Calvin was responsible for "cleansing" Christianity of icons[130] and some reports go so far as to suggest he would pay for evidence of broken statues, destroyed paintings, and other ruined religious imagery. I don't point this out merely to suggest that Christianity has as many reasons to be ashamed as radical Islam, but to lay the foundation for why there is still such reluctance toward the inclusion of the arts within our present context.

We're afraid.

We're afraid to create art because it is provocative and open to misinterpretation—this, after all, is at the root of iconoclasm. We destroy images and artwork about God for fear that those images might somehow lead us astray.

---

[129] Hatra, Nimrud, and large portions of Palmyra. See http://www.bbc.com/news/world-middle-east-31779484; http://www.cnn.com/2015/03/09/world/iraq-isis-heritage/index.html; https://www.theguardian.com/world/2015/sep/02/isis-destruction-of-palmyra-syria-heart-been-ripped-out-of-the-city.

[130] Kuckuk, John William, *Out of the Cocoon: Rethinking Our Selves*, 34.

We're afraid to take creative risks because others may hate it; because others may scream about it; because others may seek to destroy what we have lovingly made. We're afraid that someone will call our art into question, labeling it "idolatrous" or "ego-driven" or "un-Christian;" and, if we're honest, we're afraid they might sometimes be correct.

We're afraid to spend money on creative pursuits because that money could be better used elsewhere (here it's always important to forget the telling story of Mary pouring expensive perfume on Jesus' feet, an act that was mindlessly loving and one which Judas roundly condemned).

We're afraid to create for fear that we make God angry as well—because our art is too raw, too honest, and our expressions of fidelity and conflict will not always have a biblical precedent.

But just because something is ugly doesn't mean it isn't beautiful. After all, the crucifixion of our Lord was a horrific scene, but as St. Augustine opined, "He hung therefore on the cross deformed, but his deformity is our beauty."

Sometimes Christian people think that if something is unpleasant to God it must be destroyed. The reason I take issue with this violence is, of course, that I frequently disagree with things that people assume God must hate. I don't think God hates secular music, so I'm certain we shouldn't force our kids to throw it away. I don't think God hates Hindus, so I'm quite certain we shouldn't advocate the destruction of their sacred places. Yet these are all things that Christians in the West are trying to do because they think that it makes them more pleasing to God. But that kind of thinking isn't Christian Spirituality; it's violent religious fundamentalism. Just because you think something is bad, even offensive, doesn't mean you can authoritatively declare it idolatrous and then smash it to bits.

Spirituality is not only about absorbing great teaching, or living well, but also about cultivating a taste for the beautiful and an accompanying distaste for the profane. The church of the future will increase her capacity to appreciate that which is truly beautiful, and to decry that which is fake, gaudy, pornographic, or ostentatious without also seeking to destroy it.

> *What does it mean to oppose ugliness without defacing it?*

PROVOCATION

SPEAKING OF HOLY THINGS IN UNHOLY WAYS

A prophet is not without honor except in his own town and in his own home.
- Matthew 13.57, NLT

Art, like prophecy, can shock us from our lethargy into obedience.

Art is what we use to go beyond ourselves. It is a means of expression beyond the cognitive, literal, calculating part of our minds. Not all art should be enjoyable—some of the best art transforms our perspective through shock, provocation, and exasperation.

> Great art is irritation.
> - Gertrude Stein

Our task is to expose the world's numbness, warning others of incumbent danger even when they would rather remain blissfully, palliatively, comatose.

We are called to be like the prophets in the Jewish scriptures who, though uncouth and offensive, nevertheless challenged the status quo. Hosea married a prostitute, Jeremiah bought desolate land[131], Ezekiel lay on his side in filth for over a year beside a model of Jerusalem, and King Saul prophesied naked. Jesus was no more orthodox than these, exemplified by his cutting down the fig tree and prophecy of the Temple's destruction, nor was John the Baptist in any way "nice."

These are the Founding Fathers of the spiritual underground—talking about holy things in unholy ways. Their power lies with the critique of *the real* versus *the ideal*.

> There are two ways of being a prophet. The first involves going to people who have been enslaved and telling them they are free. That is the path of Moses. The second involves going to people who believe they are free and telling them they are slaves. That is the more difficult path of Jesus.
> - Unknown

---

[131] A cultural gaff in the ancient world, tantamount to inviting a curse upon your life.

We must persist in sanctified subversion. The church of the future will be freed from the common misconception that the Kingdom of God is about keeping Christians happy.

Our task is to harness creative restlessness. We must use this energy to generate new ideas, new applications, and new experiences for the glory of God.

> The human soul needs actual beauty even more than bread.
> - D.H. Lawrence

It is common for Christians to divvy up art into the too-clean categories of the sacred and the secular, perhaps best articulated in Francis Schaeffer's book, *Addicted to Mediocrity*. But scripture never speaks in these terms.

Art, like conversation or money, always belongs to someone. Art is worship, whether of God or of some counterfeit; and, when the people of God expropriate from sources in rebellion against God, that commandeering consecrates, and the art is sacralized. So, when we play a secular song in church for example, we're not glorifying un-Christian art; we're sanctifying it, reminding us that God will speak to his children through any means possible. As Oswald Chambers famously declared, "All truth is God's truth, regardless of where it is found."

The church of the future will expand her understanding of beauty to include those things that must shock us into action, bolstering our convictions about *the ideal* Kingdom God intends to create.

Who do you know that best typifies the provocative prophet?

NINE.EIGHT

COMPOSITION

UNDERSTANDING PRIMARY AND SECONDARY IMAGINATION

Another shapes wood, he extends a measuring line; he
outlines it with red chalk He works it with planes and
outlines it with a compass, and makes it like the form
of a man, like the beauty of man, so that it may sit in
a house.
- Isaiah 44.13, NKJV

> *There are two ways to imagine the future: with your mind or*
> *with your hands.*

When W.H. Auden gave his Inaugural lecture in Oxford he spoke of the difference between Primary and Secondary Imagination.

Primary Imagination refers to our contact with all that is sacred. We know the spiritual world exists, but we cannot see it, so we imagine what it must be like. We are full of wonder and awe and so feel a need to respond. Primary Imagination manifests in two ways: ideas that run themselves, and ideas we must perpetuate. The former includes things like delirium, worry, dreams, daydreaming, or mental complexes driven by martyrdom or inferiority. These are all things that happen without any concerted effort on our part; our thoughts just run. The latter class—those imaginations we must perpetuate—include things like speculative imagery *("What would it look like if...?")*, reproductive imagination *("Have I seen anything like this before that I can reproduce here with a few tweaks?")*, structural visualization *("How would this look in a three-dimensional space?")*, "bridging" or vicarious imagination *("How can I help others see or think or experience what I'm perceiving?")*, anticipatory imagination *("What will we do once...?")*, or creative expectancy *("In order to _____, we must first...")*. Here, we are forcing ourselves to think certain thoughts in certain ways; we set our minds to work, aiming our imagination so that our generative capacity is applied along new pathways.

> Imagination is not only the uniquely human capacity to envision that which is not, and therefore the fount of all invention and innovation; in its arguable most transformative and revelatory capacity, it is the power that enables us to empathize with humans whose experiences we have never shared.
> - JK Rowling[132]

---

[132]   Rowling, JK, *Very Good Lives*, 41.

Secondary Imagination refers to what we do with our thoughts, our wonder, and our awe. It is how we give shape to our awareness—how we incarnate it, so to speak. We take our thoughts and make films and songs and pictures and words.

In the First Imagination we sense that there is more to our lives than what we really see. Everyone has this Imagination, because we all know intuitively what quantum physics has now proven empirically: the fundamental building blocks of the universe are invisible. The truest parts of our reality cannot be seen, but function like vibrating strings of energy. Our intentions matter more than our arguments, our beliefs manifest more strongly than our education, and our loves and fears override all but the most absolute barriers to getting what we want. The First Imagination allows us to perceive this invisible world, to operate it and play with it, however fleetingly or briefly. In the Second Imagination we do something with our thoughts. We make stuff. We achieve things that echo our longing for life to be different.

Westwinds has had some success in creating new works of art that manifest common ideas. For example, people are often overly concerned with their own fragility, so we wanted to underscore that frailty doesn't necessary have to be the focal point of breakable objects. To whit, we hired a glass blower to make four special bowls. We filmed the process and added a voiceover, talking about the beauty of fragile things, and emphasized that God can do more with us than simply keep us from getting broken. We then used those bowls directly after the video to invite our people to anoint one another with oil, as a symbol of their power as kings and priests. We wanted them to know they may be fragile, but that they could overlook their frailty and stop being afraid if they would, instead, focus on God's calling in their lives to bless others. After the service, the videographer[133] created a cross that housed one of the bowls and put it on display in our cross garden as a constant reminder that beauty can be more prominent than brokenness.[134]

The church of the future will not be content with Primary Imagination, but will create artifacts, exhibits, and experiences designed to inspire thoughts about God.

> *Who do you know with the best Secondary Imagination?*

---

[133] Jacob McGarry, a staff member at Westwinds and freelance filmmaker. http://www.jacobtmcgarry.com

[134] The Cross Garden at the main entrance to Westwinds is one of my favorite places. Modeled after the Hill of Crosses in Lithuania (see https://en.wikipedia.org/wiki/Hill_of_Crosses), there are dozens of crosses and crucifixes from all over the world, in a variety of styles, on display year-round.

NINE.NINE

NOVELTY

REFUSING TO RETURN TO OUR BAG OF TIRED TRICKS

See, I am doing a new thing! Now it springs up; do you not perceive it? I am making a way in the wilderness and streams in the wasteland.
- Isaiah 43.19, NIV

Repetition is the soil of contempt, but novelty brings forth life and health.

In my years at Westwinds we have created some incredible experiences. We once took all the chairs out of our auditorium and filled it with thousands of pillows, inviting people to wander, cluster, and recline during church as though we were Bedouins. We once hosted the percussion section from the Symphony and explored "the theology of rhythm," allowing our people to clap, stomp, and play classroom instruments along with the pros. We once created sound-domes that hung from our ceiling, creating aural environments that allowed people to hear prayers sung in other languages as they moved from station to station throughout our performance space. We once set up computer terminals with access to our pastor friends all over the globe, providing private space for virtual confession. We once set up tricliniums in place of chairs, giving our people the experience of dining in the Roman style of Christ at the Last Supper. We once set up dozens and dozens of 4-person dinner tables and crafted our entire service around meals. We once allowed our people to vote on which songs they would sing, and then performed only their requests. We once taught through the book of Titus using Pecha Kucha, a Japanese oratory style employing 20 slides, each shown for 20 seconds.

The key word in all these experiences is *once*. Because we never repeat an experience. We might stretch that experience out for a short season (twelve weeks at the outside), but when we dissemble our environments we know they will never be reassembled. Sometimes we may resurrect an idea that didn't work, adding something significant to make a fresh experience un-recognizable from the first iteration. Or, we may take the experience into a new environment, with new participants and designers, for a new audience. But even with these caveats, we're a "one and done" kind of place.

That means we struggle with perfecting the experience for our people, since it's difficult to accurately conceptualize how crowds will act, react, and interact once you put everything together. But the risks inherent in experimentation are never fully rewarded in repetition. If we took the time to get absolutely everything absolutely perfect, we'd lose the spark that made the risk special in the first place. We still aim for perfection, but expect something unforeseen will prohibit us from fully realizing it. So we intensify our preparatory efforts, scrutinize our walkthroughs, and keep contingency plans in place to make changes on the fly for each experience.

I have never, in over twenty years, preached the same sermon twice.

Why?

Because some of these experiences are so meaningful, so provocative, so emotional that our people want them again. And again. And if left to our own devices, it would be the easiest thing in the world to go back into our bag of tricks and pull out same amusements every year. Every Christmas could have trees made entirely from hardcover books. Every Easter could have elaborate hand-cut lilies hung off our walls. Every Good Friday could be a Liturgy in Blues.

They could be, but they won't. Because every time you repeat an experience, you diminish the impact by half. The first time, it's amazing. Unbelievable. Incredible. But the next time, it's only great. Then it's only cool. Then it's only good. Then it's a little stale. Then it's tired. Then we're afraid to change because it might hurt someone's feelings (they've worked so hard!). Then it's too much work to change. Then it's simply what we do. Then it's what we have to do. Then we can never stop.

There is nothing more destructive to a relationship than doing what you've done before in hopes of getting what you got before. Candlelight dinners may sometimes result in romantic trysts, but beware the idiot husband who makes spaghetti and hopes for sex "because it worked last time." A Father's Day tie is a nice gift—once. But if every Father's Day you offer Papi another $10 bargain from JC Penney, he's going to tire of your carelessness.

Do we suppose our relationship with God is any different? That we could sing the same songs and go through the same motions mentally disengaged, emotionally absent, and socially wayward without God feeling as though we're paying our tithes just to make him enlarge our territory? This-then-that religion is offensive. God will not bark when we say speak, nor provide because we prayed the right psalm.

> I hate, I despise your religious festivals; your
> assemblies are a stench to me.
> - Amos 5.21, NIV

The church of the future will always be trying new things. Always. We will experiment with new experiences. We will explore new avenues of worship. We will read the Bible in new ways. We will develop new tools for the integration of study and prayer. We will use new technologies. Some will try new things thoughtlessly, recklessly, perhaps even harmfully. But only some. The best will critically engage as they innovate, thoughtfully working to articulate the opportunities, imperatives, and offerings of each new expression.

Creative experimentation doesn't only generate beautiful ideas, but beautiful people, also. The very process forms and funds our understanding of Christian spirituality, catalyzing both our personal development and our missiological future.

Our mistrust of glitz and glam has made us scared of healthier, holier creativity. Why not see if God is still in the business of making things new?

> Your Creative Batting Average equals hits divided by total ideas, with ideas calculated as the ideas per notebook, the number of ideas recorded in your notebook over a few months ... for the hits, count the great ideas that not only got sold and produced, but also made you proud."(34)
> - Dave Kuhl[135]

Whenever we're generating new ideas, I think it's helpful to consider whether we're "on the hunt" or "working the change." The hunt is a search for something new, whereas the change is the synthesis of existing materials.

If you're on the hunt, you will soon realize that ideas are born from association, continuity, and contrast. New ideas require incubation as we create and resolve inner tension. So, when you're trying to solve a puzzle, think about it really hard, and then think about something else.

Play with it, let it marinate.

Ideas can come from rearrangement, reversal, and combination. We can rearrange elements from what we already have—music, oratory, the visual arts, congregational participation, etc.—and put them together in new ways. We can also flip things inside out, or backwards and forwards, leading us to consider how we might "bring our church to friends", for example. But perhaps the most provocative ideas are generated

[135] Kuhl, Dave, "What's your creative batting average?" *Communication Arts Photography Annual* 2016, 34. In this interview, the best "pro" average was 0.006.

from the combination of multiple disciplines, overlapping and complexifying one another. Westwinds has had great success with these layered experiments, including this past Sunday when we mixed a live DJ, drummer, and marimba player to soundtrack a silent film. The film, however, was not one storyline played on one screen, but two intersecting storylines displayed on seven different screens, each weaving together and coming apart as the story unfolded. Such mashups may include what legendary producer Jimmy Iovine claims is the "key to revitalizing the entire music industry, bridging the worlds of art and technology,"[136] or it may include disciplines from much further afield.

One of my long-term ministry ambitions is to adapt the theory of inventive problem-solving for Christian ministry. First articulated by Soviet scientist Genrich Altshuller (1926-1998), iTriz (as it is more commonly known) posits there are roughly forty different kinds of solutions to common problems across varying disciplines (such as manufacturing, medicine, transportation, and design). The solutions are simply named, such as "try heating things up or cooling things down" and could easily be adapted to help pastors, leaders, and innovators think around corners. Like so many other multidisciplinary theories, iTriz has almost immediate ministry application and we could greatly assist the church of the future by adapting, modifying, or substituting the basic tenets according to the demands of ecclesial life.

One basic application from iTriz demonstrates that ideas result from addition, subtraction, division, and multiplication. What would happen if, for example, we added something to the water of our baptismal font to color it red? What would happen if we subtracted all the light from our auditorium and worshipped in the dark? What would happen if we divided our

---

[136] Tanz, Jason. "Relentless", *Wired Magazine*, 65.

congregation according to gender, to recall more antiquated traditions? What would happen if we multiplied our service times, inviting new cadres of people to experience God in new ways?

These possibilities and many more besides are at the root of my ambition to open a center for the holistic integration of art, work, and faith much like Andy Warhol's Factory in the seventies. In case you're unfamiliar with the backstory, the Factory was an artistic haven where photographers, designers, models, and fashionistas gathered with movie stars and music moguls to play, to create, and to party. By all accounts, it tended toward the libidinous, but the purest essence of the Factory involved the cross-pollination of ideas, expertise, and backgrounds. Such an environment, sanctified, would place men and women working together to help make the invisible visible, to see what cannot be otherwise seen, and hold up a mirror to the distortions present in our world.

That's what the church of the future will be like: a great collaborative smorgasbord of ideas, generativity, and love.

What is one thing you have always wanted to try?

TEN | WE
SEE
A
CHURCH

that **POUNCES** JOYFULLY *on* NEW OPPORTUNITIES, **CONFIDENT** *in* HER ABILITY TO MAKE MID-COURSE CORRECTIONS;

a **CHURCH** *that* PROTOTYPES, ITERATES, *and* **IMPROVISES** *as we progress* IN STEP *with the* SPIRIT.

TEN.ONE

DESIGN

DOING THE SAME OLD THINGS IN (RE)NEW(ED) WAYS

If we live by the Spirit, let us also walk by the Spirit.
- Galatians 5.25, NASB

> *The future is an ongoing experiment in which design and intention are woven together.*

John Maeda, famed media-artist and former President of the Rhode Island School of Design, was one of my earliest influences as a creative leader. His writing demonstrates the convergence of an artist's capacity with the strategies of an administrator. His thinking is atypical of peers in both arenas, and that's why it is so valuable. He's not spouting platitudes or rehashing old concepts. Instead, he maintains that the combination of artist and leader results in a designer, someone "who solves problems through making and iterating."[137]

> Artists don't distinguish between the act of making something and the act of thinking about it— thinking and making evolve together in an emergent, concurrent fashion. As a result, when approaching a project, an artist often doesn't seem to plan it out. She just goes ahead and begins, all the while collecting data that will inform how she will continue. A large part of what drives her confidence to move forward is her faith in her ability to course correct and improvise as she goes.
> -John Maeda[138]

Maeda's work has helped me form the passion and confidence with which I am able to pursue many large-scale projects at once. Whether writing fiction, designing curriculum, or crafting an artifact, I know that if I patiently follow my instincts all of my answers will ultimately reveal themselves. That's a sharp contrast from the majority of leadership literature that recommends we develop comprehensive plans for projects before we begin.

Don't get me wrong—I'm a planner, but especially in creative endeavors we cannot foresee all the roads ahead and must

---

[137] Maeda, John, *Redesigning Leadership*, 10.

[138] Ibid, 11.

always rely on our ability to adjust. When creating the future, we must expect the process to be an ongoing experiment in which design and intention are woven together, where goals and outcomes are discovered *en route* rather than perfectly articulated at the outset.

The church of the future will be committed to innovation and experimentation, understanding that our imaginative work amounts to cooperation with God. This requires that we think differently about ministry—not exclusively about different topics, but equally through different means of consideration. But isn't that the essence of holiness? Not doing new things from everyone else, but doing the same things as everyone else in (re)new(ed) ways?

> *How can you learn to stay more malleable at work, at home, and in your heart?*

TEN.TWO

EXPERIMENTATION

CELEBRATING THE FREEDOM TO CONSTANTLY TRY WITHOUT THE PRESSURE TO ALWAYS SUCCEED

See, I am doing a new thing! Now it springs up; do you not perceive it? I am making a way in the wilderness and streams in the wasteland.
- Isaiah 43.19, NIV

> *Just because some ideas don't work the way we intend doesn't excuse us from the requirements of experimentation.*

Recently I read an article in *Harvard Business Review* about Lego and their commitment to innovation. If you have children you're probably already aware of Lego's mastery of childlike fascination, and also of their relentless release of new themed sets. Lego Batman, Ninjago, Lego Friends, Lego Star Wars … apps, video games, devices, augmented reality toys. The Danish company seems obsessed with newness, seeing growth as "one testimony of whether we're sufficiently innovative."[139]

But as much as Lego is obsessed with innovation, they are driven by something deeper. They care about how children play.

> [Lego has been performing] deep ethnographic studies of how kids around the world really play … If you want to understand how animals live, you don't go to the zoo, you go to the jungle.
> - Jonathan Ringen[140]

I suppose I am partial to Lego because it has provided such enjoyment for my children, perhaps never more so than when my daughter staged her bedroom as a "house church," only to excommunicate her brother for playing Lego during the sermon. "Get those out of God's house!" she demanded, to which he replied, "God's home is in my heart; plus, the Lord told me he loves Lego." Unfortunately, my daughter had no one to assist her in removing her unruly congregant, as I had already been kicked out of "Hope Faith Chapel" for not wearing pants.

The church of the future will care about how people pray and play at the same time.

---

[139] Ringen, Jonathan, "When it clicks, it clicks," *Harvard Business Review*, February 2015, 77.

[140] Ibid, 76.

How? Through experimentation. Sometimes we'll need to try things just to see if they work, or work well. We don't necessarily do this because our current strategies and methodologies are failures, but because we know that everything has a shelf-life and by the time it hits its expiration date, the opportunities for another successful foray have greatly diminished.

Opportunity originates from the Latin phrase *ob portum veniens*, which means "coming into port." It was a term sailors used to reference favorable winds that made for safe harbor. If you wait too long, the wind will shift and the things you want to do will be more difficult, more perilous, and less pleasurable.

One of the most important lessons I've learned in life is that it's not the strong that eat the weak, but the fast that eat the slow.

What do I mean by that? I mean if you don't react quickly when opportunities come your way, you'll miss out. So file the paperwork. Return the message. Bid on the house. Move!

The church of the future will respond quickly to situations and circumstances where others can be introduced to Christ, challenged by the Spirit, or deepened in their understanding. She will not quibble endlessly about how to proceed, but move forward boldly into the opportunities God provides.

> Whatever turns up, grab it and do it. And heartily!
> This is your last and only chance at it.
> -Ecclesiastes 9:10a, MSG

We have to be constantly experimenting, constantly innovating, and yet we do these without the pressure that they have to be successful. This doesn't mean we are free from ever producing meaningful results, merely that we ought to provide time for tinkering. Ultimately our lives, our businesses, and our churches must prove themselves, but the path to lasting satisfaction and meaning at work involves trying new ideas "just to see"; then, if the results are good, we can continue down the path.

Consider, for example, the success of manufacturer 3M, who gave their employees time off to explore their own products long before Google or Hewlett Packard followed suit. This "15% time" is an initiative at 3M that allows employees to "use a portion of their paid time to chase the rainbow"[141] and has resulted in such tremendous successes as Post-It notes, masking tape, and cellophane (Scotch) tape.

One of the great failures, if I can call it that, at Westwinds was our one-time approach to spiritual formation called "Causemology." We designed a gamefied version of discipleship in which we invited everyone in our church to participate in something for their soul, something for their relationships, something for their church, and something for their world. We wanted them to be intentional about their spiritual development, and also to understand that their spiritual development neither centered on church nor wholly away from it, either. We wanted to authenticate all that God was doing through secular organizations, teaching our people to engage when and where and to what degree they felt was appropriate. To help, we gave them suggestions about what they might do every month and invited them to either change what they were doing or reject the newest suggestion in favor of tracking along with their present "rule of life."

[141] Goetz, Kaomi, "How 3M Gave Everyone Days Off and Created an Innovation Dynamo," *Fast Co Design,* February 1, 2011, https://www.fastcodesign.com/1663137/how-3m-gave-everyone-days-off-and-created-an-innovation-dynamo, accessed August 25, 2017.

For example, in September of 2009 I decided I would do *lectio divina* for 20 minutes each morning (something for my soul), call my mom every Thursday (something for my relationships), serve in our children's ministry as a helper on the two Sundays I wasn't preaching (something for my church), and volunteer on an ecological clean up dive (something for my world). Others would make different choices, but the grid was always the same.

It was such a good idea, with such good thinking, and at the time I felt like the execution and branding was done very, very well. But it never worked. Not really. Not like we wanted. Somehow it always came back to giving our people new things to think about, and in its worst moments it began to feel like there were thousands of spiritual practices our people were rejecting. Consequently, those that participated felt tired and those that opted out felt exhausted and ashamed.

And I still don't know why.

> Failure is just part of the process, and it's not just okay; it's better than okay. God doesn't want failure to shut us down … It's more about how God helps us dust ourselves off so we can swing for the fences again.
> -Bob Goff[142]

I can autopsy the entire six-year span of the experiment and outline every tweak we made along the way to reduce the negative consequences; but, in the end, I can't figure out why it didn't revolutionize spirituality for our church or our people. And so, after iterating that sucker to death, we let it go.

Because some experiments don't work.

---

[142] Goff, Bob, *Love Does.*

That's not to say we learned nothing, or that our people didn't benefit. In fact, I think Westwinds has maintained a healthy holism noticeably absent in most congregations. But I thought it was going to be better. I thought it could really matter.

And I was wrong.

Thank God we ultimately abandoned it once we realized there were no more tweaks to be reasonably made. And thank God we've got other ideas that have grown out of Causemology and that the Spirit was able to bring something new to bear in our church. And thank God we've maintained our commitment to experimentation.

Because the church of the future will know she must keep tweaking everything along the way instead of digging in our heels and telling people to toughen up. She will perceive failures as setbacks rather than defeats, and continue to change and grow in step with the Spirit.

> *What area of your life would benefit most from some time back at the drawing board?*

TEN.THREE

ITERATION

LEARNING NOT TO DEFEND WHAT WE THINK WE'RE DOING RIGHT

> Blessed is the one whom God corrects; so do not
> despise the discipline of the Almighty.
> - Job 5.17, NIV

> *We must pursue the truth and be cautious our small successes do not*
> *create arrogance, blindness, or an unwillingness to keep learning.*

298

The church of the future knows there are certain things we'll never get totally right, but they will continue to try anyway, knowing that "our desire to please God does, in fact, please God."[143] And as we continue to make changes, mid-course corrections, and adjustments we get closer and closer to what God wants.

And of course God won't always want the same thing, and the moment won't always bear the same characteristics, so our relationship with God and God's mission will always be like a dance. He's leading, we're following. We move with God. We adjust. Which means we've got to stay malleable. Editable. We need to stay in step with the Spirit, realizing there's few things in this life that are ever going to be black and white.

We grow spiritually much more by doing it wrong than doing it right. Like skaters, we move forward by actually moving from side to side.

We'll never get discipleship totally right, because the actual ways God forms us and grows us are myriad, circumstantial, and individual. It should be no surprise that churches have a difficult time formulating discipleship strategies and pathways. Sunday school classes, small groups, Bible studies, missions trips, etc. All those things are good, but in the final evaluation it is the Spirit that makes disciples. God grows us using everything—predominantly pain!—so the things we do intentionally in our churches are good but never sufficient to shore up the movement of the Spirit in the life of a believer. We do everything we can to help people recognize the Spirit, listen to the Spirit, respond to the Spirit; and we do everything we can to help people understand the Scriptures, live by the Scriptures, come under the authority of the Scriptures; but the ultimate responsibility for spiritual development belongs with

---

[143]   Merton, Thomas, *Thoughts in Solitude*.

each person. And it will always be hard for us to accept this. It will always be impossible for our churches to systematize spirituality. But we should try to put up some guardrails. We should teach and model maturity. But we should also be released from the expectation that discipleship is something we can provide independent of the Spirit's guidance. We're just supplying opportunity for our people to recognize God.

Likewise, **we'll never get liturgy totally right**. Because worship is like romance. You can't legislate it. You can't script it. You can't boil it down to a repeatable process. There has to be some spontaneity. There has to be some verve. And the fact that we're all participating in worship together makes these qualities more elusive.

Worship is also like watching baseball. It can be tedious and disinteresting until something exciting happens to galvanize the fans, and then they're no longer observers, but a force unto themselves.

But this, too, is strange. Since we know there are things that will often generate that kind of excitement and we are appropriately wary about falsifying it.

So we walk the line. We balance. We pay attention to the Spirit, trying to figure out if our worship has become too formulaic. Too stale. Too try-hard. Too ambitious. Too obscure. Too lifeless. And we'll never get it totally right. We might have a great experience one week, but that hardly guarantees the next week will feel the same. For us or for God. And what may have been wonderful for one group of people may feel overly simplified for another. Or too zealous and spastic. And we realize we won't keep everyone happy. But we try because we know the true manifestation of worship is our attention to the Spirit in each moment as we endeavor to please God.

Every day God invites us on the same kind of adventure. It's not a trip where He sends us a rigid itinerary, He simply invites us. God asks what it is He's made us to love, what it is that captures our attention, what feeds that deep indescribable need of our souls to experience the richness of the world He made. And then, leaning over us, He whispers, "Let's go do that together.

- Bob Goff[144]

We'll never get our theology totally right (though no theologian would ever agree). But the truth is that when we stand before God he will reveal entirely new ways of reconciling theological distinctions. The old arguments about free will and predestination will evaporate. The old lines we've drawn between Reformers and Wesleyans, Catholics and Lutherans, Charismatics and Contemplatives will dissipate as God patiently reveals we are all, partly, wrong. I imagine we'll find out we're mostly right, too—especially given the wide-scale agreement between us—but the things about which we're so passionate are often the issues about which the Bible is especially unclear. I suspect that's where our passion comes from, feeling like we've figured something out that you couldn't discern just by reading it off the page. Isn't that why people get so fascinated with eschatology? With angels and demons and spiritual geography? With gifts and manifestations and miracles and prophecy? We become excited when we think we've solved a complex metaphysical quandary, and threatened when we realize others are unconvinced. We entrench ourselves with rhetoric and reason, fortified by likeminded folks, and wage silly wars over sideways sectarianism.

---

[144] Goff, Bob, *Love Does.*

We'll never get our stance in the world totally right. Being "in the world but not of the world" guides us, but not perfectly. How are we to discern the difference between enculturating the gospel, being missionaries to our culture, and simply capitulating to the prevailing spirit of the age? How can we ensure we do not conform to "the pattern of this world?"[145]

Serious followers of Jesus who are eager to evangelize will acknowledge this is a trickier balance than most would care to admit. Are we always on the right side?

Are we too separate? Too close?

Again, the key here is to listen to the Spirit and move back and forth as the Spirit gives guidance. It will be impossible to get the balance just right for long because the culture changes, and we change. We are raised in our own worldview with its own blind spots, and we will always carry with us some degree of anxiety about whether we have done enough, gone too far, or have lost our way on either end of the spectrum.

There are other things we'll get wrong, too. We'll never get our **financial models** totally right. We'll never get our **ministerial credentialing** totally right. We'll never get **ecumenism** totally right. We'll never figure out how to support **government** without controlling it, how to defend the weak without sanctifying **war**, how to challenge **sin** without alienating sinners. But we'll try. And by trying, stay nimble. And humble. And correctable. And nuanced. And in that nuance the world will see that the church of the future is not an iron gauntlet, but the open hand of love and friendship.

---

[145] Romans 12.2.

What areas do you most suspect you'll never totally get right?

CORRECTION

ALTERING OUR THINKING, OUR HABITS, AND OUR PERCEPTIONS

But the Advocate, the Holy Spirit, whom the Father
will send in my name, will teach you all things and will
remind you of everything I have said to you.
-John 14.26, NIV

*The Holy Spirit does now what altars did in the Jewish Bible—helping
us make things right between ourselves, our God, and our people.*

Altars were God's provision for the fact that none of us are perfect, that none of our efforts are sufficient, and that sometimes we need a way to begin again. The altar wasn't for God, but for us. Altars altered our thinking, our habits, and our perspectives. They forced us to slow down, perform rituals, and focus on things gone wrong with the hope that future decisions will be better.

The altar is God's acknowledgment that things don't always go according to plan, that we will need a way to get back on track, and that our last mistake is not the end of the world.

Consider the story of Abraham and Isaac in Genesis 22. God spoke to Abraham and asked him to sacrifice his son. So the old man took his boy far away to the top of a mountain. Isaac was confused, and Abraham gave him chores to take his mind off circumstances. Then, Abraham tied his son to the stone altar, intending to sacrifice him. But, God sent an angel to intervene, sparing the boy and honoring Abraham's obedience.

It's a crazy story. And we're probably wise to remember that the Bible very rarely tells us these stories because we're meant to imitate the protagonist. In fact, most of the stories are told "flat," meaning without any moralizing or commentary. The reader is meant to make up their own mind about whether Samson was good, or Saul was ever fit to be king, or Cain's punishment was just. We're invited into these stories as God's conversation partners, and many times we must acknowledge God wants us to recoil.

Like here.

Abraham believed God, obeyed God, and was honored by God. But it's a little disconcerting he never argued with God, right?[146] Most of us would have put up a little fight if God suggested we harm one of our children. Why didn't Abraham?

Maybe he did and it wasn't recorded. Maybe Abraham had lost other such arguments. Maybe Abraham had enough prior experience with God to know something was going to happen to interrupt the plotline. Who knows? But, as far as I'm concerned, Abraham missed the mark.

Human sacrifice is wrong, and God is the reason I know it; so, if God suggests human sacrifice, I've got a pretty good hunch that there's a bad connection, and I'm gonna work on getting our wires uncrossed before I do anything I cannot later undo.

Why didn't Abraham operate on the same assumption? How could he have been so wrong about God?

These questions will likely remain unanswered; but at the very least, this story is important because it illustrates no one is going to the grave free from grievous error.

You're never going to get it totally right the first time. Not in life. Not in your career. Not in marriage or relationships or parenting. Most people think that means you have to quit, walk away, and start over. But many times, all you need to do is make a course correction. Figure out a new communication pattern. Apologize. Level up. Get some training. Acknowledge your failings. Make changes. And go back into your life with a renewed purpose and confidence that this can still work. Your marriage isn't over. Your job isn't the worst. Your house probably doesn't need to be condemned.

---

[146]   This issue is the central motif of Len Sweet's remarkable book *Out of the Question Into the Mystery?* as well as a favored conversation among rabbis.

The entire sacrificial system in the First Testament demonstrates God's provision for failure. After the Garden, God knew we wouldn't get it right. He knew! He also knew we wouldn't totally get the sacrificial system right, either, which was why he had to personally get involved with the ultimate sacrifice of his son.

But don't miss this: *then*, if we sinned, we knew exactly what we had to do to make things right with God and with other people. There's some relief there. Because when we make mistakes—either intentionally or accidentally, either morally or socially—we feel terrible. We know we did something wrong. And, apart from the few sociopaths who always seem to get the most press, when we do something wrong we want to make it right. We want to atone. We want things to go back to the way they were before we made them worse. And the sacrificial system gave us clear guidelines on how to do that.

It was useful. It was helpful.

But over time those prescriptions were robbed of their power because they became mindlessly automatic and therefore meaningless. Maybe not to everyone. Maybe not all of the time. But certainly God seems to have become frustrated with the inability of his people to prioritize obedience over sacrifice.[147]

> These people come near to me with their mouth
> and honor me with their lips, but their hearts are far
> from me.
> - Isaiah 29.13, NIV

Thus the story of Jesus' sacrificial atoning death, reconciling God and God's people for all time.

---

[147] Isaiah 1.11; Malachi 1.6-14; 1 Samuel 15.22.

But here's what many of us today miss: there's no longer a clear way for us to *feel better* when we sin. Maybe at the beginning, when we first encounter Jesus and we experience grace. But the longer we serve Jesus, the more we're forced to acknowledge that we still wrestle with sin against God and we still sin against others. And we don't know how to make the little course corrections that ought to get us back on track. We promise God we won't ever do those things again. We make the necessary changes in our lives to ensure those promises aren't empty. But then we sin once more. Again. And again. So much that we lose hope that we can ever please God through our behavior. Then we realize that we can't. Then we're brought back to our need for grace all over again, this time sprinkled in humiliation. And then grace comes upon our humiliation and we once again experience the fresh breath of God. But it's a long process. And it's arduous. And it's unclear.

And it still doesn't help us make things right with other people.

> If you are offering your gift at the altar and there remember that your brother or sister has something against you, leave your gift there in front of the altar. First go and be reconciled to them; then come and offer your gift.
> - Matthew 5.23-24, NIV

We're adrift when it comes to sorting out our horizontal issues. Because we can't pray to our neighbors and ask for their forgiveness. And when we do ask forgiveness of others, it's puzzlingly ineffective. Even if they grant it, it's not like they forget our misdeeds. They remind us later. Sometimes they're passive aggressive. We wonder why they won't extend grace to us like God does. As if they could. And so our apologies and our repentances don't repair our lives with others the way they do with God. We don't know the way forward; we just know things won't ever go back.

But here's the solution: in place of a clear, sacrificial system we now have the guidance of the Spirit. The church of the future will forgo her need for a rule book and will follow instead the much more complex, more precise, more individualized guidance of God himself as he helps us navigate life's complications.

Do you see why this is better?

God knows exactly what to do to make things right between us and others, and he wants to teach us, but the process is slow. Perhaps by design. Perhaps God's guidance is only revealed bit by bit because our relationships with others can only be healed slowly, over time, without rash promises or grand gestures. God knows he has our attention when we feel guilty, so as we're agonizing in prayer, desperately begging him to fix the mess we've made, God can reveal to us the errors in our hearts and minds that caused these crummy circumstances in the first place. And we actually listen, because we're desperate, and so we actually change. The people we've hurt begin to wonder if the changes they think they see in us are genuine. And slowly God's guidance and God's transforming power work in us until they flow out of us, and with wisdom and patience we are able to repair what we have destroyed.

The church of the future will attend to the Holy Spirit as God's allotment of course correction. Conviction is the altar in our hearts. Jesus is our ultimate High Priest. The Spirit-filled life is about the sacrifice of our very lives.

This is the Law of Love.

Is there anything the Spirit is currently leading you to fix?

TEN.FIVE

REVISION

EDITING OURSELVES TO PLEASE GOD

My son, do not make light of the Lord's discipline,
and do not lose heart when he rebukes you.
- Hebrews 12.5b, NIV

God's ultimate provision is himself. God's ultimate guidance is the Spirit.

When I was studying happiness, one of the most interesting lessons I learned was that—whether in business, family, romance, or sport—the best way to create love, harmony, and success was to avoid defending what you already think you've got right. A defensive posture sets you against others. A defensive posture prohibits you from listening to reason. A defensive posture ensures you will take things personally, get stung, and hold onto offenses. A defensive posture sets others on edge, confuses them, and awakens their aggressive impulses.

So learn to listen. Hear your critics. Attend to their recommendations. And take what's useable. It won't all be good feedback. You might hear 200 bits of nonsense for every one useable truth. But that's okay. The point is that you know your work is unfinished. You know you're working on your next iteration. And there will always be revision. Even after the final revision has been submitted. Even after the final product has been launched. Even after you say, "I do." There will be more changes to make.

Keep changing. Keep iterating. Keep growing. Be willing to learn. Be willing to listen. Be willing to change.

Sharks die if they stop swimming forward. Keep moving. Be a shark.

Writers recognize the powerful tool of revision. All good writing is rewriting, and rarely have any successful authors followed the path of "first time write." Instead, authors know they have to "commit to really sh*tty first drafts"[148] and keep hammering away at their work until it works. Take, for example, the obsession with which bestseller Patrick Rothfuss attacks his prose:

---

[148] Lamott, Anne, *Bird by Bird*.

> I employ a host of beta-readers, who read my early
> draft, my middle draft, and my late drafts. I do
> hundreds of drafts … I probably run through more
> drafts than any living writer, and I don't say that glibly.
> - Patrick Rothfuss[149]

The church of the future will constantly be revising and
revising and revising until she gets it right because Christ's
story is too important to be submitted as a rough draft.

God knows we won't get it right all the time. But the purpose
of starting over is not to keep the slate clean but to renew our
efforts, revitalized and with the confidence that God has not
abandoned us. Like us, our work must be made new.

We have to stay in step with the Spirit, but we also have to stay
in step with our context. And, of course, if we stay in step
with the former we will be driven to do so with the latter, also.
If we obey Jesus' command to "go into all the world"[150] and
model ourselves after St. Paul who "became all things to all
men,"[151] then we know contextualizing the message is critical.

The business world learned these truths long ago. Take, for
example, Tarun Khanna's article on Contextual Intelligence in
the September 2014 issue of the *Harvard Business Review*.

> Most universal truths about management play out
> differently in different contexts. Best practices don't
> necessarily travel. Global companies won't succeed
> in unfamiliar markets unless they adapt—or even
> rebuild—their operating models. The first steps in that
> adaptation are the toughest: jettisoning assumptions

[149] Shivener, Rich, "Patrick Rothfuss: Worldbuilder," *Writer's Digest*, July/
August 2015, 45.
[150] Matthew 28.19-20.
[151] 1 Corinthians 9.22.

about what will work and then experimenting to find out what actually does work.[152]

Khanna goes on to specify that "[managerial knowledge] is specific to a market or culture," and any student of Christian missiology knows this is true, also. Whether the dress and habits of Hudson Taylor in China, or the Christian Ashram movement of E. Stanley Jones in India, or even the adventurous nobility of David Livingston in Africa, missionaries have always understood that the gospel can be placed in a cultural container without damaging the essential truth that God became one of us to redeem all of us.

The church of the future will continue to think like missionaries, constantly iterating her presentation and manifestation of the gospel in order to persuade others to meaningfully engage Jesus Christ. And when her critics speak up and speak out, she will not silence them. Instead, she will authenticate their concerns and work tirelessly to refine her presentation of Christ in the world.

Which aspects of your life are in greatest need of revision?

---

[152] Khanna, Tarun, "Contextual Intelligence," *Harvard Business Review*, September 2014, 61.

ELEVEN

WE SEE A CHURCH

where **STORY, IMAGE,** *and* **METAPHOR**
are **THE DEFAULT APOLOGETIC;**

a **CHURCH** COMFORTABLE WITH PARADOX
that **DOGGEDLY** PURSUES THE TRUTH
and **REGARDS** EASY ANSWERS
WITH SUSPICION.

ELEVEN.ONE

STORIES

STUDYING THE SECRET LANGUAGE OF THE HUMAN HEART

> Then he told them many things in parables, saying: "A farmer went out to sow his seed …
> - Matthew 13.3, NIV

We see truths in fantasy we cannot perceive in reality.

When I was writing and researching *Nativity and Kingdom*,[153] I learned there is a surprising amount of science fiction nestled within Christian tradition—a tradition that, historically, predates science and vilifies fiction. In my work, I discovered stories about monsters being sent to kill the Holy Family, only to fall in adoration at the feet of the Christ. There were stories about stone statues coming to life and turning on their pagan worshippers, shaming them for denying the One True God. There were stories about animals speaking, trees uprooting, and birds plucking feathers from their own breasts in order to praise Elohim. Some of these stories are loosely based on historical fact—like those that tell us the origins of the Magi— and some of the stories are fabricated entirely—did I mention the Romanian werewolves of Advent?—but they all betray a fascination with God.

Stories, images, and metaphors make up the secret language of the human heart. They make us tick. They move us forward. Stories can inspire us. Galvanize us. Interest us. Stories educate and inspire us, motivate us to achieve, and harden us so we might endure. True stories do this, but so do faerie tales. As J.R.R. Tolkien was fond of saying, myth and history are largely analogous, since they both force us to wrestle with good and evil, love and loss, destiny and grace.

> Talented storytellers have always found a way to make [people] care … if you give a good idea to a mediocre team, they will screw it up. If you give a mediocre idea to a brilliant team, they will either fix it or throw it away and come up with something better.
> -Ed Catmull[154]

---

[153] McDonald, David, *Nativity and Kingdom: Rumor, Myth, and Legend in the Advent of Christ*.
[154] Catmull, Ed, *Creativity Inc*, 74.

We live in an economy of stories. There are Story shops and Story conferences, Story nightclubs and Storytelling cafes. We love a good story, since the man with the best story wins. And the stories we love most are those of valor, true love, and self-sacrifice. They are the good stories, stories that demonstrate we can be better than we are.

I love to tell stories to children, and whenever I do, they never ask me if the story was real. On the contrary, children first ask the important questions like, "Was he good?" Or, "Did they live happily ever after?" Children are much more concerned with understanding right and wrong than with dates and times, and in this regard, theology and fiction are in step. As G.K. Chesterton said, "Fairy tales do not tell children that dragons exist. Children already know that dragons exist. Fairy tales tell children the dragons can be killed." C.S. Lewis said something similar when he observed, "We do not despise real woods because we have read of enchanted woods; the reading makes all real woods a little enchanted."[155]

The world is full of terrors, both real and imagined, but true Christians—bold Christians—know that faith overcomes fear. Fear is the prelude to courage—you cannot be brave if you're never afraid. And because we know that God's Spirit in us surpasses any horror in the world, we can advance in power and confidence with Christ.

The church of the future will help her people rediscover the magic and the mystery that exists in every moment, right before our very eyes. She will penetrate our fantasy-obsessed culture, helping them to see that God still works in surprising ways.

---

[155] Lewis, C.S., *On Stories: And Other Essays on Literature*.

A myth is something that never was but always is.
-Leonard Sweet

What story has most impacted you?

ELEVEN.TWO

APOLOGETICS

THE SHIFT TO PRIORITIZE EXPERIENCE OVER INFORMATION

As it was in the days of Noah, so it will be at the coming of the Son of Man. For in the days before the flood, people were eating and drinking, marrying and giving in marriage, up to the day Noah entered the ark; and they knew nothing about what would happen until the flood came and took them all away. That is how it will be at the coming of the Son of Man.
- Matthew 24.37-39, NIV

> *In our culture, the power of stories is greater than the power of arguments; that doesn't mean our faith should discard intellectual rigor, only that our polemic should be nestled within narrative.*

I recently returned from an 8-day tour of biblical Turkey—a land replete with sites right out of the book of Acts, so much so there were times it felt like I was tripping over the Apostle Paul.

I didn't go to Turkey in hopes of acquiring new information. With the ease and access of the Internet, you can learn everything there is to know about a given location, its history, and its significance to the biblical story. Even the pictures available online are better than anything you would see while on site. But when you go, you get the pleasure of walking on the stones, breathing the air, listening to the bees in the wildflowers, being startled by the snake in the grass, feeling the warmth of Turkish tea in your belly while the cold air makes your nose run.

It's the experience, not the information, that matters.

And though I had a wonderful time with my friends Jason and Becky, and though my travels were chock-full of adventurous escapades, those good things occurred in spite of, not because of, our tour guide and academic tutor. Both men were intelligent and kind. Both men were very knowledgeable. But they wanted to talk (while standing still) for 10-15 minutes at a time, all the time. It was like being invited to a buffet, only to have the chef explain all the ingredients before you were allowed to taste the food; and, once you were permitted to eat, the meal had already gotten cold and you were instructed to move onto the next course.

Somewhere, somehow, we've bought into the notion that serious study is preferable to joyful encounter, that critical thought is better than exuberant laughter.

Could that be why so many churches are dying?

Could that be why so many churches are greying?

Could that be why so many Christians are perceived as loveless and harsh?

I spent eight days touring the sites of seven churches from the Book of Revelation, but the only times I truly enjoyed were those when I snuck off with my friends to explore.

The church of the future will privilege adventurers over academics, giving her people a hands-on experience with Christ that allows us all to get caught up in the Story of God.

> Stories trump statistics. It's more important to convey the reason why you are presenting the numbers instead of the intricacies of the numbers themselves. Telling a good story isn't a quantitative skill, but it is a skill that requires intuition about what your audience wants to hear and how to tell it in a compelling manner.
> -John Maeda[156]

Apologetics is the art of defending our faith and providing reasons for why we believe as we believe. In the late twentieth century, apologetics had become a kind of intellectual pugilism, most prominent on college campuses, where our smartest folks dueled atheists for the cognitive supremacy of undergrads. I have attended many such events, and many times the Christians felt as though we won. We never did. There was always a vote, and somehow it always skewed toward the other side. We wondered if someone tampered with the tally or miscounted the raised hands.

But the truth is we never captured the heart of our audience. For all our intellectual superiority, we forgot the cardinal rule

---

[156] Maeda, John, *Redesigning Leadership*, 23.

of postmodern America: the best Story wins. We won the argument, but forgot the narrative, and as a result we lost the war.

Stories can be experienced as much as they can be heard, read, or imagined. That's why the church of the future will capitalize on immersive storytelling to construct her liturgies, and also why we've worked so hard at Westwinds on our Atlas Project.

I've spoken openly about Teaching Atlases at Westwinds. These began as sermon manuscripts and have since evolved into full-length manuscripts (like the one you're reading now) that accompany our weekend teaching and introduce our people to the history, theology, and backstory of why we believe as we do. Similar to its teaching counterpart, the Design Atlas is a collection of all our blueprints, aesthetic ideals, liturgical planning, and music for each series. Rather than being bound and printed, though, our Design Atlases are available for free online.[157]

The goal is total immersion in an image, story, or metaphor, almost as though we're emulating the experience of virtual reality in low-fi. "The secret sauce of VR is, in a word, immersion … in a matter of seconds, the world around you disappears. You plunge into a new dimension."[158] Similar experiences have been created using projection mapping, wherein multiple projects are shot onto 3-D surfaces. "I could render projected images of 3-D worlds that could work on every angle inside the spherical architecture of the dome and beyond."[159] This was also a hallmark of Tolkien's fiction. His secondary worlds create space "into which both designer

---

[157] https://www.pinterest.com/WestwindsDesignAtlas/.

[158] McMillan, Sam, "Virtual Reality is Virtually Here," *Communication Arts Advertising Annual*, 2015.

[159] McMillan, Sam, "Obscura Digital," *Communication Arts Photography Annual*, 2014.

and spectator can enter, to the satisfaction of their senses while they are inside; but in its purity it is artistic in desire and purpose."[160] Apps are another new medium for immersive storytelling, whether via augmented reality portals or the method of using Instagram and Snapchat stories as discovery games, inviting users to swipe right and up in order to guide the participant through a narrative map.[161]

Again, this is all so much richer when experienced than when taught, which is why our design team is constantly trying to layer the presentational elements of our service. So, we're not just using music, but music and images and olfactory senses, together with participatory elements from the congregation. And we're not just teaching, but layering our teaching with visual flourishes and mnemonic aids upon which our people write or draw or stamp or fold. Sometimes this begins with a text, but others the text is the final element we include (especially given the ease with which I can adapt my teaching, versus the complexity of adapting music and lighting and graphics and everything else).

> Everything begins with a text. But I find myself more than ever returning to the idea of the theater as a meeting place for architecture, music, dance, literature, acrobatics, play and so on. In all my shows, this is what has interested me most of all: gathering artists together, combining different styles and disciplines.
> - Robert LePage[162]

---

[160] Tolkien, J.R.R., *On Fairy Stories,* 64.
[161] McMillan, Sam, "Interactive Instagram: Just Add Stories," *Communication Arts Illustration Annual,* 2017.
[162] LePage, Robert, *Connecting Flights,* 22.

The church of tomorrow will intensify her fascination with stories, and thus provide endless opportunities for the church of the future to preach, teach, and engage the world in the Story of God.

What would you most love to learn?

ELEVEN.THREE

IMAGERY

TRACING THE SENSORY DIMENSION OF THE SCRIPTURES

This Book of the Law shall not depart from your mouth, but you shall meditate on it day and night, so that you may be careful to do according to all that is written in it. For then you will make your way prosperous, and then you will have good success.
-Joshua 1.8, ESV

> *When we mix the Story of God into our own, smaller story, we are fertilized with the Spirit and grow stronger.*

The prophets employed stories, images, and metaphors as their default apologetic. Nathan, for example, knew he wouldn't have success confronting King David directly, so he told the King a parable about a wicked neighbor.[163] Likewise, many preachers and writers use personal illustrations and anecdotes to make these presentations interesting. Why? Because our minds work primarily in images. Our thoughts are a complex activity "encompassing reasoning, intuiting, and feeling,"[164] and if we want to go deep within the Story of God we have to work with images—both actual images like photographs, graphics, etc—and word-pictures, like metaphors, similes, and comparisons.

> The sensory dimension of the Scriptures, in which God's self-revelation to us is expressed, is encompassed in the term 'imagery.' Imagery includes pictures and images, such as 'God is my rock', but also includes the sensory qualities of individuals and groups, the physical environment, comparisons, metaphors, and similes. Imagery is another dimension of the world of specific persons and events in which our faith is revealed to us.
> -Patricia Wilson-Kastner[165]

One of the least explored methods of studying the scripture is to look for imagery and trace it throughout as much of the biblical literature as possible. Something as simple as a seed, for example, could be used to talk about the lineage of God's people (the seed of Abraham), the unbroken promise of God's plan to heal the world (the seed of Promise), the faith required to become vested in Christ (faith like a mustard seed), and the ultimate connection we enjoy with the Father (the seed which grows into the vine and the branches).

---

[163] 2 Samuel 12.

[164] Wilson-Kastner, Patricia, *Imagery for Preaching*, 15.

[165] Ibid, 12.

When we trace these images throughout scripture, we begin to make connections between authors and genres that would not otherwise have been obvious or accessible.

Len Sweet refers to this as the Apple Method of exegesis.[166] Why? Well, think about how we eat apples in comparison to how we eat oranges. Oranges come apart in segments, and we eat them one at a time. Apples, on the other hand, we bite through the middle. Oranges are enjoyed bit by bit. Apples are enjoyed in huge chunks.

Most biblical scholars feel strongly about the importance of "Orange Exegesis," recommending we stay within genre, audience, author, and epoch. But this is a relatively late invention in biblical interpretation. The Apostle Paul and Jesus both sampled wide swathes of scripture in their retelling and retooling of the First Testament, as did the Patristics, the Mystics, and the Reformers. It was only in Late Modernity that we privileged Orange Exegesis over the Apple. And don't get me wrong—we need a strong comprehension of the segments that make up the whole—but we've lost something if we can no longer get a sense of the Big Story in Scripture, or the overarching promise of God to heal the world.

> It is information technology that has enabled this new creative era, dramatically expanding the space for speculative thought. Information technology is evolving into the technology of relationships, facilitating the flow of creative interaction through computer-based communication networks, groupware, increasingly intelligent agents, knowledge representation and management systems, videoconferencing systems, and the convergence of difference forms of traditional media ...

---

[166] Exegesis is the academic term for biblical interpretation.

> Information technology has become a business's single
> greatest path to wisdom and inspiration—to digital
> remembrance of things past.
> - John Kao[167]

The Internet has given us amazing tools for drawing these
connections through scripture, and the church of the future
will deepen her exploration of God's Word in order to better
understand who God is and how God is at work in the world.

But make no mistake: we will never move beyond scripture, for
the Bible is our anchor. We must always be able to trace any
"new" theology in, at least, the Pentateuch, Prophets, Gospels,
and Epistles.

A significant component of my work as a post-doctoral
fellow at Portland Seminary was the creation, compilation,
and publication of *The Story Lectionary*. A Lectionary is a
compilation of sermons designed to be preached weekly in
local congregations, and our students crafted 52 sermons that
re-tell the Story of Scripture from "the Garden to the Garden
City." Len Sweet and I each wrote a short accompaniment
to the students' work, and I learned a great deal through the
embarrassing comparison between my work and his.

Len's work felt more substantive. Whereas I was bringing my
best thoughts on a particular passage, ensuring each section
connected to the larger thesis, Len was always roping in other
thinkers and writers. Consequently, Len's accompaniments felt
like a three-way conversation between himself, the reader, and
the intellect to whom he was introducing the reader. I imagined
his work like a conversation at a cocktail party, "David! Have
you met St. Anselm?"

---

[167] Kao, John, *Jamming: The Art and Discipline of Business Creativity*, 4-6.

After comparing our work, I realized that part of the great gift of the Christian tradition is the tradition itself—we are neither the first people to believe as we do, nor the first to struggle for fresh expression of those beliefs. By getting specific and varied, Len was able to provide richness and freshness to material that had already begun to feel well-worn.

> A kite cannot fly unless it's anchored. If you let go of the string, the kite falls to the ground. Great preaching needs to be anchored. With an anchor, you can roam and wander and the kite will still soar. What's the anchor? A controlling image in the scriptures.
> -Len Sweet

Do you tend toward reading the Bible as an orange or an apple?

TWELVE | WE SEE A CHURCH

that EMBRACES *the* LONELY *and* BROKEN PEOPLE
OF OUR COMMUNITIES,
PROVIDING AID *and* COMFORT *as though*
CHRIST HIMSELF HAD SHOWN UP IN RAGS;
that EMPLOYS OUR UNEMPLOYED;
that EDUCATES OUR UNDER-SERVED;
that ELEVATES OUR DOWN-TRODDEN;
that TRAINS OUR UNSKILLED;
that WON'T TURN A BLIND EYE
WHEN ONE OF OUR OWN
STRUGGLES OR STARVES;
that REFUSES TO ALLOW
OTHERS TO GLORY IN
THEIR VICTIMIZATION.

BROKENNESS

CELEBRATING CHRIST'S RENEWAL IN OUR LIVES

But he was pierced for our transgressions, he was crushed for our iniquities; the punishment that brought us peace was on him, and by his wounds we are healed.
- Isaiah 53.5, NIV

Our scars demonstrate God has healed us

Kintsugi is a Japanese technique that involves mending broken pottery with exotic lacquer. The seams of the smashed pots are filled with gold, so that break lines become highlights in the design. It is the art of treating repair as the glory of an object rather than something to be hidden within it.

Kintsugi reminds me of the strange episode after Jesus' resurrection when he appeared to Thomas, the Doubter. Thomas refused to believe Christ had truly conquered death until he placed his fingers in the holes in Jesus' side and hands. When he did, Thomas exclaimed "My Lord!"[168]

Despite being made new, Jesus retained his scars, and it was those scars that revealed Christ's true identity.

Perhaps, instead of hiding our old hurts and trying to look as though we're perfect, we ought to share them with one another. Perhaps, it is our past battles that best reveal our present character.

But there's an important caveat here: Jesus didn't let Thomas touch an open, festering wound. Scars are a sign of completed healing. The church of the future will not fetishize her wounds, endlessly reliving the hurts we've endured. Instead, she will revel in God's healing, restoration, and regeneration.

Kintsugi shows us brokenness is no longer an issue. We are filled with gold.

> *What has been most beautifully healed in your life?*

---

[168] John 20.24-29.

TWELVE.TWO

AID

RISKING OUR WELLBEING FOR THE SAKE OF OTHERS

We love because he first loved us.
- 1 John 4.19, NIV

From the earliest days of our faith, Christians have been helping those in need at great personal cost.

Cyprian of Carthage was an African bishop in the third century AD who rose to prominence during a massive plague. Because Carthage was so weakened by sickness, barbarians took advantage of the circumstances and sacked the town, enslaving many of the residents. The reduction in workforce—both from the plague and from the barbarian attacks—left few to work the fields and care for the livestock, thus resulting in drought and famine.

The citizens believed their gods had sent the plague as punishment for so many people converting to the Christian faith. Consequently, persecution ensued for followers of Jesus. Nevertheless, Cyprian and his fellows developed a plan of medical relief, recruiting workers to nurse the sick and bury the dead. They boldly assisted the very people who proclaimed they were at fault.

> It is a bad world, Donatus, an incredibly bad world. But I have discovered in the midst of it a quiet and good people who have learned the great secret of life. They have found a joy and wisdom which is a thousand times better than any of the pleasures of our sinful life. They are despised and persecuted, but they care not. They are masters of their souls. They have overcome the world. These people, Donatus, are Christians. . . and I am one of them.
> - Cyprian[169]

Christians ought to be involved in helping others, loving those around us precisely because Christ loved us first.

Why? Because if we truly comprehend what Christ has done for us, the natural outpouring of our energy will be to pass on that which we have received. We are all sinners; and, if there's

---

[169] Cyprian, *Goodreads*, https://www.goodreads.com/author/quotes/812837, accessed August 22, 2017.

anything we know for certain about Christ, it is that he holds those who do not acknowledge their sinfulness in contempt.

If we focus on knowing Christ more personally, more deeply, we will be overcome with charity because we were overwhelmed with grace.

Our strategy, then, isn't to pressure one another to be more helpful because charity is good in and of itself. That strategy only ever results in guilt and shame, since we can never do enough to fully heal the world on our own. Instead, the church of the future will devote herself more fully to Christ, trusting that a better comprehension of his love will naturally result in helping, and loving, others more.

> *How have you carried on the good work of Christians who help the less fortunate?*

RELIEF

OFFERING SHELTER AND SHADE TO A WORLD THAT'S BURNED OUT

You have been a refuge for the poor, a refuge for the needy in their distress, a shelter from the storm and a shade from the heat. For the breath of the ruthless is like a storm driving against a wall.
- Isaiah 25.4, NIV

The church of the future will help, heal, and hear everyone, everywhere. We are the antibodies to neglect, depression, and apathy.

The world has become very good at caring. Consider, for example, the featured section in *Architectural Record*'s June 2015 issue, "Design for Social Engagement." This section highlights pro bono work in six communities across the world that must "deal with the peculiarities of culture, climate, and convention."[170] If the world loves with this much extravagance, how much more can we muster?

Perhaps more than we think. And the more socially conscious our world becomes, the more the church of the future must rise above the level of care demonstrated by the world. It is noble competition.

Our commitment to helping others has motivated Westwinds to give a yearly Christmas Eve offering to fund our needs assistance program.[171] Run by our deacons, this program accepts requests from people within our community to help pay their bills, purchase essentials, and secure repairs. There are limits on how much, and how often, we're able to help; but I love the spirit of this ministry, which says we will absolutely help anyone who comes to us.

The same spirit motivated my wife and her friends to host a great event pampering single mothers on Mother's Day. They arranged for free oil changes while the women received massages and manicures, and each of the participants was given a gift basket of treats and goodies to let them know we care. They called the event "Reprieve," and it was so meaningful to so many that we have since offered something similar many times.

---

[170] "Design for Social Engagement," *Architectural Record*, June 2015, 81-112.

[171] This is just one of approximately a dozen social initiatives Westwinds annually undertakes.

The church of the future will do more of this, not once or twice, but as a matter of course, because she is meant to provide aid and relief to a world that's been burned. And, our world needs some place to escape from the heat and pressure of life.

We need shade.

Consider the metaphor: the sun is good, but if we're too long exposed we get burnt. Dehydrated. Our skin becomes overly sensitive and everything hurts. We can't think clearly. We become confused and cannot tell where we are going. It's difficult to speak, and we do not want to continue the journey. All we can think about are our basic needs, or the basic needs of those with whom we travel. We bicker. We blame.

God provides shade to refresh us and rejuvenate us.[172] In this shade, we find solace and comfort. Our head clears. We can see the path forward. Now that we can safely rest, we can gather our strength for the journey to continue.

> People will dwell again in his shade; they will flourish like the grain, they will blossom like the vine— Israel's fame will be like the wine of Lebanon.
> - Hosea 14.7, NIV

In the book of Jonah, God provides this kind of reprieve in the form of a plant. Knowing Jonah's heart was troubled, the Lord gave him a place to rest. He brought relief. But then he took that relief away as a means of exposing what was in Jonah's heart.

> Then the Lord God provided a leafy plant and made it grow up over Jonah to give shade for his head to ease

---

[172] Psalm 121.5; Isaiah 4.6.

> his discomfort, and Jonah was very happy about the
> plant. But God also arranged for a worm! The next
> morning at dawn the worm ate through the stem of
> the plant so that it withered away.
> - Jonah 4.6-7, NIV

God always deals with our heart. Always. Too often we
think the real problems in our churches result from either
our financial lack or overabundance. But that's gross
oversimplification. Like Jonah's plant, once those who need
shade receive it, their heart-issues come to light. A lifetime of
hunger, hurt, and humiliation can create a heart filled with fear,
anger, or even deep self-indulgence. The first taste of shade
won't heal that heart instantaneously, but it will allow the real
work of examining the heart to begin.

Of course, shade provides more than just relief, and the church
of the future won't simply hand out help, but also seek to
provide delight. Shade is delightful, and church can be, too.

In Nehemiah's day, the Israelites stayed in temporary shelters,
observing the festival of booths. These booths were made
from shade trees (Nehemiah 8.15), designed to last only a short
while. It was precisely their temporary nature that made them
valuable, showing us that some pleasures spoil, like fruit, if
we try to hold onto them for too long. We are meant to enjoy
those things that are in season, without demanding those
seasons endure. And the church of the future will celebrate
these delights, inviting others to enjoy all such pleasures
appropriately.

> From the days of Joshua son of Nun until that day,
> the Israelites had not celebrated it like this. And their
> joy was very great.
> - Nehemiah 8.17, NIV

Likewise, the Song of Solomon graphically describes the pleasures of life in the shade. When we find our delight in God, it is also easier to delight in one another. We do not simply "obey", since obedience is rarely the path to delight. We must, instead, explore and appreciate; investigate and wonder. We must be curious creatures, eager for new knowledge, new connection, and new expression.

> Like an apple tree among the trees of the forest is my beloved among the young men. I delight to sit in his shade, and his fruit is sweet to my taste.
> - Song of Songs 2.3, NIV

The church of the future will offer new hope, new opportunities, and new life to those in need. She will not pity them, but love them as they find rest and rejuvenation among her people.

How are you providing relief and reprieve to those who are burned out, exhausted, and feel abused?

TWELVE.FOUR

COMPASSION

WELCOMING MISFITS AND MISCREANTS

Do not forget to show hospitality to strangers, for by so doing some people have shown hospitality to angels without knowing it.
- Hebrews 13.2, NIV

> *We must perceive Christ in every stranger.*

There are two signs outside of our church. The north entrance says "Welcome Rabble Rousers and Rebels" while the east entrance proclaims "Welcome Misfits and Miscreants." When we first made these signs, we thought people would read them and chuckle as they came into our building. But, for some, these signs are a gospel unto themselves.

"Misfits" perceive our church to be a safe haven in a way I never could have imagined. Because misfits could be anyone, anyone at all, who feel as though church would never be a hospitable environment: strippers, addicts, teens, millionaires, unicorns ... you name it. If there's someone who feels out of place in society, then seeing our "Welcome Misfits" sign has been like a lighthouse on a wet rock.

How do we pastor these people? How do we help them move beyond identification primarily through their inability to fit in, and instead incorporate them into the family of God? How do we help them take the next step, and the next, and the next as they mature and grow in Christ?

I don't know. The Bible is not sufficiently specific to function as a policy for many of today's complex issues. So, we take it a step at a time, case by case, heart by heart, person by person, trusting the guidance of the Spirit. We provide reprieve for those who need it and work alongside them until God illuminates the way forward.

That's how the church of the future will proceed: carefully, in constant communication with the Spirit, welcoming everybody.

Everybody.

Imagine that Christ himself is in disguise, standing in front of you as the person who makes you most uncomfortable.

351

Imagine this is a test, and your character is being evaluated and your worth appraised.

Do you pass?

There are many such tests in the Bible. Jesus appeared as a gardener, though Mary didn't know it (John 20.11-18); Jesus appeared to Mary and Clopas, though they didn't recognize him on the road to Emmaus (Luke 24.13-34); Jacob wrestled an angel, and was unaware of whom he fought (Genesis 32.22-30). Such tests reveal our blind spots, allowing God to remind us that we are not as perfect as we imagine.

The church of the future will not only take these tests, but will endure them again and again and again until her people pass with flying colors. We will sing with the dying and laugh with the aged; we will offer redemption to inmates and extend innocence to prostitutes; we will listen to the confessions of evil and accept hugs from pedophiles; we will absorb the fury of the righteous and endure the scorn of the elite; we will anoint the scabs of the afflicted and dry the tears of the aggrieved; we will be ridiculed by family, mocked in the press, and groped by the desperate as we carry burdens and resurrect dreams.

The church of the future will hope everything changes, will pray everyone recovers, will work tirelessly with God to heal the world, and will thank her people for the privilege of serving.

But, some will object, what about the sinners? What about the blatantly rebellious? What about the people whose lifestyle is totally contrary to the witness of the scripture? What about the people who are in dire straits precisely because they have foregone the clear moral teaching of the Word?

We will never reject them. They may not like what we say or what we believe, but they are still welcome. Like a recalcitrant child sitting sullenly at supper, there will always be a place at the table for rabble rousers and rebels, misfits and miscreants.

Because the church of the future will perceive Christ in every stranger.

We believe that every person has been made in the image of our Creator. So even if they're weird, strange, unsettling, or off-putting, we will choose to search for and to see the image of God in them. Everyone has value, even the weirdos. Maybe even especially the weirdos. Human beings matter to God, and therefore human beings matter to us. Before someone is ever defined by gender or ethnicity or capability or orientation, they are defined by their humanity. That's our starting point—we are all human.

How have you shown love and friendship to outcasts?

TWELVE.FIVE

SOLIDARITY

LOVING OTHERS WITHOUT "FIXING" THEM

Therefore, as God's chosen people, holy and dearly loved, clothe yourselves with compassion, kindness, humility, gentleness and patience.
- Colossians 3.12, NIV

> *Solidarity is charitable commitment with another person absent the accompanying burden of having to "fix" them.*

Compassion is not a bottomless reservoir. Helping can hurt, deplete, and exhaust. At some point, after you've been helping and helping and helping, you despair. You wonder how many starfish you can throw back into the sea. How many drops of rain can you catch before giving up, knowing the ground will remain wet regardless?

There was a man, who I will here refer to as Martin, who used to come to our church service at the pub. People would eat, drink and laugh while we were preaching and singing. It was a lot of fun and, though it ultimately ran its course, I fondly remember those days.

Martin is homeless, and once the word got out that Christians were at the pub he started hanging around, asking for free meals. At first the owner shooed him away; then we convinced him to allow us to look after Martin. But after ten or twelve weeks it became apparent that Martin had no interest in God, or church, or us. He just liked getting a meal worth $40 or $50 every Sunday night.

Each week people would engage Martin about his plans to get back on his feet and each week Martin would assure us he would get cleaned up, bathe, and apply for a job. But he never did. We bought him toiletries and furniture, clothing and food, groceries and sundry goods for his home.
But Martin never changed because he didn't want to.

Eventually we stopped buying meals for Martin. We welcomed him and sat with him, and maybe someone would share a plate of fries. But that's the key here: they would *share*, not give. Once Martin realized he'd received everything he was likely to get, he stopped coming. I still see him around town and we stop and chat, but I am under no illusions about whether

Martin will take steps toward becoming self-sufficient. He likes his life just fine the way it is.

I tell this story because it's a good microcosm of the limits of charitable action. When we've got a front row seat observing how our donations get discarded, abused, or ignored we realize that not every problem can be solved by our good acts toward others.[173] At some point, everyone has to accept responsibility for where they are and decide to do what's necessary to move forward.[174] That doesn't mean we shouldn't help—we absolutely should—but it does mean we ought to invest in the people themselves before we ever try and purchase a solution for their problems.

My friend Amanda suggests the issue here is the difference between charity and solidarity. Charity tries to fix the problem, whereas Solidarity commits to the person. Charity sometimes bullnoses into a situation with the assumption we know what's best for someone else. Solidarity, on the other hand, enters into a relationship, willing to bless as the relationship progresses.

> We are not called to look at someone, decide what "better" would mean in their life, and force them into our definition. We are called to solidarity within community, where we ask the person what it is that they need and, without judgment, provide it to the best of our capacity without causing harm. That means we ask what they need and want and we provide that if we can. If they want notebooks to write in and we think they need shoes – we give them notebooks to write in. Honoring the choices of those we seek to help is critical. We get tired when we try to force people (through our charity) along pathways that

---

[173] Matthew 7.6.

[174] Proverbs 24.30-34; 1 Timothy 5.8.

> they don't want to go. Poorly done charity sucks the
> life out of both the giver and the receiver. It sets up
> the equation so that one side always bears the burden
> of the encounter. Solidarity reaffirms the humanity
> of both sides of the equation and equalizes them –
> bringing them back into Shalom.
> - Amanda Zentz-Alo, in conversation with the author

This is the plight of many charitable workers. There's just no
end to the problems and suffering around us. And when we are
trying to make a difference, we often feel like Mr. Incredible—
the cartoon superhero—who, after saving the world again and
again exclaimed in frustration, "I just want it to stay saved, you
know?"[175]

We do know. We have access to the Savior of the World,
and, like Peter in Matthew 14.31, he keeps hauling us out
of the storm and into the boat. But in some strange feat of
multidimensional irony, the boat itself is full of waves and
once again we begin to drown.

And so we must be rescued all over again; and we must also
continue to rescue others. This requires we work to put
solutions in place that help people move forward. Something
that helps them cover their basic needs, develop self-
sufficiency, and progress. This is no small project. But the
church is in a unique situation, for we are able to hold people
accountable for both their cooperation and their development.

So we work to employ our unemployed, knowing there's likely
a reason they were jobless in the first place. We follow up with
their new employers and learn they don't show up on time. We
follow up with the formerly-and-soon-again-to-be-unemployed
and tell them they're in danger. And, sometimes, they sort

---

[175]   *The Incredibles*, Pixar Animation Studios, 2004.

out their issues and keep their job. But when they don't, and they complain the church wasn't there for them, we kindly stand with them, determined to be the church they need. And sometimes, they keep their next job. Or the one after that. But the only thing that keeps the cycle alive is the goodwill of the Church. One Christian can't do it. One employer can't make it happen. You need a hundred Bible-believing, Jesus-loving, Spirit-attending Christians working together to truly make a difference.

Hence the need for sustainable systems that provide protections and early warning signs. So that the employer who has one job to offer is given an employee from among our ranks we're confident won't botch the job. And then we get to celebrate with them. Then we get to thank the employer for their investment and willingness to risk. But it starts with relationship. It starts with community. It starts with Church.

This, I think, is one crucial finding of the "Rat Park" experiment.[176] In it, rats were first placed in a cage with two water bottles, one of which was filled with narcotics. The rats quickly became addicted and died. However, in a follow-up experiment, rats who were already addicted were placed within a Rat Park—full of games and wheels and other, healthy rats— and all quickly recovered from their addiction by choice and went on to live normal rat lives. The experiment demonstrated that, although addiction is a complex issue, there is more at work than chemical biology. Relationships, families, and even amusements have power to help us overcome even the most crippling ailments.

If it's true that it takes a village to raise a child, then thank God it can also be true that a church can redeem a miscreant. The church of the future will love and embrace addicts and

---

[176] https://www.youtube.com/watch?v=sbQFNe3pkss&feature=youtu.be.

vagabonds, criminals and haters, profiteers and peddlers, with such genuine love and grace that even the worst can find new life in Christ.

> No one can have God for his Father, who has not the Church for his mother.
> -Cyprian[177]

The church of the future will realize that no one gets into heaven without a reference letter from the poor. She will lovingly engage the world, offering great love and great hope till the end.

How have you shown solidarity with your community?

---

[177] De Ecclesiae Catholicae Unitate (AD 251), ch. vi.

CHARITY

TAKING THE OATH OF COMPASSIONATE SERVICE

My command is this: Love each other as I have loved you.
- John 15.12, NIV

Charity is love and friendship among brothers and sisters.

All church work is collaborative. Liturgy, for example, is the "work of the people." It isn't one or two people that put our church services together, but dozens of teams and hundreds of opinions formed over thousands of years. Charitable work, likewise, is not simply a matter of us "doing things for someone else." It is a matter of us coming together. It isn't favors for strangers, but love among brothers.

> Collaboration … requires three distinct kinds of concerted effort: cooperating (acting purposefully toward a common goal), coordinating (synchronizing efforts and sharing resources), and cocreating (producing a novel outcome together) … Collaboration isn't just about achieving a goal or joining forces; it's about creating something together that it would be impossible to create alone.
> - Jane McGonigal[178]

The church of the future will come together, not simply for clustering or conversation, but to spur one another on. As iron sharpens iron[179], so, too, will we spur one another on to greater works of love and faithfulness.[180]

I think Robert Lupton's book *Toxic Charity* has the healthiest framework for how the church of the future will engage in social issues. Because we must engage. We must wade in. But we cannot fool ourselves into thinking that we should be saviors, or even that the world desires us to try.

> Religiously motivated charity is often the most irresponsible.
> -Robert Lupton[181]

[178] McGonigal, Jane, *Reality is Broken*, 268.

[179] Proverbs 27.17.

[180] Hebrews 10.24.

[181] Lupton, Robert, *Toxic Charity*, 4.

Here is Lipton's *Oath for Compassionate Service*, a guideline for how the church of the future will work to help those in need.

- Never do for the poor what they have (or could have) the capacity to do for themselves, since "giving to those in need what they could be gaining from their own initiative may well be the kindest way to destroy people."[182]
- Limit one-way giving to emergency situations.
- Strive to empower the poor through employment, lending, and investing, using grants sparingly to reinforce achievements.
- Subordinate self-interests to the needs of those being served.
- Listen closely to those you seek to help, especially to what is not being said—unspoken feelings may contain essential clues to effective service.
- Above all, do no harm.[183]

The church of the future will be as innocent as doves and as shrewd as serpents, committed to helping others while simultaneously ensuring their help doesn't hurt.

How can you simultaneously engage those who need help and ensure you do not enable their helplessness?

---

[182] Ibid.

[183] Ibid, 8-9.

INJUSTICE

OFFERING MORE THAN OUR OUTRAGE

> Truly I tell you, at the renewal of all things, when the Son of Man sits on his glorious throne, you who have followed me will also sit on twelve thrones, judging the twelve tribes of Israel.
> - Matthew 19.28, NIV

Injustice requires more than outrage in order to be repaired.

On Sunday, August 13, 2017, I came home after church and learned there was a car crash in Charlottesville, Virginia at a white-supremacist demonstration. The first report I read made it seem as though an African American driver had accidentally collided with a group of neo-Nazis. It took me thirty minutes to learn that 20-year-old James Fields Jr., a member of the alt-right Vanguard America, had intentionally driven his car into a group of protestors, killing 32-year-old legal assistant Heather Heyer, and injuring 19 others.

Later, at church, I responded with shock and shame but refrained from making any statements on social media. But some questioned my slow response, wondering why we don't address these issues from stage or from Westwinds' social media more frequently or more immediately?

There are three main reasons. First, because we cannot always trust the information available. Consider, most of my thirty-minute investigation into those events involved weeding through unhelpful screaming matches about terrorism, Nazism, and snowflakes. Even after I learned what happened, I spend another several hours checking alternate-sources to sidestep the inherent bias of each source. Such suspicion is warranted, and more people would benefit by taking more time to be more certain of their information.

Second, because Westwinds' primary audience is local; and, sometimes when we reach beyond our sphere of influence to make dramatic proclamations, we only succeed in exposing our ignorance. We simply cannot guarantee we either understand or anticipate correctly the feelings, needs, and reactions of people from other parts of the world. Especially concerning sensitive issues. Especially during times of increased hostility.

But the biggest reason we don't address more of these issues more publicly, more quickly is because we cannot always trust our first reactions, especially when our first reaction is outrage.

Make no mistake—racism and bigotry are undeniable evils, and Christianity has always been characterized by widespread multi-ethnic diversity, as evidenced in the Asians, Africans, and Middle-Easterners of the early church. And scripture indicates that not only will diverse ethnicities come together in Christ, but that we will cooperatively rule with him in the New Creation.[184]

Racism may justifiably incite our anger, but that doesn't mean our responsibilities end with outrage. Fury is both easy and natural; meaningful action is neither.

In place of only outrage, I propose the work of Kings and Priests, which includes justice, ingenuity, and rehabilitation.

JUSTICE

True justice moves beyond the condemnation of evil action and into the provision of systemic healing. Take, for example, Starbucks Coffee Co. In the last decade they have made two significant commitments to rebuild hurting American communities. First, in response to the underserved population of the US military, Starbucks made their "hiring and honoring" commitment to employ 25,000 veterans and military spouses by 2025.[185] But Starbucks' second major commitment was to open 15 stores in hurting communities nationwide, like their

---

[184]   Revelation 5.9, 7.9, 13.7; Daniel 7.14; 2 Timothy 2.12.

[185]   Their original goal was 10,000 by 2018, but that goal was met 3.5 years early, so the company increased their commitment. This story is told in Howard Schultz' book *For Love of Country: What our veterans can teach us about citizenship, heroism, and sacrifice*, which was itself accompanied by a $30 million donation from the Schultz Family Foundation for job training and PTSD research.

pilot store in Ferguson, Missouri.[186] In each venue, the company hires local contractors and vendors owned by minorities and women, works in tandem with local government and civic leaders, and partners with nonprofits to offer young people free, on-site job training.

Initially, Starbucks was ridiculed for their social investment, most notably by those who claimed the last thing Ferguson needed was a "four dollar cup of coffee." But the company believes their social responsibility outweighs both the scorn of their accusers and the loss of their profitability.

And here's the good news: Starbucks' heroic efforts have inspired significant emulation. In fact, since the Ferguson store opened in April 2016, 41 other businesses have followed suit.[187]

INGENUITY

Not all responses to injustice can leverage the resources of a global brand. Some, by contrast, rely on the cleverness of the local populace. For example, citizens in the German town of Wunsiedel have become increasingly dissatisfied with their routine subjugation to neo-Nazi marches.[188] Rather than protest the rallies, however, the Center for Democratic Culture in Germany (ZDK Deutschland) has found donors who will give €10 per rally participant to EXIT-Deutschland, an organization that helps right-wing extremists transition out of

---

[186] They have since opened stores in Jamaica, Queens, and Long Beach. Starbucks' social-impact agenda also aims to hire 100,000 opportunity youth (men and women between 16 and 24 who are not in school or working) by 2020.

[187] In contrast to the 37 businesses damaged during the riots of 2014, 17 of which were completely destroyed. Valby, Karen, "Starbucks Digs In," *Fast Company*, September 2017.

[188] This is on account of Nazi leader Rudolf Hess once being buried there, though his body has been exhumed.

their radicalism and build new lives. That means every time the Nazis march, they are raising money stop fascism!

The event has been dubbed "Germany's most involuntary charity walk," and has raised over €10,000 since 2014. But the best part of the endeavor is the signs and placards that greet the neo-Nazis as they march, thanking them for being "Nazis against Nazism." Such signs include "Generous like Never Before" and "If only the Fuhrer knew."[189]

REHABILITATION

One additional response to injustice involves the determination not to give up hope for the redemption of evil men. A good model here is Baptist preacher Carlyle Marney (1916-1978), who went "into the midst of the KKK and converted some of them to true faith, honoring their personages but not their positions or prejudices."[190] Mahatma Gandhi, also, wrote a personal letter to Adolf Hitler calling him "his sincere friend" and pleading with him on the basis of this friendship to stop his monstrous activities, even though Gandhi claimed he knew Hitler himself was not "the monster described by his opponents."[191]

When I say we need to offer more than outrage, I intend for us to employ the biblical definition of healing. We are kings, concerned with justice, but we are also priests, concerned with healing. We fully manifest God's purpose in us when we are Kings and Priests simultaneously, never surrendering justice in favor of healing, or vice versa.

---

[189]   https://thinkprogress.org/german-town-pranked-neo-nazis/.
[190]   https://www.facebook.com/lensweet?fref=search; https://groups.google.com/forum/#!msg/soc.religion/t2HB1IDqWeo/mg5AES_ij2gJ.
[191]   http://www.mkgandhi.org/letters/hitler_ltr1.htm.

The Kingdom moves through love and friendship; it begins with names and handshakes, coffee and basketball. The church of the future will model and embody ethnic harmony and diversity through our actions and relationships; showing our children that diversity is healthy, normal, and desirable.

What is your biggest opportunity to participate in the work of healing social injustice?

THIRTEEN | WE SEE A CHURCH

that **BURSTS** *with* THE POWER *and* PROVOCATION OF THE SCRIPTURES,
where **GOD'S WORD** IS NOT ENDURED *but* EMBODIED;

a **CHURCH** WHERE EVERYONE CAN HEAR THE GOSPEL *in their* VERNACULAR
at **ALL** TIMES,
across **ALL** PLATFORMS,
through **ANY** MEDIUM;

that **TRANSLATES** *the* WISDOM OF YESTERDAY *into* THE FOUNDATION FOR TOMORROW.

PREACHING

SPEAKING SO THE AUDIENCE UNDERSTANDS

To the weak I became weak, to win the weak. I have become all things to all people so that by all possible means I might save some. I do all this for the sake of the gospel, that I may share in its blessings.
- 1 Corinthians 9.22-23, NIV

> *The gospel message must always be contextualized.*

Anthony of Padua (1195–1231) was a Portuguese Franciscan priest who earned the moniker "The Hammer of Heretics" because of his fierce defense of orthodoxy. He was a powerful preacher, close friend of St. Francis of Assisi, and champion for the unfortunates of his society.

> Actions speak louder than words; let your words teach and your actions speak.
> - Anthony of Padua[192]

My favorite story about Anthony concerns his first sermon. Through a long and winding series of events, Anthony was press-ganged into preaching during an awkward moment when no one else was available. Having been called out on the spot, Anthony stood up and amazed his audience with not only his content but also his delivery. He was the dark horse no one expected, come from the back with little to commend him. When others imagined he would be adequate, Anthony proved to be outstanding.

Anthony was a master of contextualization, understanding the best connection points between his audience and his Abba. Like him, we must render the timeless work of Christ for our time, in our towns. We will need to attach people to the words of God, so they can experience the Word of God.

> Men will surrender to the spirit of the age. They will say that if they had lived in our day, faith would be simple and easy. But in their day, they will say, things are complex; the Church must be brought up to date and made meaningful to the day's problems.
> - Anthony of Padua

---

[192]   Anthony of Padua, *AZquotes.com*, http://www.azquotes.com/author/23000-Anthony_of_Padua.

The church of the future will always consider her audience when presenting the gospel. She will not be content to expound, but seek instead to inspire, elevate, and persuade.

What do you think your audience would consider good news?

SCRIPTURE

SUBMITTING TO THE FINAL AUTHORITY

> For the word of God is alive and active. Sharper than any double-edged sword, it penetrates even to dividing soul and spirit, joints and marrow; it judges the thoughts and attitudes of the heart.
> - Hebrews 4.12, NIV

Scripture keeps us tethered to Christ and prevents us from inventing a new religion.

Spirituality must, of necessity, involve every part of who we are—our thoughts, our feelings, our intentions, our bodies, our relationships, our experiences, etc. However, any portion of us can be contaminated, most notably and commonly through self-deception. For example, we convince ourselves that our intentions are pure when our desire to lead is simply a desire to control; we convince ourselves that the hurts we have endured are so grievous as to justify retribution; we convince ourselves that our experiences are so profound they excuse our moral inconsistencies as we relentlessly pursue deeper satisfactions.

What can correct us, when our thoughts and feelings and experiences lead us astray?

The Bible.

The church of the future will find strength and power in scripture, protecting her from the collisions of culture and circumstance, and will keep her from becoming just another Instagram account endlessly posting platitudes in memes.

Every revival in history has begun with a fresh reading of scripture in the common parlance of the people. People hear the Word, they read the Word, they discover the Word, they sing the Word, and the Word transforms them. But the Word, remember, is not the words of the text, but the Story of God as manifested in Christ Jesus. Jesus is the Word, and the words of the Bible are his chosen means of telling us about himself.

There are portions of this book that strongly affirm Jesus as the Word of God, ensuring that the church of the future is not so biblically minded she cannot be of any Christological good. However, the church of the future must also affirm the scriptures as the safeguard for our souls.

Some, of course, will let their Biblicism run rampant. They will enjoy arguing and debating far more than they enjoy applying the deeper truths behind the words on the page. Some will use the Bible as a weapon to isolate, damn, and manipulate others. Some will justify their own prejudices, citing verses out of context in order to provide the impression they are mature when, in fact, they are malicious. But we cannot let the aberrations of some distort God's design for all.

The church of the future will recognize the Bible provides guardrails for life's scenic highways. No one drives with their eyes focused on the guardrails, but we need them, lest our attention be so fixated upon the wonders of the ocean that we fail to abide by the most basic concerns and drive into the waves. We need the Bible's guardrails to ensure we do not become so enamored with wonder we neglect the mundane. We live by the Spirit, but if it weren't for the scriptures, we'd never accurately discern how the Spirit moves in the first place. Reading the Bible gives us the confidence that we're heading in the right direction, safely, and can therefore be liberated to enjoy all God has provided without worry.

Similarly, the Bible provides speed bumps to ensure we proceed slowly in places we would otherwise like to accelerate. Parking lots, for example, are often filled with speed bumps in order to ensure impatient shoppers do not collide with exhausted mothers and their enthusiastic children. We need the Bible to provide cautions and impediments to our quest for making changes *now!*, and finding new perspectives *right away!*, and redefining the tenets of Christian spirituality *at this second!* to accommodate a culture that has only been prevalent for a decade.

> All Scripture is God-breathed and is useful for teaching, rebuking, correcting and training in

righteousness, so that the servant of God may be thoroughly equipped for every good work.
-2 Timothy 3.16-17, NIV

I'm always nervous when I meet a Christian who has ideas about God I cannot find in scripture. Because there are lots of neat ideas about God out there—or gods, or the gods, or the spirits—but I have some boundaries in my thinking that separate what I can hang onto firmly and what I can only entertain as "pipe and bar" talk.

If I cannot find evidence for my beliefs in the scriptures, then I cannot trust what I believe. If I think God must be a certain way, or behave in certain patterns, and yet cannot substantiate those claims from the Bible, then I'd better hold them loosely. On the flip side, if I find scriptural examples that contradict my thoughts about how God is supposed to be, I should let go of my opinions immediately.

Because I'm not the final authority.

I'm not more moral than God, and if God decides to do things I don't like or behave in ways that embarrass me, I'm the one out of line. Not God. And the only way I have to adjudicate whether I'm wrong is scripture. I can block out the voice of the Spirit and deny the conviction God sends. I can deceive myself and others. But I cannot eliminate what the scripture teaches. It's there, in black and white (and sometimes red or green), for the entire world to see. And when I depart from it, there are millions of believers who cry foul.

Can you think of a useful guardrail the Bible provides?

THIRTEEN.THREE

AUTHORITY

LIVING IN AND WITH AND FROM THE STORY OF GOD

> Do not merely listen to the word, and so deceive
> yourselves. Do what it says.
> - James 1.22, NIV

*The Bible we have is the Bible God intended for his people to know,
to use, and to enjoy as we cooperate with him in his ongoing work of
Creation.*

The church of the future has to be filled with Christians who want to play fair with God on God's own terms, not coopting God's Word for their own agenda, position, or power. She will be filled with serious students of the Bible who begin and end with questions like:

- "What does it mean for me to live as a faithful follower of Jesus Christ?"
- "What did this mean to its original audience and how did they respond?"
- "Am I coming under the authority of God as I study this text, or am I trying to bend the text to my own purposes for my own benefit?"

The church of the future will embrace scholarly, critical methods for understanding scripture and yet never lose hold of its sacred understanding that the Bible is the inspired word of God, sent to us by God, compiled and authored by God, containing the full revelation of God, outlining God's plans to heal the world.

Famed biblical scholar Tom Wright makes this point brilliantly, asserting that our task will not be so much to quote the Bible as to imaginatively discern the ongoing story of the Bible in our context. Wright suggests we compare the Scriptures to a Shakespearean play whose fifth act has been lost. The first four acts are so compelling that the play is staged, but rather than ghost-writing a fifth act the actors agree to improvise. Remember, these are trained Shakespearean actors, so they must consider the beginning four acts authoritative, and consider the larger body of Shakespeare's work, also, as they mount the performance. Wright concludes:

> This 'authority' of the first four acts would not consist in an implicit command that the actors should repeat the earlier pans of the play over and over again. It

would consist in the fact of an as yet unfinished drama, which contained its own impetus, its own forward movement, which demanded to be concluded in the proper manner but which required of the actors a responsible entering in to the story as it stood, in order first to understand how the threads could appropriately be drawn together, and then to put that understanding into effect by speaking and acting with both *innovation* and *consistency*.[193]

Wright's point is well taken. We are not meant to repeat past episodes of the scripture. Instead, we enjoy entirely new episodes of God's Story, working to engage the world consistent with our spiritual ancestors and with some innovative flourishes all our own. This will require us to both know the Bible more comprehensively and to pay attention to the Spirit's promptings more holistically.

Such an understanding may require more complex theological engagement on our parts, but it is important to note that even though our theology may complexify, our faith should not concretize into an intellectual pursuit. On the contrary, many intelligent people are attracted to the faith precisely because it affords us the opportunity to be thinkers and feelers, to experience God emotionally and sensually, rather than just cognitively and consciously.

---

[193]   Wright, N.T., http://ntwrightpage.com/2016/07/12/how-can-the-bible-be-authoritative/.

Our theology may complexify, but our faith will get simpler. Our minds sharpen as our hearts soften, for both capacities faithfully represent the image of God.

How does this understanding of the "Bible's fifth act" change how you view scripture?

STUDY

PLAYING AND PRAYING WITH GOD'S WORD

Your word is a lamp for my feet, a light on my path.
- Psalm 119.105, NIV

It is insufficient for us to simply read the Bible. Instead, we must pore over it, talk it over with friends, and allow the scriptures to both fund and form our ordinary lives.

In 2007, the Willow Creek Association published their "Reveal" study, calling into question all previously-held beliefs about the efficacy of small group ministry. One of their findings was that many Christians had abandoned the virtue of reading the Bible and no longer pored over the text with friends, speaking from the heart about the tensions and crossovers between their own lives and the Story of God.

The problem with small groups wasn't that conversation and friendship were unimportant, but that they inherently lacked the power to help believers mature. If, however, the conversation centered about the scriptures—what they said, what they meant, what those stories might imply for us in our ordinary lives—then the results were very different. Instead of dealing with the importance of relationships, the scriptures tell us about David and Jonathan, Ruth and Naomi, Jesus and Peter, inviting us to draw our own conclusions. To speculate. To wonder. To appraise. And the more we wrestle and talk and suggest, the more God's Story is rooted deeper and deeper into our hearts. It infiltrates our imagination. It saturates our consciousness. So that in those crossover moments where we see points of similarity between what happens now and what happened then, we feel empowered and ennobled to act differently, think differently, and respond differently.

Westwinds, for all our nontraditional weirdness, holds to the inspiration and authority of the scripture and is committed to helping people understand what it means in our contemporary context. Every year we publish a new tool for our congregation to better understand the scriptures. Our first volume was called *The Crux,* and it was a harmony of the gospels, wherein all the stories of Jesus from the New Testament were compiled together into one chronological volume (much like Tatian's *Diatessaron*). Because we wanted our people to recognize Jesus as a Jewish figure, we also placed the full text of any citations from the Old Testament next to their occurrence in the New, so the context was easy to see (and then we provided some small bit of commentary, if needed, to explain its significance).

The following year, we published *The Crux of Victory*, which compiled all the scriptures that dealt with the conflict between good and evil, beginning with the Garden of Eden and ending in the Final Battle. Then we published *The Crux of Revelation*, of which I was particularly proud, that placed every Old Testament text next to its referent in the final book of the New Testament (as well as including any Jewish or Christian apocalyptic references from outside the Bible). The last two years we have published an adult coloring book highlighting the major covenants, called *Designs for Contemplation and Meditation*, followed by *Sixty Second Scriptures*, which are daily prayers from the Bible that can be read aloud in one minute or less. In 2018 we will publish *The Crux of the Old Testament*, which will place key stories from the scriptures and Apocrypha in their chronological order to help our people understand how we got from Eden to the Second Temple Period, during which time Jesus' ministry occurred.

Why do we do these things?

Because it takes tremendous effort for us to see and understand the scope and sequence of the Bible, and most of us do not invest ourselves sufficiently. With a little prodding, and a lot of extra work, we've been able to reintroduce our people to the Bible again and again, making the familiar fresh and the unfamiliar commonplace. We want our people to get caught up in the Story of God and his plans to heal the world, and there's no better mechanism for doing this than to give people new access to the scripture.

We often teach through biblical books expository-style, which means we go line by line and verse by verse. There are some strong benefits to doing this, most notably that it forces us to wrestle with all sorts of texts we would rather avoid and find difficult to explain. This discipline results in a church that takes the Bible seriously and isn't afraid to ask hard questions, both of ourselves and of our God. In my tenure at Westwinds we have done this with Genesis 1-2, Nahum, Nehemiah, Jeremiah, Mark, Hebrews, Ephesians, Colossians, Titus, Revelation, and Jude; but my favorite experience with any of them was with Ecclesiastes.

Ecclesiastes is the ultimate postmodern treatise. "Everything is meaningless" could be the title of an unreleased Nirvana EP, and the tone of Koheleth, the preacher, sounds like a marriage of Dark Horse comics and Tim Burton films. But we wanted our people to move past the inherent coolness of the text and into a deeper appreciation for the questions, dissatisfactions, and ultimate faith Koheleth possessed. So we printed the entire text of Ecclesiastes on six 4x8 sheets of Plexiglas and mounted them over wooden frames filled with incandescent lights. We displayed these back-lit panels as tables, waist-high, so our people could lean over them. During the months that we taught through the book, we invited our people to get up at any time during the service and comment on the book using Sharpie markers. And they did. Hundreds and hundreds of comments were written—some loving, some frustrated, some hurting, some hurtful—over the text and covering all of the margins. That's how scripture is meant to be used. Not simply read and remembered, but engaged, argued, considered, rehashed, personalized, questioned, adapted, parsed.

How would you evaluate your familiarity with the scriptures?

THIRTEEN.FIVE

APPLICATION

PRACTICING THE RELIGION OF AMATEURS

> How, then, can they call on the one they have not believed in? And how can they believe in the one of whom they have not heard? And how can they hear without someone preaching to them? And how can anyone preach unless they are sent? As it is written: "How beautiful are the feet of those who bring good news!"
> - Romans 10.14-15, NIV

> *Applying the scriptures requires not only linguistic translation, but also cultural translation.*

Everyone needs to hear the Story of God in a way that makes sense to them. Our responsibility isn't to ensure, primarily, that others enjoy the Story, nor even that they choose to participate in the Story—for if we prioritize either their amusement or their acceptance we run the risk of compromising the integrity of the Story. No, our primary concern is that people hear and understand the Story so that the Spirit can continue to press and pull and tug on their hearts.

The church of the future will work to bring the scriptures into contact with more and more people in more and more meaningful ways. She will gamify our devotion and share our ongoing education via open resources, nonlocal and asynchronous discussion, streaming, and public dialogue using such diverse mediums as apps, interactives, comics, films, cards, books, games, and images.

If there is a way the Story can be told, there is a responsibility the Story must be told. How? However we can. Where? Wherever we can go. When? As soon as possible.

Christian spirituality has always been best understood as a religion of amateurs. Whether we were the peasants of communist Russia, the hideaways of pre-Constantinian Rome, or monks hiding in the desert—we have always been at our best when our faith was lived out in the streets, rather than thought through in ivory towers.

One of the great gifts from the Internet to our world is that it has given people back their own voices. In blogs and chatrooms, via email or online forums, people have begun to sound like themselves again. Whereas once we all spoke with false formality, whether at work or at church, now we've all begun to sound a little more real regardless of the situation. Thankfully, much of our world has grown tired of seeing people act one way at home and another at church, or school, or work, or whatever. We want one another to speak truthfully, with our own voices. We want that for ourselves.

> Speaking the truth in love, we will grow to become in every respect the mature body of him who is the head, that is, Christ.
> - Ephesians 4.15, NIV

This idea of communicating the gospel in the language of the people is an old idea. The gospel, after all, was first articulated in Aramaic (a.k.a. NOT the voice of the common people in 1st Century Rome). While the message remained in the language of one ethnicity within the Empire it remained isolated and ineffectual. It was only when the Second Testament began to be circulated in *koine* Greek—street slang—that it took off, and Christian spirituality began to spread like wild fire.

We must retranslate the gospel into our shared language, our *koine*, which is the language of pop culture.

Consider that there are far more references to genuine spirituality and true spiritual curiosity in our world today than ever before. People are fascinated with the invisible life, the nonmaterial world, the human soul, the eternal spirit, and the possibility that they have within them the spark of something special, something divine. Pop culture gives us more possibilities for spiritual conversation than any tract, any Christian book, and any politic combined. You just have to interpret what people are really asking.

Contrary to popular belief our world is not a world run by atheists and agnostics. It is a world full of spiritually curious people who happen to be woefully disenfranchised with organized religion.

The task ahead of us is to embrace this shared language and speak it with others out of love and deference to Christ, in love and respect for our fellows. The question ahead of us is whether or not we are willing to learn how to do so.

> How shall we sing the Lord's song in a strange land?
> -Psalm 137.4, NIV

Where do you see the most obvious connection between Christian spirituality and popular culture?

THIRTEEN.SIX

CONTEXTUALIZATION

SETTING ASIDE OUR PREFERENCES IN FAVOR OF OUR MISSION

> With the tongue we praise our Lord and Father, and with it we curse human beings, who have been made in God's likeness. Out of the same mouth come praise and cursing.
> - James 3.9-10, NIV

We must present the message of Jesus in a culturally-meaningfully container at all times.

Common among creatures like octopus, chromatophores are pigment cells that reflect light, useful both for camouflage and communication with other octopodes. There is no compromise on their oceanic function in the food chain, or in their reproductive habits, or in their social strata. They camouflage to stay alive. That's what we need to do, also.

The church of the future will recognize she needs to both blend in and avoid predation. And make no mistake, there are plenty of predators hunting the church. There are organizational predators seeking to consume our resources. There are political and special-interest predators seeking to consume our platforms and our constituency. And there are actual, violent predators who want to see Christianity wiped off the map. So let's make ourselves so much a part of our surroundings that they cannot pick us out to pick us off.

Again, this doesn't mean we dilute our message. On the contrary, the underground church in China used this kind of camouflage to escape the persecution of communism for many decades. Their faith was not compromised, but their visibility was.

Chromatophores are also used for communication with other octopodes. These are hyper-intelligent creatures that can manipulate their bodies to tell others what's happening.[194] Again, this is camouflage, not compromise. In some instances, we must become culturally invisible—there, but impossible for predators to locate. In others, we must become culturally indistinguishable—focusing on relevance without reducing our commitment to orthodoxy. We must prioritize connection over tradition.

---

[194]   Schweid, Richard, *Octopus*, 18-19.

We see this kind of camouflage in the Bible, though it appears by another name: tongues. Most nations and ethnic groups, in scripture, were delineated by their use of other tongues. Tongue was the term for language, and the requirement of learning other tongues, speaking in other tongues, and welcoming other tongues was essential in any geopolitical or economic relationship.

A tongue is a symbol of the whole person. "Out of the abundance of the heart, the mouth speaks."[195] The tongue betrays us, reveals us, and defines us. There are some who seek to hide behind their tongues, but the truth will eventually come out. The tongue has the power of life and death; it is an arrow; it is a fire; it is gold; it is a spring.

To "speak in other tongues" means to communicate in something other than your native language. And though the miracle of Pentecost has meant many other things to the Charismatic movement of the 20th century, we have often overlooked the simplest truth of all: when the apostles spoke in other tongues, people understood what they were saying.

Isn't that the goal?

Yes. Partly. But the tongue is also meant to indicate taste. And, here again, there is something for us to understand about the church of the future. It isn't just our language that must change, but our preferences. The church of the future will set aside her own preferences for terminology, musicology, and ethnology in favor of contextualizing the gospel into her zip code. Isn't it possible we are meant to enjoy something other than our primary preferences?

---

[195] Luke 6.45.

Nourishment is necessary only for a while; what we shall need forever is taste.
-Robert Farrar Capon[196]

Is it possible to camouflage without compromise?

---

[196]   Capon, Robert Farrar, *The Supper of the Lamb*, 40.

FOURTEEN

WE
SEE
A
CHURCH

where **THE SIZE** OF THE GIFT *is* WEIGHED LESS *than* **THE HEART** *of* THE GIVER; *not* **ACTING** *as a* RESERVOIR, *but* A RIVER OF GENEROSITY, *where* **WE** ALL *give* **ALL** WE ARE *in* **SERVICE** TO OUR KING;

a **CHURCH** *through which* GOD'S PEOPLE COOPERATE IN HIS MISSION TO HEAL THE WORLD.

GENEROSITY

ALLOWING GOD'S RESOURCES TO FLOW THROUGH US

There is a river whose streams make glad the city of
God, the holy place where the Most High dwells.
- Psalm 46.4, NIV

*We channel God's generosity when we give money, when we offer our time
and expertise, and when we share our resources.*

We all know what rivers are like. There's one near my house, the fountainhead of the Grand River that later bursts into a massive waterway through Michigan. Rivers create life. Rivers nourish entire valleys and ecosystems, and riverbanks are always filled with healthy trees and wildflowers.

But the river isn't ours. By design, we are forced to share. And though some may try and regulate the river or dam it or redirect it, at the end of the day you can only ruin the river by trying to control it.

There is no better understanding of the life-giving effects of generosity than the image of the river—a biblical symbol of God's peace,[197] sustaining power,[198] provision,[199] and blessing.[200]

As the river of God's generosity passes through us, we can choose where to direct that generosity, but we cannot hold it in. We are like culverts. We can channel God's generosity to provide barren areas with much needed relief, ensuring that those who might be otherwise ignored are now swimming in grace. We can help others grow, providing refreshment as we facilitate the distribution of God's resources, delivering his goodness where our unique passions meet the world's great needs.

There are significant rivers in the scripture that speak about the nature and character of God. Three times God broke open the river so his people could walk across on dry land.[201] Naaman was cleansed by water from the Jordan.[202] There were four

---

[197] Isaiah 48.18.
[198] Psalm 46.4-5.
[199] Joel 3.18.
[200] Psalm 36.8-9.
[201] Exodus; Joshua 3.14-17; 2 Kings 2.7-8.
[202] 2 Kings 5.

rivers in Eden, and since four is the number of the earth[203], and waterways were the chief means of transportation, we know God intended those rivers to export his goodness, creativity, and peace from Eden to the rest of the world. There is a river that flows through the middle of the New Jerusalem, with orchards of life-trees on either side; and in Ezekiel's temple,[204] an eternal river teems with life.

My friend Jeff Baxter recently released a book on church leadership entitled *From Broken to Beautiful: What Repairing Streams Has Taught Me about Healing the Church*. In the book, Jeff explores the metaphor of fixing broken streams, a geographic term I'd never heard employed until he sent me his manuscript. The logic is obvious: sometimes streams are blocked, and when that occurs, life is arrested. This happens in churches sometimes, and in the lives of Christians as they wade into generosity.

God is the river. He gives and sustains life. He is powerful and can appear temperamental. His river provides renewal,[205] and baptism,[206] and a private location for prayer.[207] And the church of the future will release the stream of God's grace and riches, lovingly directing the flow of his goodness into the world through charitable contributions, financial gifts, and systems for sustainable help.

How are you directing God's generosity to benefit others?

---

[203] Four winds, four corners of the earth, four cardinal points of the compass
[204] Ezekiel 47.
[205] Revelation 22.1-2.
[206] Acts 8.36-38.
[207] Psalm 137.1-3.

PHILANTHROPY

LOVING WHAT IT MEANS TO BE HUMAN

> Which of you, if your son asks for bread, will give him a stone?
> - Matthew 7.9, NIV

A deep appreciation of the gospel expands our concern beyond purely "spiritual" pursuits.

> The Church is the one institution that exists for those
> outside it.
> - William Tyndale[208]

William Tyndale (1494-1536) is most famous for his outlawed
translation of the Bible into English from its original Greek
and Hebrew manuscripts. He was dogged by religious
authorities his entire life before finally being martyred for his
insistence that Englishmen read the good news in their own
tongue.

But one of the oft-overlooked features of Tyndale's character
was his generosity. He was passionate about scripture,
but equally devoted to those in need. He was startlingly
philanthropic, a word which literally means "possessing a love
of what it means to be human." And Tyndale's philanthropy
was rooted in his understanding of the gospel. "Evangelion
(that we call the gospel) is a Greek word and signifieth good,
merry, glad and joyful tidings," said the man, convinced that we
were meant to share that which "maketh a man's heart glad
and maketh him sing, dance, and leap for joy."[209] For Tyndale,
our goodness sprang from the ultimate goodness of God, for
"God's goodness is the root of all goodness."[210]

Tyndale was a good example of a spiritual conduit, delivering
God's river of goodness to communities and people that he
felt needed it most. Not stopping it, not hoarding it. In short,
he practiced what he preached.

> On Monday he visited all such poor men and women
> as were fled out of England, by reason of persecution,

---

[208] Tyndale, William, *Christian Quotes*, https://www.christianquotes.info/quotes-by-author/william-tyndale-quotes/#axzz4jKrU5Tn8.
[209] Tyndale, William, *AZ Quotes*, http://www.azquotes.com/author/14900-William_Tyndale.
[210] Ibid.

into Antwerp, and these, once well understanding
their good exercises and qualities, he did very liberally
comfort and relieve; and in like manner provided for
the sick and diseased persons. On the Saturday, he
walked round about the town, seeking every corner
and hole, where he suspected any poor person to
dwell; and where he found any to be well occupied,
and yet over-burdened with children, or else were aged
and weak, those also he plentifully relieved. And thus
he spent his two days of pastime, as he called them.
And truly his alms were very large, and so they might
well be; for his exhibition that he had yearly, of the
English merchants at Antwerp, when living there, was
considerable, and that for the most part he bestowed
upon the poor.
-John Foxe[211]

The church of the future will be filled with men and women
who understand that their love for God must overflow into a
love for God's people.

How do you share God's love, tangibly, with those in need?

[211]   Foxe, John, as quoted in https://www.wayoflife.org/database/history_of_the_english_bible_tyndale.html.

FOURTEEN.THREE

GIVING

BECOMING GENEROUS AND
OPEN-HEARTED

> Instruct those who are rich in this present world not
> to be conceited or to fix their hope on the uncertainty
> of riches, but on God, who richly supplies us with all
> things to enjoy.
> - 1 Timothy 6.17, NIV

Generosity results in joy but begins in obedience.

The gospels record the tale of Jesus witnessing two people giving offerings at the temple: a rich man and a widow. The rich man gave a significant sum representing a pittance of his wealth, whereas the widow gave all she had, and Christ commended her big-heartedness.[212] This story illustrates a compelling feature of Kingdom economics: it's not about equal giving, but equal sacrifice.

Jesus celebrates those who provide generously and expects his followers to be open-handed.

I want to become more generous. I want to give more money to our church. I want to give more money to missionaries, Christian organizations, Christian charities, and nonprofit groups. I want to pay for dinner more frequently, maybe even for everyone in the restaurant. I want to give gifts that are meaningful and memorable. I want to include others on excursions and share adventures that others wouldn't be able to experience otherwise. I want to set aside time to think creatively about how I might bless others, and then follow through on my best ideas to let them know they are loved, protected, and enjoyed. I want my spirit to enlarge, such that I perceive everyone around me as part of my family and I understand my responsibilities to them as a God-given mandate to take care of their wellbeing. I want to embrace them. I want to laugh with them. I want to include them in my plans.

But make no mistake: my generosity isn't natural. I have foolishly prayed that God would make me more generous, and, eventually, have to experience the benefits of an open-handed life. Now, there are times when I feel so much love I will burst if I do not share it.

---

[212] Luke 21.1-4.

The church of the future will be full of generous, open-hearted givers. It has to be. We have no future without them.

> You care for the land and water it; you enrich it abundantly. The streams of God are filled with water to provide the people with grain, for so you have ordained it.
>
> You crown the year with your bounty, and your carts overflow with abundance. The grasslands of the wilderness overflow; the hills are clothed with gladness. The meadows are covered with flocks and the valleys are mantled with grain; they shout for joy and sing.
> - Psalm 65.9,11-13, NIV

How is God inviting you to become more generous?

CONTRIBUTION

SHARING, BECAUSE GOD FIRST SHARED WITH US

> The Lord will grant you abundant prosperity—in the fruit of your womb, the young of your livestock and the crops of your ground—in the land he swore to your ancestors to give you.
> - Deuteronomy 28.11, NIV

God allows us to enjoy Creation and to share our enjoyment with one another.

One of the preeminent biblical scholars of the twentieth century, John Dominic Crossan, suggests that God is best understood in light of an Ancient Near Eastern householder. "The father as (pro)creator of the household," says Crossan "becomes model and metaphor for God the Creator as divine father of humanity."[213] He goes on to remind us that householders were responsible for the protection and provision of their estate, its inhabitants, and its workers.

Once we perceive God as a householder, it becomes obvious that much of God's action in our lives is designed to give us the opportunity to cooperate with him in the administration of the earth. We are stewards on God's land, and we are permitted to enjoy everything the earth produces so long as we first serve the Lord. Which is to say, God won't pick the apples for us, but he'll give us permission to eat as many as we retrieve.

Likewise, we must share the fruit of our labors with God—in tribute, or tithe—and also with one another. Not everyone can pick apples, so we bring them back to the kitchen, knowing we will later enjoy apple pie, clean clothes, and a warm hearth. We are members of God's *oikos*, his earthly "household," which is the Greek root of the word ecology, and as such we should behave with consideration and care for the other members of the household.

We want to be generous contributors to the abundant provision of God and his people because our wellbeing is connected to the wellbeing of others. That's why the church of the future will involve us all giving all we are in service to our King.

There's a fascinating detail in Exodus 30.12-13 about our limitations and responsibilities. Having led the Israelites out

---

[213] Crossan, John Dominic, *The Greatest Prayer*, 41.

of Egyptian bondage, Moses must organize them into a new people, and this will require a census. Normally a census was viewed as something terrible, since Israel was always the smallest of the nations and their numbers were guaranteed to depress. Yet God instructs Moses that each adult must make an atonement offering, demonstrating that the strength of God's people will not be measured by their numbers but by their contribution.

The offering is not much—just a half-shekel, which, in today's currency, is about three dollars. Moses was pointing out that even our offerings are not whole by themselves—just "half" an offering—and we need the contributions of others for even our own gifts to add up.

In what ways might you consider your generosity part of God's provision for others?

FOURTEEN.FIVE

OWNERSHIP

LIVING IN THE TENT-CITIES OF GRACE

Honor the Lord with your wealth, with the
firstfruits of all your crops; then your barns will be
filled to overflowing, and your vats will brim over with
new wine.
- Proverbs 3.9-10, NIV

God owns all, and shares.

God's economic philosophy is presented in the tithe. Ultimately, God tells us that everything belongs to him, yet God chooses to share. In fact, he allows us to keep the great majority of whatever we earn.

God is like a sharecropper, loaning out a portion of his fields in exchange for a percentage. Since most of us don't work with the natural environment directly, and since most of us spend most of our financial energy on banks and loans and deeds and rights, it's easy to forget that God has prior claim to everything. Consequently, when God raises the issue of what belongs to him we have a hard time getting the math to work. We've already allocated 100% of our resources, so when God reminds us that at least 10% is his according to our original agreement, we get feisty.

But the result of our negligence is that we function like squatters, hiding from our landowner. We become dirt-diggers and profit-smugglers, scrabbly hobos living in the tent cities of grace. We imagine if God knew accurately how much we had, he would rob us of it all. But God is always beside us, scratching his head, wondering why we choose to live like this. Because if we would open our hands, if we would open our hearts, we'd find that God is inviting us to live like him. God wants us to enjoy life the way he does, by sharing it with others.

We share what we have. The refusal to share is the decision to isolate and, ultimately, to starve.

There is a word in Hebrew, *simhah*, that we often translate as "joy." But that's not quite right. *Simhah* refers to the happiness we share and the happiness we make by sharing. It is a word about companionship and friendship, solidarity and laughter, trust and tears.

Generosity yields happiness. When we hold our possessions loosely, eager to share with others, our lives become a wellspring of joy.

God asks for only a small portion because it's important for him to see what we do with the rest. God delights in variety, so our choices are delightful to him insofar as they are neither negligent nor sinful. God is interested to see what we buy, and what we hold, and what we do.

God wants to know if we've yet figured out how to share happiness.

How do we best encourage one another to give?

FOURTEEN.SIX

STINGINESS

LETTING GO OF WHAT WAS NEVER OURS

Give and it will come back to you. A good measure,
pressed down, shaken together, and running over. For
with the measure you use, it will be measured to you.
- Luke 6.38, NIV

The refusal to give brings grief.

To model generosity, one Sunday our staff placed $50 bills
under three seats in our auditorium. Not even our elders knew
the money was there, taped to the bottom of the plastic chairs
upon which our people sat. When we told the congregation to
look under their chairs, we also told them that if they found
the money they couldn't keep it. They had to give it away. We
weren't giving them $50; we were giving them the opportunity
to give someone else $50.

Who knows if they did? Two of the recipients thanked us
and promised they would, but I can't recall if either of those
people came back and let us know how things went. But the
third $50 I remember very well. A young girl, no more than six
or seven years old, found the money under her chair and began
screaming with excitement. Since she was so little, she hadn't
been paying attention to our instructions and only checked
under her chair at her father's insistence.

But dad forgot to mention she couldn't keep the money.

Consequently, when he did tell her, those excited screams
turned into bitter wails. And I mean *wails*. Howls of betrayal.
Shrieks of disconsolate rage.

Her father tried to explain, as we had, that she was no worse
off. She didn't have $50 when she walked in the door, and
she wouldn't have $50 tomorrow morning after she'd given it
away, either. All she would take with her was the joy of having
blessed another person.

Nope. She wasn't having it. Until my dying day I'll be certain
that little girl thinks we cheated her.

Aren't we all like that, just a little? We've been blessed with
much we have not earned, and we squeal when told to share

what we've never truly owned. By choosing not to be a culvert for God's generosity, we run the risk of damming the river only to have the water flow out of our eyes.

But the church of the future will break this cycle entirely. She will help her people rise above their momentary concerns and give as freely as they have received.

Can you think of a time when you dammed the flow of God's generosity?

BENEVOLENCE

LEARNING FROM RIVERS, WADIS, SWAMPS AND RAIN

Whoever believes in me, as Scripture has said, rivers of living water will flow from within them.
- John 7.38, NIV

We must intentionally keep the stream of God's generosity flowing.

Several years ago, we called all our local high schools and asked how much money would be required to present a scholarship to a student for outstanding Christian character. John Voelz, my co-pastor at the time, learned it was only $500 and set up an endowment. He then attended the local graduation ceremonies and was able to present the award to the candidates. For $2,000, we made a significant impact in the lives of both the schools and the four award-winners.

The church of the future will see more people giving more scholarships to more causes. Why? Because this is a simple way we can perpetuate God's generosity.

Several months ago I was reading Teresa of Avila, and her thoughts on prayer made me think of philanthropy, also. She likened prayer to watering a garden, and with every subsequent activity our efforts become gradually less onerous.

Like prayer, when we first begin to give it's as difficult as pulling water from a well. But this gets easier with repetition, so that each subsequent time we give the flow comes more naturally, as though we were using a hand pump or, eventually, an irrigation system. Eventually, generosity becomes second nature. We give and give because there is a natural spring inside us that flows up and out.

We must become like the river. We must invite others to play and be refreshed. Too many Christians are like wadis, dry river beds made entirely barren by their refusal to give. But the church of the future will experience a massive season of rain, during which time the wadis will transform into raging torrents.

Sadly, other Christians are like swamps. Water comes in, stops moving, and as a result of having nowhere to go, stagnates.

The putrefaction invites disease, until swamps are fetid and huffing murks where nothing lives and nothing good can grow.

But the church of the future will live by the maxim that God's gifts flow to us so they can flow through us. Of course, in order for that flow to occur, some elevation is required—a place from which we can begin.

Teresa of Avila's book, *The Interior Castle*, describes a "place" of consciousness in which we find sanctuary in order to commune with God. This is not an escape, but an elevation, allowing us to observe the conflicts around us without being overrun. Such perspective means we can recharge even as we are being depleted.

That's what God's generosity does to us—it constantly refills us, even as we are pouring out everything we have. Thus the old adage "you cannot out-give the Lord." Why? Because he replenishes the generous faster than we can emulate his generosity.

Like a river, God's relationship with us is almost entirely one-sided. He gives us everything, requiring only that we don't interrupt the flow of life-giving goodness.

How much easier do you find giving now as compared to, say, five years ago?

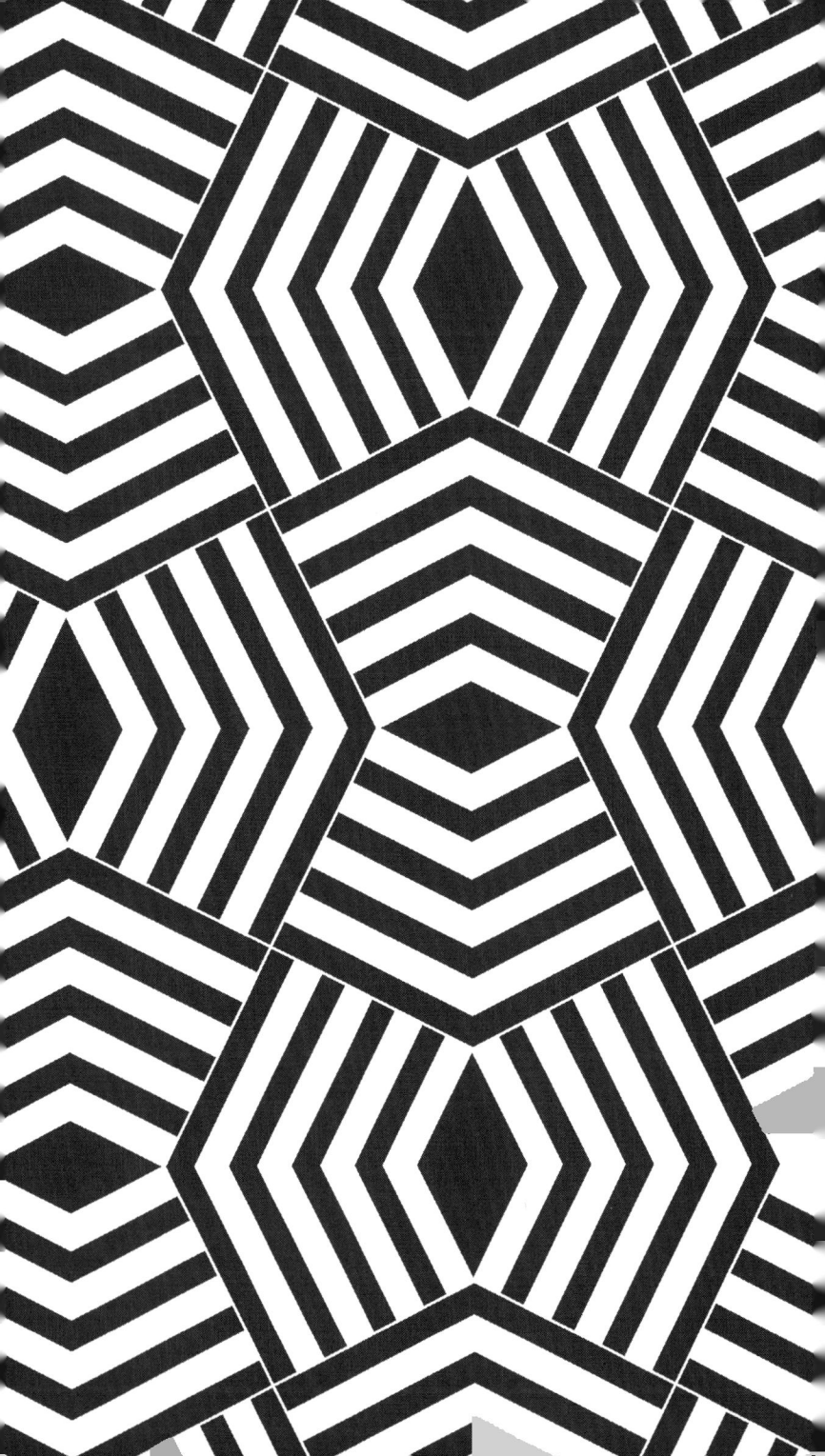

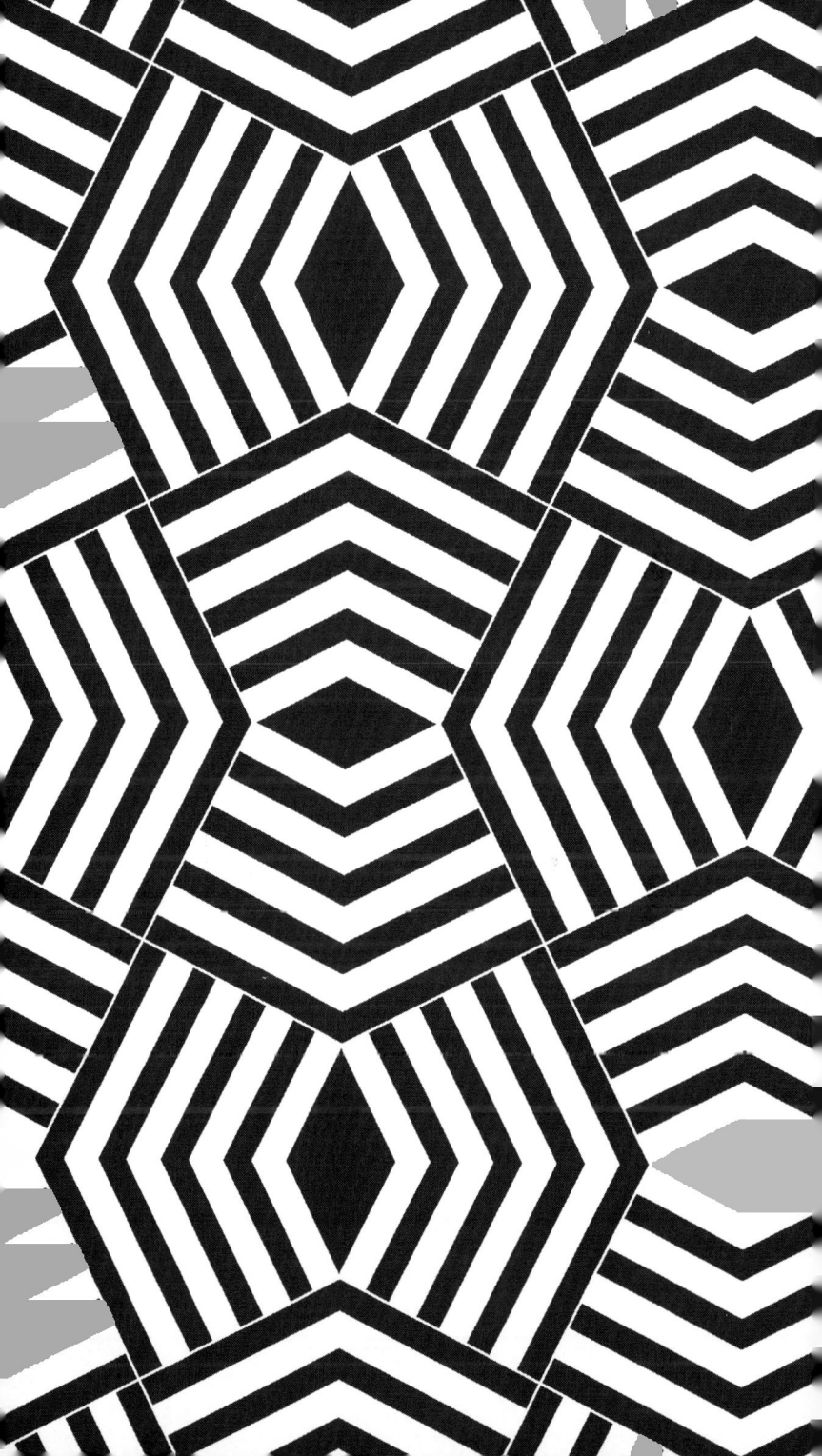

FIFTEEN

WE SEE A CHURCH

that **DOES** A LOT *with* A LITTLE;

that **LEVERAGES** POWER *and* INFLUENCE *without* CATERING TO THE PREJUDICE *of* PRIVILEGE;

a **CHURCH** *that* SPENDS FRUGALLY *and* SACRIFICES JOYFULLY, **ANNOUNCING** GRACE IS FREE *and* GOD IS HERE.

FIFTEEN.ONE

INGENUITY

WORKING AROUND LIMITED RESOURCES

> Your beginnings will seem humble, so prosperous will your future be.
> - Job 8.7, NIV

> *There will never be enough money for us to satisfy all our godly desires.*

One of my earliest impressions in Christian ministry was "we don't have money for that." I heard it often, from a wide variety of sources. Sometimes it was for liturgical elements (communion glasses instead of plastic cups), sometimes for presentational ones (a complete drum set); sometimes for outreach opportunities, sometimes for local missions; sometimes for office supplies, sometimes for staff.

We never had the money.

So I began doing what I wanted without the money. Without the required resources. Without the proper equipment. I began to tinker. To repurpose. To make do. And that's how the church of the future will operate.

Not: *I wish we could* …
        But: *Let's try this* …
Not: *If only* …
        But: *Watch this* …

We will never have sufficient resources to fund our ideas. Ever. Especially not among our wildest and most passionate innovators. The people on the fringes will always be unknown and therefore under-resourced. It's only after we see them unleash their creativity that they will attract any potential sponsors.

So if that's you, quit stalling. Quit waiting.

Of course, you're probably already in a garage somewhere making a smoke machine, or in the church basement looking for crucifixes on Good Friday. You're probably putting Bondo on an old van so you can drive three states north with your teenagers to put on a camp. You're probably incubating the church of the future without even realizing you're the embryo of awe. If so, excellent—keep aggressively pursuing this path. Thank God that what you presently lack in finances, you make up for in abundant ingenuity.

> *What's stopping you from getting started on your next great idea serving God?*

FIFTEEN.TWO

PARITY

BRINGING RICH AND POOR
TOGETHER AT THE LORD'S TABLE

Rich and poor have this in common: The Lord is the
Maker of them all.
- Proverbs 22.2, NIV

> *We must allow our people to deal with one another as Christian brothers*
> *and sisters, first, and share their love, their knowledge, their expertise,*
> *and their noble ambitions before they share their cash.*

The church has an often-puzzling attitude toward wealth. There are those who seek to exploit the wealthy for Kingdom purposes, always asking for more and more money to assist "the Lord's work." There are those who perceive the rich to be "blessed" by God, and their riches are the substantiation of their righteousness. There are also those who blast the rich for their wealth, imagining that it represents greed or materialism or corruption. But the church of the future will perceive wealthy people as, first of all, people. We will love and serve them just as we do the poor and all those in between.

Like the church in the New Testament, the church of the future will bring rich and poor together in friendship. Not simply so the rich can fund the poor; nor simply so the rich can employ the poor; nor simply so the rich can see the poor, feel guilty, and solve all of the problems associated with being poor. The rich and the poor will first come together in fellowship, across the table, to pray and learn and grow in the Lord Jesus. From that common cause, it may very well be that those with greater means respond to the prompting of the Holy Spirit; but—and this is crucial—the church of the future will no longer dictate the rules of engagement. We will not guilt the rich. We will not excuse the poor. We will not glamorize wealth. We will not fetishize poverty. We will not be predators of privilege. We will not be enablers of ease.

When we gather, there will be innumerable socioeconomic strata represented. Too often, the church has only acknowledged the very top and the very bottom, and everyone on the top feels like everyone in the middle is waiting for them to fix those on the bottom. Those on the bottom wonder why they aren't getting taken care of like they were promised. Those in the middle are confused.

But the church of the future will not demand the ideal from the outset. We will persist in helping those who exploit her, refusing to succumb to bitterness, resentment, or cynicism. We will balance the need for systemic checks and balances with our commitment to boundless and extravagant love. We will cooperate with God to take the next steps, and then the next steps, at the pace and discretion of the people being required to move forward. Sometimes that will be the rich, but sometimes God may not be speaking to the rich about their resources. Because there's more to a person than how much money they have. Sometimes God may be speaking to the rich about their relationships, their dreams, their brokenness, and the church of the future will support the rich as they listen to the Spirit and grow in the Lord, regardless of the direction that development takes.

Likewise, there may be more at work in the lives of the poor than simply the fact that they are poor. Extreme poverty is a reality in our world, but for many in North America our relative poverty is nothing like the desperation experienced by those in refugee camps, shantytowns, or U.N. townships. Consequently, we are "poor" but still have iPhones, three daily meals, automobiles, Internet access, satellite television, and entry to free community college.[214] Please don't misunderstand: I do not want to minimize anyone's suffering, for our suffering always counts, regardless of what someone else might endure; but I do think it's important to acknowledge that when the Lord speaks to us, he may very well be addressing some other issue than our lack of financial resources.

The church of the future will leverage our resources toward gospel ends. Sometimes that will mean raising capital; sometimes that will mean generating ideas and putting them

---

[214]   See http://www.npr.org/sections/ed/2017/06/11/532003646/ free-community-college-for-all; http://money.cnn.com/2017/04/08/pf/ college/new-york-free-tuition/index.html.

to work. But she will not treat the offerings of her people as an endless resource. She will set aside funds for the future. She will wisely assign tightly controlled allotments to specific tasks, projects, and initiatives that have both an immediate and a long-term payout. And, despite the lack of resources within the church, she will not rely upon wealthier Christians as the solution to her collective problems. Instead, she will work to ensure our communities do not become predatory, withholding or compromising the gospel in favor of treating those with means like substitute saviors or false gods.

How can you "set a table" for both the haves and have-nots in your life?

FIFTEEN.THREE

FRUGALITY

SPENDING EVERY DOLLAR TWICE

The Kingdom of heaven is like yeast that a woman
took and mixed into about sixty pounds of flour until
it worked all through the dough.
- Matthew 13.33, NIV

> *We must be good stewards, not only employing our talents,*
> *but investing them.*

Having travelled extensively, I can attest to the can-do attitude of most indigenous pastors and overseas missionaries.
They know they won't have the resources they need, so they make drum sets out of Tupperware and learn to rewire old projectors; they've learned that a microphone can be run off a car stereo and that you can syphon gas from a lawnmower back into your moped if you need to preach out of town; they know that fruit makes a better snack than pizza, and that commemorative t-shirts are a waste. They stretch their money. They know what an American dollar is worth. They have an inborn sense of what's valuable, profitable, and useable for the Kingdom.

What if we began running our churches the way we require our missionaries to run theirs?

The church of the future will function like a missions outpost, or a hidden cell of believers underground, or a fledgling operation without an American benefactor.

We will do a lot with a little, because a little can go a long way.

Like yeast.

Yeast is the little ingredient causes exponential multiplication. Jesus' use of yeast-imagery was profound, especially given that every prior time the prophets had used that term it was in the negative, and Jesus himself often employed the metaphor to refer to the corrupted teachings of the Pharisees. And yet, the principle remains—yeast breaks down starch into sugar, then into expansive gas. Yeast causes something to blow up from the inside. A "bad" yeast, like bad teaching, will result in a catastrophic increase of error and misbehavior; a "good" yeast, like the Kingdom, will result in an overflow of love and faithfulness.

Thus, the Kingdom of God, when planted within us, bursts forth in abundance. It is the power that multiplied the loaves and the fishes; that transformed the water into wine; that perpetuated the widow's daily oil and flour.[215] Consider that in the story of Jesus feeding the 5,000, there were leftovers. In the story of Mary anointing Jesus' feet with perfume,[216] the value of that offering was a years' wages.[217] What else is that, if not extravagant? What does that tell us about God? About his riches? About his proclivity for abundance?

In the Kingdom of God, there is always more than enough, because grace is free and God is a giver.

Of course abundance does not always manifest in material goods, increased financial capacity, or an improvement in your standard of living. However, God's Kingdom multiplies both in us and around us. His generosity results in a life of increased means and satisfactions—both materially and in the more valuable immaterial Kingdom of God.

This yeast, at work in our churches, teaches us to think about multiplying what we can get out of our investments. So if someone else had a budget to, say, decorate their auditorium for $500, we might begin to work with only $150 and immediately think about how these decorations might later be repurposed, recycled, or transformed into something that could be used in another part of our building.

Take, for example, the project we completed in the summer of 2017: The Garden Path.[218] Our church designer, Melissa Evans, recruited seven teams of architects, engineers, and laborers to create prayer spaces for our front lawn. The spaces

[215] 1 Kings 17.
[216] John 12.2.
[217] Mark 14.6.
[218] https://www.facebook.com/WestwindsGardenPath/.

were constructed using mostly recycled materials and laid out along a labyrinthine path to encourage our neighbors to take prayer walks and learn how they might commune with God. The installations were then re-purposed as obstacles in our children's adventure race, The Sheep Dog Splash & Dash.[219] After the race, the installations were dissembled and stored, with each later being rolled out as an aesthetic piece within either our lobby or our auditorium.

Much of this repurposing we learned while running a local missions initiative we referred to as Beyond 1000, indicating that we intended to take our church off-site, away from 1000 Robinson Road (our church address). Instead of trying to convince our people that they should bring their friends to church, we encouraged them to bring their church to friends.

Part of the motivation for pressing into local missions was due to the imbalance between our overseas efforts and our local initiatives. We realized we were more intent on blessing people in other countries than we were on blessing those in our zip code. Because Jesus instructed his followers to be his witnesses in Jerusalem, Judea, Samaria and the ends of the earth we felt like it was important to do something at home, in our "Jerusalem."

So every quarter we gave each department $1,000 to invest in healing our community. Sometimes our people did service projects like provide free oil changes or renovate bathrooms or replace the heating and cooling systems of people outside the church; other times our people did educational projects like partnering with local art schools and literacy foundations to provide extra-curricular learning environments.

---

[219] http://sheepdogsplash.com/.

The truth is that running the Beyond 1000 initiative was exhausting, since our people didn't always want to get involved in the community. Those relationships take a lot out of you and sometimes the people you help aren't grateful, kind, or even benefit from your service. But the church of the future will be generous, regardless of the miserliness of her beneficiaries. We will be givers, regardless of what the world gives back.

When we give generously and sacrificially, we exorcise our bitterness. Selfishness is septic, but generosity is the algorithm of joy.

> *How can you reduce, reuse, and recycle your resources to better honor God?*

FIFTEEN.FOUR

TITHING

BECOMING SACRIFICIAL GIVERS

Remember this: Whoever sows sparingly will also reap
sparingly, and whoever sows generously will also reap
generously.
- 2 Corinthians 9.6, NIV

> *If we give generously and sacrificially it will cost us more than simply
> tithing, but the rewards will be far greater than if we give only to fulfill
> an obligation.*

There is a difference between generosity and obligation. Obligations rob us of our joy, whereas generous offerings and contributions enhance it.

This is the problem with tithing. Despite its widespread advocacy within the contemporary church, tithing in the Bible was neither unilaterally applied nor enforced. For starters, there was more than one tithe (sometimes requiring as much as 23%, sometimes only being paid once in a lifetime like Abraham to Melchizadek[220]), and we never see the New Testament church enforcing the tithe among Gentile converts. When we advocate tithing today, we are introducing a new legislation that requires our people to give.

The old paradigm of hoping for more tithers—people who are adamant about giving the first 10% of their income every paycheck, every week for the rest of their lives—will ultimately bankrupt us. Why? Because tithing is ultimately rooted in obedience for its own sake. Most people cannot tithe. Most people will not tithe. Those who can and will, do so … sometimes. But when we tithe, at best we feel relief that we are finally in step with God's demands. If we fail to tithe, we feel like we've incurred a debt that must be repaid before we can ever truly be free of our guilt.

That may be true.

The problem is not that our people give, but that we *require* them to give. That requirement robs us of the joy inherent in giving generously and replaces it with a satisfaction for fulfilling our obligations. So, even if you're suspicious about my conviction that the Bible doesn't advocate tithing among New Testament Christians, the point I want you to consider is that tithing is insufficient as a paradigm for financial church

---

[220] See http://cldibillings.org/wp-content/uploads/2011/11/Tithe-Verses-and-NT-Giving.pdf.

management. Why? Because less than 0.6% of the 247 million American Christians claim to tithe.[221] Simply put: no one does it (except, apparently, me and my friends).

From the standpoint of church administration, tithing is a flawed paradigm. It makes a good floor but a bad ceiling. Giving 10% is a good place to start for a serious follower of Jesus, but the real beauty lies in giving generously. In realizing that you've set aside a significant portion of your income to love and serve others. In this light, all that money becomes play money. It's your investment capital in the Kingdom of God. You can give it wherever you like, redirecting the flow of God's generosity, like a culvert in a river. You can place it wherever you wish, so long as you place it back within the hands of the Lord. It's exciting. It's liberating.

In the same way that we are meant to be generous with our finances, we are also meant to be generous with our homes, our churches, and with Christ himself. We ought to be sharing Christ with everyone; and by this I don't intend for us to perform our prepared spiels about sin and redemption, but that we would invite others to share the life of Christ, the light of Christ, and the joy of following Jesus.

The church of the future will be filled with Christians who understand their role as evangelists. They will recognize that the good news is too good to keep secret, and will spread the message of Christ and his church throughout their networks. In our culture, ironically, it is actually consumers who tend to make the best evangelists. For example, in his article "Making Freemium Work," management guru Vineet Kumar says "the primary value of a Free user is in their ability to generate referrals."[222] Essentially, Kumar is suggesting companies give away a portion of their product in exchange for the natural outpouring of "evangelism" that results.

[221] See http://www.sharefaith.com/blog/2015/12/facts-christians-tithing/.
[222] Kumar, Vineet, "Making Freemium Work," *Harvard Business Review*, May 2014, 29.

Could there be a better metaphor for all we've received than to consider Christians "Freemium users" of God's grace, God's gifts, and God's cooperative plan to heal the world? We share in something we cannot afford, to which we have no earned right, and from which we benefit immensely. The church of the future will find new ways to celebrate this and to invite others into this Freemium celebration, also.

This will require something on the part of our leaders and pastors. Adapting Chris Anderson's FREE principles,[223] here are four ideas for how to make this work:

> 1. Build church community around free information and advice on helpful topics ranging from marriage and family advice, to biblical theology, to money management, and how to be happy and have fun.
> 2. Invite the church community into the process of designing products that people want, and return the favor by making the products free in raw form.
> 3. Let those with more money than time/skill/risk-tolerance buy the more polished version of those products (that may turn out to be almost everyone).
> 4. Do it again and again, leveraging profits to both fund future innovation and fixed church expenses.

The church of the future will be more concerned with what she gives than what she keeps; what she offers than what she obtains. She will be filled with extravagant evangelists who offer joyful generosity born of reckless love.

How will you cultivate more generosity with both your finances and your faith?

---

[223] Anderson, Chris, *Free: How Today's Smartest Businesses Profit by Giving Something for Nothing*, 69.

FIFTEEN.FIVE

EXPERTISE

GIVING MORE THAN JUST MONEY

May the favor of the Lord rest upon us; establish the work of our hands …
- Psalm 90.17a, NIV

We must invest in our innovators, thereby reclaiming the spiritual discipline of mentoring others at work.

The church of the future will put her resources toward assisting, inspiring, and motivating amateurs to innovate. We will recognize that our best ideas will come from the margins, not the center; from the undiscovered, hungry passion of new people rather than the stoic professionalism of the existing institution.

As such, I suggest we look to the model of crowd-funding to consider how we might source and support new ideas, initiatives, and experiences. Not only concerning the "pitch an idea, and if we like it we'll fund it" sense, but more importantly in the sense that once an idea is funded the people who provided the funding are now invested in the success of the new venture.

Isn't this what our giving is meant to feel like anyway? Not paying tithes with the same lifeless efficiency as paying bills, but investing into the people, into the mission, and into the future of our church?

> By connecting enthusiastic makers with enthusiastic investors, crowd-funding has the power to keep people motivated—right through what, in a 9-to-5 job, might be career-ending missteps or failures—so that they can stay focused on realizing their vision.
> - Jack Hitt[224]

Rather than just having a congregation (or denomination) vote on which ideas they like best and then supply the necessary resources to see it done, such a model would place key business people, economists, and organizational leaders around innovators as coaches and mentors to ensure their ideas are executed with the utmost competence. In such a relationship, rather than relying on the wealthy for monetary donations, we would be asking them for something even more valuable:

---

[224] Hitt, Jack, "A Nation of Tinkerers," *Wired Magazine*, June 2012, 20.

their help. By giving the opportunity to share their wisdom and expertise, we would be affording successful people the joy of "teaching a man to fish."

I remember hearing New Song Church's[225] pastor, Dave Gibbons, speak of a similar concept years ago that he referred to as an A-B-C model, where Artists, Business People, and Community Leaders are brought together on local projects. It's a problematic mix in reality, since artists get along with almost no one and community leaders tend to get trampled by the go-get-em urgency of successful professionals, but the idea is well-intentioned. Artists often have great ideas. Community leaders often have a front-row seat to great need. Business people understand great execution. And we need to be great in all three directions in order to make a lasting impact. Since we'll rarely have the appropriate resources to purchase such greatness, we're left to our own devices for how to bring the best out of the people we have already gathered. But the good news is we have more than enough right in front of us, so long as we remain teachable and coachable. We need to be willing to work with others, acknowledging that we don't have to align on every single issue so long as we're working together for something significant.

> To love is to will the good of another.
> - Thomas Aquinas

True love means we want good for others for their own sake, not for any residual benefit to ourselves. It means wanting your wife to be happy—not so your home will be less stressful or your life will be easier, but because you want your wife to experience the wonder of joy. It means wanting your children to grow up and flourish—not so you can avoid embarrassment or make comparisons or rely upon their benevolent care, but because you want them to live life to its fullest measure of

---

[225] http://newsong.net.

satisfaction. And true love, in crowd-sourcing the future of our faith, would involve mentoring and coaching others only because we want the church of the future to flourish.

How can you invest in others' ideas, initiatives, and experiences through your wisdom, insights, and expertise?

SIXTEEN | WE
SEE
A
CHURCH

CONCERNED *with* PASTORING THE PLANET,
DRAWING TOGETHER RESOURCES *to*
BRING WISE ORDER *to our* WORLD;

a CHURCH *that* MAKES NO DISTINCTION
BETWEEN HONORING GOD *and* HONORING
GOD'S CREATION;

that WORKS *to* RESTORE CITIES *and* SPECIES,
LANDSCAPES *and* ECOLOGIES,
NEIGHBORHOODS *and* ETHNICITIES,
ECONOMIES *and* CULTURES,
so that EVERYTHING
FLOURISHES IN THE PRESENCE
of GOD.

SIXTEEN.ONE

ECOLOGY

UNDERSTANDING OUR ROLE AS PLANETARY STEWARDS

The Lord God took the man and put him in the
Garden of Eden to work it and take care of it.
- Genesis 2.15, NIV

*The Hebrew words for "man" and "earth" share a root: a'dam (man)
and a'damah (earth) demonstrate the relationship-by-design of people
and planet.*

I spent the first three decades of my life in Vancouver, one of the most environmentally conscious cities on the planet. When I moved to small-town USA in 2005, I was stunned to learn there were no green initiatives. There was no recycling pickup. There were no separate trash cans for aluminum or cardboard. People in our county routinely threw bags of McDonald's out their windows to land on the side of the road.

Up until that point I had always mocked environmentalists, but it only took a few short months of this new disregard for me to change teams.

At that time, Dave Midkiff was the groundskeeper and handyman at Westwinds. Dave approached our church leadership about installing the first ever recycling station in Jackson, and with our blessing, had it done. We poured a concrete slab, coerced a local waste management company into figuring out how to sell cardboard and aluminum, and announced to the neighborhood there was a new way to get rid of their recyclables.

It was a great moment, and one we often celebrated, because it gave us the sensation that we were—in our own little corner of our own little town—doing what God intended his stewards to perform: taking care.

The ecological teaching of the Bible is inescapable. You cannot read scripture and come to any other conclusion than the fact that God made the earth, intended for us to care for it on his behalf, and has long term plans for the planet that care at least as much for it as for us. The eschatological promise of a New Earth might be better understood as a (re)New(ed) Earth, for all literary cues point to the fact that the New Earth is still This Earth after Christ has "made all things new."[226]

---

[226] Revelation 21.

Consider that with the rebellion of Adam and Eve in the Garden of Eden, sin entered the world.[227] Consider, also, that sin had a corrupting influence that spread beyond people and into the created order itself. Sin ruins everything,[228] and the corruption of sin is at least partially responsible for the deterioration of the physical world—either directly, through some as-of-yet-not-fully-understood metaphysical undoing of Creation's harmony, or indirectly—as a result of the sinful condition of humanity and our disregard for the planet.

Take, for example, the plight of the world's oceans. We're everywhere made aware of the pollution—at both a high level and at the lowest, day-at-the-beach scenario. When I was in Mumbai, people routinely threw their trash off the ferries into Back Bay. The water was so covered in garbage it looked like the scene from *Star Wars: A New Hope* when Luke and Han try to rescue Princess Leia. It was incomprehensible, and made me realize the challenges involved in getting world citizenry on board with cleanliness, sanitation, and sustainability were much larger than I'd imagined.

> Every day is World Oceans Day. Small changes can make a big difference. Eat sustainable seafood. Recycle and minimize plastic in your world. Become a citizen scientist. And meet the ocean—set a date with the sea.
> - Stephen Frink[229]

And, of course, we are not the first Christians to recognize both the significance and the challenges for our stewardship of the planet. Hungarian Christians have acknowledged this in their celebration of Vizkereszt, which means "water cross." They believe Christ's baptism foreshadows his crucifixion (a connection the apostle Paul explores in Romans 6.3-5 and

---

[227] Genesis 3.
[228] Romans 8.
[229] Frink, Stephen, "Conscious Conservation," *Alert Diver*, summer 2014, 12.

Colossians 2.12) and participate in a crucessional (a parade with a giant cross at the head, carried by the bishops and fathers of the church) through the city streets to the banks of a river. The giant cross is then blessed by the bishop and heaved into the sub-zero water. Many burly (presumably sober) men then strip down to their underwear and wrestle for the lumber. The man who returns the Water Cross to the bishop receives a blessing for his family for that year, and hopes no one is around with a digital camera.

Why bother? In part, this tradition harkens back to an even older set of beliefs. Consider that in the ancient Near Eastern world—comprised of Israel, Assyria, Babylon, Mesopotamia, etc. —the commonly held assumption was that our planet existed in a kind of water womb. We were encircled by water, and we were brought up out of the water onto dry land, as if God (or the gods) had built a palace on a falling tear drop.[230] Our spiritual ancestors often thought of this water as anything but pleasant and gentle. The water was churned up, chaotic, a perpetual threat to human existence.

What God does for Creation, he does for us also.

God brings order out of chaos, patrols the seas with angelic horses, and presides over Creation. He calms the churning tempests of our lusts and ambitions, and when the tumultuous storms of our past memories and associations threaten to scuttle and down us, God is there to bring us safely home.

God's plan to heal the world is very much a plan to heal every aspect of the world and his rescue mission begins with the sacrificial death and resurrection of Jesus Christ.[231]

---

[230] Psalm 104.2-3, 5.

[231] 2 Corinthians 5.

That is why the Hungarians toss the cross into the water: they're preaching to it.

God instructed us, first, to fill the earth and to subdue it, and to have dominion. We have done a poor job. We've filled the earth and subdued it, sure, but our dominion has borne all the hallmarks of a fascist dictatorship. What we need to do next is discover a way to undo our damage and repair the planet.

One of the more entertaining imaginings of this kind of ecological repair was recently featured in Horizon Zero Dawn, a video game for the PlayStation 4. This post-apocalyptic adventure story tells of humans sharing the earth with mechanized animals. As the narrative progresses, the player learns these animals were created by earlier humans as an elaborate system designed to renovate the earth.[232] The robot birds recycled the air. The robot fish and alligators cleansed the waters. The robot animal herds tilled the fields. It's a brilliant concept, beautifully executed, that demonstrates our use of the planet doesn't only have to subtract from Creation, but can also draw resources together to replenish Creation.

That kind of rejuvenating work is inherent in the term "dominion," which literally means "the territory of sovereignty or government." It is the land for which a King is responsible. Since we are Kings and Priests, and have been entrusted with the ongoing administration of God's well-ordered Creation, we must likewise repair it as much as we inhabit it.

The church of the future will celebrate ecologically regenerative technologies as our scientists and engineers continue to find new and better sources of energy and clean fuel.

---

[232] See https://www.youtube.com/watch?v=_FSbZC2Kn4.

Human beings, while capable of the worst, are also capable of rising above themselves, choosing again what is good, and making a new start.
- Pope Francis, encyclical on climate change

How can you better observe your responsibilities as a steward of God's earth?

SIXTEEN.TWO

CONSERVATION

LOOKING AFTER THE NON-HUMAN
INHABITANTS OF GOD'S CREATION

How many are your works, O Lord! In wisdom you
made them all; the earth is full of your creatures.
There is the sea, vast and spacious, teeming with
creatures beyond number-living things both large and
small.
- Psalm 104.24-25, NIV

> *The church of the future will acknowledge that conservation is a godly*
> *pursuit, and the way we engage with nature is a manifestation of our*
> *holy calling.*

In 2017, I traveled with a group of scuba divers to the Siccorro Islands, 200 miles south of Cabo San Lucas, to dive with some of the most rare and elusive sharks on the planet. Whale Sharks, Great Hammerheads, and Black Manta Rays accompanied us on almost every one of our twenty dives, and I was profoundly affected by the experience of being so close to these beautiful animals. When you're inches away, you realize how fragile they are. Mantas, for example, are covered with an inch-thin mucus membrane that, once touched, ceases to perform its primary function as a barrier against disease. The problem is that mantas are playful and want to be touched, so they constantly hover over your face eager for your bubbles to tickle their bellies. The only thing protecting them from their own playfulness is the loving caution of human beings. Sharks, likewise, are curious about all the commotion and will eventually screw up the courage to investigate. Here again, sharks are surprisingly gentle creatures—much more like cats than the rabid wet-werewolves we're made to believe in the movie theater. Because we've been told sharks are vicious killers, the first reaction of almost every new diver is to panic. But this panic puts the shark at risk, since it senses the divers are distressed and becomes anxious. The sharks' fear feeds the divers' fear, and as the tensions mount something unpleasant is bound to occur—usually on the part of the diver, who will hit, kick, or stab out of mad terror. Here again, the only thing protecting the shark is the calm sense of self maintained by human beings.

> Up to 25 percent of the world's sharks and rays are threatened with extinction, according to the IUCN Shark Specialist Group.
> - Tiffany Leite[233]

---

[233] Leite, Tiffany, "Year of the Shark," *Sport Diver*, August 2014, 34.

In his award-winning documentary *Sharkwater*, diver Rob Stuart catalogues the devastating effects of the shark-fin trade that removes an estimated 150 million sharks each year from our oceans. Among the many problems associated with this mass harvest is that sharks are unable to adequately perform their function as the ocean's top predator, keeping the populations of smaller creatures contained. This effect trickles down the food chain, until the bottom-level fish breed disproportionately high numbers and eat too much plankton. That plankton recycles more carbon monoxide than trees, which means the oxygen supply of our entire planet is suddenly at risk.
As long as this planet is our home, earth care is self care. The earth is the Lord's and everything in it, and we are his people, called to shepherd his Creation.

We know that God's plans to restore Creation do not merely include humanity, but also the non-human inhabitants of this world (animals, plants, etc.) and the world itself.[234]

To help reinforce this, last summer Westwinds held our first ever Blessing of the Animals. People brought dogs, cats, goats, chickens, turtles, ferrets, and even an albino boa constrictor to be blessed, and we both blessed them collectively and (if desired) individually by anointing them with oil. A blessing is an "impartation of life," and expresses goodwill and care on the part of both the clergy and the congregant.[235] We did this in imitation of the service held yearly at St. John the Divine in Manhattan, but also to walk in step with St. Francis of Assisi, who frequently preached to animals.

> My brother and sister birds, you should praise your Creator and always love him: He gave you feathers for clothes, wings to fly and all other things that you need.

[234] Isaiah 65, 66; Revelation 21.
[235] See http://www.letallcreationpraise.org/worship-services/blessing-of-the-animals.

It is God who made you noble among all creatures, making your home in thin, pure air. Without sowing or reaping, you receive God's guidance and protection.
- St. Francis[236]

How can you "preach the gospel" to the animals like St. Francis?

---

[236] St. Francis of Assisi, *Franciscan Media*, https://www.franciscanmedia.org/stories-about-saint-francis-and-the-animals/.

SIXTEEN.THREE

STEWARDSHIP

SERVING 'OUR HOUSEHOLDER, WHO ART IN HEAVEN'

> Thy Kingdom come, thy will be done on earth as it is in heaven.
> - Matthew 6.10, KJV

> *By pastoring the planet, we don't just mean that the church of the future will be ecologically responsible, but that our responsibilities extend to culture, society, and government also.*

The church of the future will be full of global citizens, people who think less about their private corner of the world and more about our shared humanity. The "earth" is not just the ecology. It is also the culture and diversity of our world. We must care for the planet, but we must also care for what happens on the planet. Our love for mountains and our love for movies are both manifestations of a healthy love of Creation; our love of city streets and our love of the Straits of Mackinac both reveal our commitment to the things God has made that we have continued to create.

Christians will consider people from the opposite half of the planet as much their brother and sister as they do people next door. Of course we do this already. It is one of the most endearing features of the faith. When we travel and meet other Christians, they embrace us warmly and call us "brother" or "sister," and there is great feeling attached to those terms.

God made the earth his home and created us as his caretakers. God is best understood as a householder, and we are his stewards and co-operants.

John Dominic Crossan is a well-regarded liberal scholar, and in his assessment of the Lord's Prayer, he asserts that we are better meant to understand "Our Father" as "Our Householder." Not, as some may assume, to remove the sting of patriarchy, but because Fathers then had very different roles than fathers do now.

In the ancient world, a householder was something akin to a modern-day rancher. They owned massive amounts of land, herds, and crops. They employed dozens of families, with jobs and responsibilities for every age of both men and women. Householders ran their holdings like a small country, and took their own responsibility seriously for the protection and wellbeing of their people.

Consider the example of *Downton Abbey*. Lord Grantham, played by Hugh Bonneville, is a British Earl whose primary occupation is running his family estate. He has no real job. He simply makes decisions about the wealth he has inherited or acquired through marriage. And yet, his job is clearly to take care of the estate and all who live on it. There are sharecroppers, workers, and serving staff that he considers family. He loans them money. He performs their weddings and funerals. He visits them. He accepts advice from them on how best to run the estate and what plans there might be for its future. When Lord Grantham does make plans for the future—such as parceling off portions of the land in order to generate some much-needed revenue—he does so with a big picture perspective on how his decisions will impact future generations. He wants Downton to remain wondrous, majestic, and noble forever, and so all his choices are weighted in light of a future that has no foreseeable end.

This is how we must imagine God making decisions for us, about us, and concerning our administration of his Creation.

The church of the future will recognize God as householder and know this entails not only ecology, but also the work of restoration in cities, economies, and cultures.

A good householder is one who ensures that there is an equal distribution among all their dependents, such that none are starving while others gluttonize themselves. It is this "distributive justice" that best characterizes God's authority and administration of the earth, and it is this ideal God intends us to adopt.

The term householder connotes three things: one who possesses an estate, one who has business to do, one who has a family of servants to employ.

Householders had responsibilities, and one of those involved knowing that companionship and inheritance were crucial to the welfare of the estate. Householders, then, placed a premium on children. Isn't this what God has done with us, first making us as his companions in order to enjoy the Garden, and then tasking us with a two-fold reproductive mandate (fill the earth; make disciples)?

Likewise, a good householder fits his family and his servants for business. He ensures that everyone has something to do so they can earn a living and contribute meaningfully to the estate. No one gets a free lunch, but neither does it fall on everyone to figure it out on their own. This is one of the many merits of Jesus' parable concerning the Vineyard Workers,[237] who are each employed and compensated for by the householder. The householder is involved in grooming and finding the right employment for each person.

A good householder never leaves, nor destroys, his estate. God is present with us, watching over us as we watch over Creation. And though we may not see God, we can be assured God sees us. He sees what we're doing and how we're doing it. He observes our disregard as well as our care. Consider the story Jesus told about the wicked vineyard tenants in Luke 20.9-19.

A good householder will protect his estate from thieves and brigands. If he senses anything amiss, he will secure the household and bring the criminals to justice. Because he cares. He cares for the estate. He cares for its inhabitants. He cares for the family. And if the family or the inhabitants should be among those destroying the estate, a good householder will remove them.

A good householder metes out justice in public, not hiding the consequences of rebellion from the children or the more

---

[237] Matthew 20.1-16.

sensitive ones. He lets everyone know that justice will be enforced so the appropriate administration of the estate can continue.

Other eastern religions have made similar connections between their respective divinities and the responsibilities we have to Creation. Hindu Grihasthas, for example, pursue a virtuous life concerned with the support and sustenance of their dependents, much like Buddhist "householders" perceive ordinary activity as their means of living harmoniously, akin to a holy man in prayer.

The church of the future will understand their primary role as care-provider for everyone, and everything, everywhere they go. At first this must seem overwhelming, but if you can imagine yourself in almost any scenario, all you're really doing is treating the world around you with respect. You're taking care of your home, your property, your car, your friends. You're minding your behaviors when you're at the beach, in the woods, on the mountains, or traveling along the roads. You're not ever engaging in mindless activity. You're recognizing that " The earth is the Lord's, and the fullness thereof; the world, and they that dwell therein."[238]

> To divide the holy from the common is a totally false distinction once you understand that everything is a sign of the presence of God.
> - Michael Mayne[239]

How would you evaluate yourself as one of God's householders?

---

[238] Psalm 24.1.

[239] Mayne, Michael, *This Sunrise of Wonder: Letters for the Journey*, 63.

SIXTEEN.FOUR

RECLAMATION

HEALING THE NEIGHBORHOOD

The Lord will surely comfort Zion and will look with
compassion on all her ruins; he will make her deserts
like Eden, her wastelands like the garden of the Lord.
Joy and gladness will be found in her, thanksgiving and
the sound of singing.
- Isaiah 51.3, NIV

*The church of the future will discover more
innovative approaches to care.*

Only the Gospel can save. The Law can curb behavior out of fear of punishment, but it can't change the heart. Governments regulate behavior. Churches change hearts. What does a ghetto need more—stop light cameras or flower boxes? Cops or teachers? DUI warnings or festivals?

The church of the future will have long-term vision, working toward inspiring others, believing that perhaps someone is learning from her example. Perhaps because the small commitments we make collectively do add up to a significant difference. Perhaps because there is value in simply not making things worse. Perhaps our shared commitment to sustainable ecology fosters enough research funding that we can solve the problem of pollution entirely through some as-of-yet undiscovered means of air filtration. Perhaps our concerns, cares, and careful activities are never wasted.

Despite the fact that most CEOs understand the reality of climate change, only "one-third believe that their companies are prepared for its disruptions," which include massive upturns in costs and heightened "risks of regulatory action and consumer backlash."[240]

Most of what we must do as adults has been taught to us as children. Don't kill. Don't litter. Don't ruin, exploit, or destroy. The problem is that those in charge of the large-scale oversight of many endeavors seem to disregard these simple moralisms, so it makes us despair of making any positive change at a local level. Why bother recycling your beer cans when factories in China are belching out more toxins in an hour than we could offset in a lifetime?

---

[240] Lowitt, Eric, "How to survive climate change and still run a thriving business," *Harvard Business Review*, April 2014, 87ff.

The church of the future will help others understand it is in their best interests to look after the planet, rather than making them feel guilty for their failure to do so.

Take, for example, the not-for-profit corporation Seacology, which is employing such a strategy based on self-interest. Seacology persuades indigenous communities to protect their threatened island ecosystems. Most of these communities thrive on tourism dollars, so Seacology's strategy is to invest in local infrastructure in order to lure increased visitor rates. The corporation provides something tangible, like paved walkways for the villages or local parks, and then tasks the locals with guarding their reefs or enforcing higher standards on the interactions between tourists and wildlife. Seacology currently has 244 projects in 51 countries on 149 islands.[241]

My mum used to run workshops helping people upcycle goods, thereby turning "trash into treasure." Long before Pinterest, mum understood that creativity and passion can provide a steady source of income. I think something similar is happening globally, not just with arts and crafts, but with business plans and sustainability initiatives.

Whether turning plastic bottles into ropes and baskets or collecting household items to be melted down and repurposed, people like Bilikiss Adebiyi-Abiola understand that garbage doesn't have to stay that way. Neither does our trash have to be disposed of by big machines and dangerous chemicals. Instead, we can put our trash to good use, bringing new life out of old items.[242]

---

[241] Gaskill, Melissa, "Seacology: Saving the world onc island at a time," *Alert Diver*, Winter 2014, 20.

[242] "How one local entrepreneur taught Lagos, Nigeria to embrace recycling," *Fast Company*, https://www.fastcompany.com/3039733/turning-trash-into-treasure.

How might you employ your ingenuity to inspire others to care for the planet, rather than shaming them for their past neglect?

SEVENTEEN | WE
SEE
A
CHURCH

INFUSED *with* PLAYFULNESS, ARTISTRY *and* INTERACTIVITY;

where the LINES BETWEEN AUDIENCE *and* ATTRACTION *are* BLURRED;

where the DECISIONS, ABILITIES, *and* BEHAVIORS *of the* COMMON PEOPLE INFLUENCE THE FORM *and* FLAVOR OF WORSHIP.

PLAYFULNESS

SCULPTING OUR MINDS WITH JOY

My command is this: Love each other as I have loved you.
- John 15.12, NIV

Church ought to be playful, fun, and energetic.

There are so many funny things that happen at church, and I used to wonder why no one ever laughed.

> When the elderly usher dropped a tray of communion, loudly exclaiming "Oh sh*t!"

> When the spinster gave her testimony, mispronouncing both Gentiles and prostrate.

> When the person creating the lyric slides invited us to worship the Loin of Judah.

In all these moments, the church of my childhood reacted with a puzzling stoicism, refusing to acknowledge that these moments were very, very funny. And my church was a fun place, filled with fun people; it's just that it seemed inappropriate to lose your composure during church.

But church ought to be a place where you can comfortably belly-laugh, especially when we experience the charm of these family-faux-pas. We should be the first people to slap our thighs and wrap our arms around each other making it okay. Why? Because playfulness is not the meaningless pursuit of frivolity. "During play, the brain is making sense of itself through simulation and testing," which means that joyful, winsome activities are "helping sculpt the brain."[243] Likewise, laughter brings people together far more than doctrine or education. The ability to enjoy another's company is one of the most profound human experiences, elevating our relationships beyond obligation and marking them with love.

---

[243] Brown, Stuart, M.D., with Christopher Vaughan, *Play: How it Shapes the Brain, Opens the Imagination, and Invigorates the Soul*, 34.

> "The ability to play is critical not only to being happy, but also to sustaining social relationships...play is what lifts people out of the mundane."
> - Stuart Brown, M.D., and Christopher Vaughan[244]

One of my favorite new things at The Winds blends well the motif of praying and playing at the same time. Part-entertainment and part-therapy, our video confession booth was modeled after the digital photo booths now common at wedding receptions, and it allows participants to send their confessions directly to our staff and elders.

> Welcome to our confessional! Sit down. Take a load off. Get something off your chest. Spew. Tell us all your problems. Gush. Vent. And then email your tales of dastardly woe to our pastors & elders (or just like, you know, your mom). REMEMBER: Anything you say can and will be used against you on the Internet (as if you didn't know). But trust us, the squad is going to love seeing you on screen during church. So #shareyoursins and #keepitreal at our #confessional
> - Posted instructions to the Westwinds Virtual Confession Booth

It's this kind of juxtaposition between heartfelt testimony and punky-gifs that not only defines today's pop culture but will also form the future of the church. Church ought to facilitate both the camaraderie and the community of genuine love and friendship, during worship and beyond it.

What's the funniest thing that's ever happened to you at church?

---

[244] Ibid, 6.

AGENCY

CREATING MEANINGFUL OPPORTUNITIES DURING WORSHIP

> But you are a chosen people, a royal priesthood, a holy nation, God's special possession, that you may declare the praises of him who called you out of darkness into his wonderful light.
> - 1 Peter 2.9, NIV

We must not abdicate our priestly role, but instead embrace our identity as God's agents on the earth.

For three hundred years the tabernacle was the earthly dwelling place of Yawheh. It was a movable tent, designed to accommodate the ritual needs of a nomadic people.[245] Countless tasks required hundreds of people just to establish the tent in a new location, which meant worship required a massive community commitment.

In some ways, the tabernacle is a better metaphor for understanding worship than the Temple, precisely because of the duties and readiness of the worshippers, the twice-daily prayers of the priests, those burning incense, plus all the occasional offerings, sacrifices, ordeals, dedications, and meetings. There has never been a more personnel-intense expression of worship than the tabernacle, and you cannot help but conclude that was by design.

The church of the future will relentlessly find even more pathways to explore the priesthood of all believers. She will help her people understand we are all equipped and ennobled by the Spirit to preach, to pray, and to prepare the sacraments.

We carry within us the image of God and can do all things through Christ who gives us strength.'[246]

The church of the future will supply increasing agency to her people. To give someone agency is to empower them to take action, exercise control, and generate their own results. And giving agency doesn't necessitate either increased individualization or a fracturing of community—far from it. Board games, sports, and virtual reality are all good examples of how individuals exercise autonomy within public contexts without damaging the social dynamics.

---

[245] Exodus 26-27.
[246] Philippians 4.13.

Ultimately there is a difference between being an agent and a patient. Agents do things. Patients have things done to them.

Consider the metaphor: Patients just show up and wait for specialists to work their magic. Patients are at the hospital. Patients are at the chiropractor. Patients need patience because they know there's nothing they can do to accelerate the process. Agents, on the other hand, are sent into the field.

They are placed on mission. We have change agents. Secret agents. Special agents.

The church of the future must seriously consider how she provides opportunities for agency. How will she provide space for ordinary people to bless? To proclaim? To sanctify? To forgive? How will she equip others to baptize, to administer communion, to anoint with oil? To act as saints, despite the fact that none of us actually are?

Perhaps my favorite example of agency concerns my friend Angela, whose younger brother had been prohibited from communion by his Catholic pre-school. Incensed, Angela came to church and gathered leftover bread and wine, snuck it home, and administered the sacrament to her sibling in their kitchen after school. That kind of black market holiness is precisely how the church of the future must operate.

This focus on agency and interactivity is partly why we, at Westwinds, have placed such an emphasis upon allowing families to baptize one another, or for parents to administer the Eucharist to their children, or why we encourage youth leaders and deacons to facilitate their people learning how to lay on hands during prayer, anoint with oil, or hold one another accountable to their commitments. But where most churches encourage these behaviors outside of the liturgy, we also make space for these activities within our worship experiences, so there is the added benefit of seeing one another function as the Body of Christ, of normalizing those behaviors, and of ensuring they can perpetuate outside of our gatherings.

One of the most profound shifts in my thinking about church came after reading Edwin Schlossberg's little book *Interactive Excellence,* in which he proclaimed, "the quality of an experience is not measured by the quality of the performance, but by the level of participation among the audience." People need to be encouraged to do things, not just watch those on stage do things. And while we love hearing exceptional music and are deeply moved by inspired preaching, the greatest opportunities for metamorphosis occur when we respond.

Sometimes that response is lifting our hands or receiving prayer at the altar—the classical Pentecostal participation—and sometimes our response involves receiving the Eucharist or confessing our sins—the classical Mainline participation—but there are endless opportunities we might create, generate, and ideate for responding within the church of the future. We can design our liturgies with the same mindset as a hands-on museum, a characteristic shared with many of the great cathedrals in Europe. These sacred sites provide space for self-directed spiritual experience—such as praying within an alcove while contemplating a work of art, lighting a candle at the altar, visiting confession, or viewing relics. There is an almost tourist-like quality to these engagements, and yet they are meaningful to the participants precisely because they get to do something, rather than just watch someone else do something.

It's hard not to be caught up in the moment when you burn a candle at Notre Dame.

It's hard not to be overcome with emotion when you sign the prayer book in King's Chapel.

It's hard not to sense your own impending mortality when you press your forehead to the bone-crucifix in Sedlec Ossuary.

> Art is that human activity that goes beyond the useful to embody in allusive color, shape, or sound, the joy or pain of being human. Art is a way of acting in the world that engages with its materiality in such a way that it illumines something about the world's depth and reality. It is an activity that involves a way of knowing as well as doing; it shows us something we can learn in no other way.
> - William A. Dyrness

The Church has always invited her people to stand, listen, sing, and give; but, we also want them to touch something, to speak with someone, to pray, to move, to write, to snap, to meditate, to eat, and to approach worship with a low-level sense that anything could happen that day, and that their willingness to jump in with both feet is directly related to their development as spiritual people.

The church of the future will be the new tabernacle, moving with God as God moves her through experiences, expressions, and stories of human metamorphosis.

How would your life change if you began engaging the world as though you were a priest?

SEVENTEEN.THREE

INTERACTIVITY

EXPLORING THE NEXUS OF LITURGICAL PARTICIPATION

> What then shall we say, brothers and sisters? When you come together, each of you has a hymn, or a word of instruction, a revelation, a tongue or an interpretation. Everything must be done so that the church may be built up.
> - 1 Corinthians 14.26, NIV

It's the participation, not the performance, that matters most.

The church of the future will discover the greatest opportunities in liturgical design revolve around "interactives." These are the things people do with one another at *the behest of* but not *under the control of* the people on stage. The simplest example would be people shaking hands with one another as they "pass the peace" or greeting the person next to them. More complex examples are littered throughout *Then. Now. Next.*, but in this chapter I'd like to explore the nexus we employ at Westwinds.

In his brilliant book *Art and Agency*, Alfred Gell suggests there are myriad ways that the artist, the index, the prototype, and the recipient work together to share an experience. I'll define those terms in a moment, but first it's important to understand Gell's book focuses on the ways communities appreciate the visual arts. And by "art" he doesn't mean high art, like what must be viewed in a gallery, but all art.[247] The **artist** is the person who creates the art, and for our purpose we adapt this to refer to "**you**"; meaning, the average Jane sitting in the chairs on a Sunday. The **index** refers to the common "**associations**" and meanings shared by all with any given object or reference. For example, a cross might be part of the index of Christianity, and include such things as piety or prayer or sacrifice or holiness. The **prototype** is the thing the artist makes—a painting, sculpture, etc. Westwinds calls this a "**token**." The **recipient** refers to the person receiving the prototype, and we replace this term with "**them**."

So the frontier of interactive excellence involves **creating** something we **share together** in the presence of the **Spirit**.

Before I expound on the nexus, allow me to give you an out. For most laypeople, the value of this chapter will diminish

---

[247] Including folk art, arts and crafts, religious symbolism, and even public statuary.

quickly, given that what follows is both highly specific and unduly technical. And yet, I include this material because the metamorphosis of worship is an area about which I am intensely passionate. If you choose not to continue reading, let me simplify this issue by asking an early question:

> *What will you do, during church, to worship God (other than spectate)?*

There is still one critical layer we must add before we begin: agency. As discussed in the previous chapter, **agents do things and patients have things done to them**. Agents are initiators, causes, and catalysts. Patients are guinea pigs, spectators, and effects. It is possible for you to be both an agent and a patient, just as it is equally possible for the associations, tokens, and other people to be agents and/or patients, also. Thus we are left with a remarkable nexus of exploration, creating fertile ground for innovations in meaningful worship.[248]

---

[248] The nexus has helped us determine why so many of our interactives once felt like "something we've done before," even if we've never tried that specific thing. And, the more we've employed this nexus to diversify our interactives, the more we've been able to craft unique, meaningful experiences for a large number of participants.

		AGENTS			
		You	**Association**	**Token**	**Them**
PATIENTS	**You**	We give you the joy of making things up as you go along, becoming spectators of your own effort.	We allow you to respond to the Spirit's guidance, asking "God what are you saying?"	We let you 'make history', creating representations, reenactments, and embodiments of spiritual events.	We provide space for you to acknowledge the good others have done, authenticating the virtue of who they are.
	Association	We encourage people to create something using common symbols, communicating without words and allowing the Spirit to fill in the blanks.	We facilitate people becoming both the creators and the artifacts, revealing something through their physical participation we would not otherwise witness.	We allow people to participate with Christian emblems, experiencing familiar rituals and sacraments in a new way.	We invite people to use their perceptions and rationalizations in order to create new interpretations of texts, events, objects, and engagements.
	Token	We ask people to make the supernatural visible, creating personifications, renderings, or manifestations of the invisible world.	We give God something to play with, allowing the Spirit to speak through uncommon goods.	We supply our people with mirrors so they can consider themselves without flattery, enhancement, or optimization.	We help our people create a symbolic substitute, imbuing that symbol with meaning and performing with it as a means of engaging that which it replaces.
	Them	We supply a platform to showcase your unique offerings and creativity to an audience.	We provide something that subverts their sense of self-possession, making them feel something they didn't choose.	We create immersive environments where they feel as though they're part of the cast, rather than spectators in the audience.	We allow them to act as patrons, enjoying their own contributions for their inherent pleasure, enjoyment, and contemplation.

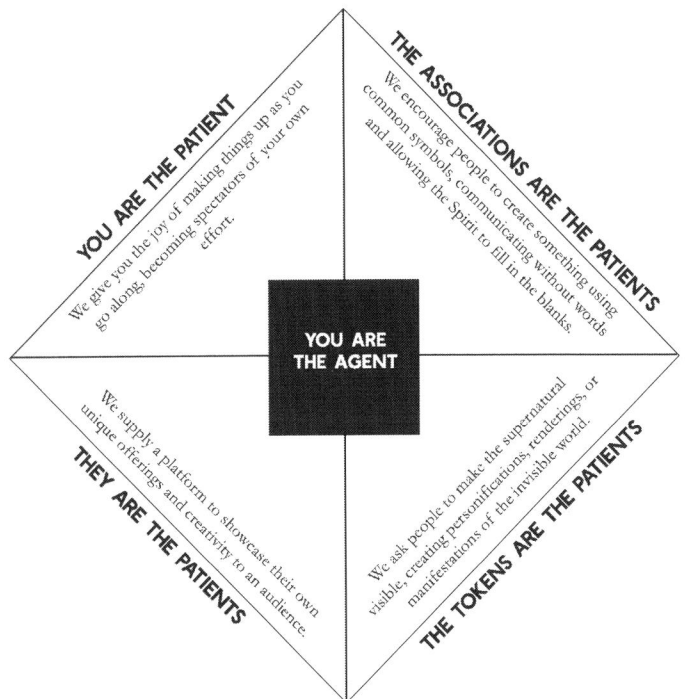

In the event that **you are both the agent and the patient**, we want to give you the joy of making things up as you go along, becoming spectators of your own effort. For example, after introducing the Christian history of rosaries, we invited people to create mala bracelets, necklaces, and other jewelry. The experience was fun, but also meaningful on account of the direct association with the teaching. It is this connection that makes interactives either a distraction or a highlight, since "meaningless" interactives will often feel like a waste of time.

Another example included peg boards, with each peg labeled according to something that made people happy (sports, relationships, food, children, etc.). Participants were given three colors of string, each representing the past, present, and future so that their final designs created a tapestry of gladness.

Here again, there is a "Choose Your Own Adventure" quality to the interactive that authenticates the choices of participants and also allows them to stand back and enjoy the collaborative exhibition as it unfolds.

There is, typically, some resistance among participants to these cosmetic pursuits on account of many feeling as though they are not sufficiently "artistic" for their work to be on display. Yet imperfect efforts have their own charms. When we give people some storied artifact—an icon, say, or bodily posture—and allow participants to experience something both ancient and settled, they will feel a sense of meaningful connection, even if the finished product is not a masterpiece. The key is to make it simple, yet still significant. We experienced something like this when we gave our people spray paint and invited them to paint 1 of 3 icons on a wall outside our church. The orthodox cross ☦ represented their desire to place others before themselves; the Greek character *Theta* ⊖ represented their ambition to cooperate with God in creative pursuits; and the book-sigil ⊔ represented their eagerness to live consistent with scripture.

When **you are the agent and the associations are the patients**, we invite you to create something using known symbols. My favorite interactive in this regard was our Instagram hashtag #WhatstheGoodNews. We invited people to take photos of anything, anywhere, they felt embodied the gospel.[249] Other times we have employed artists to illustrate our sermon notes, filming them in real time and projecting those images onto our screens.

---

[249] This was several years ago, and the hashtag has been used many subsequent times for unrelated endeavors, but during our three-month exploration of the gospel we enjoyed high participation and had a lot of fun.

Memes are good fodder here, employing emojis to communicate clearly without words (i.e. ✝=♥). In order for this to work, you must use common symbols with widely understood referents—a swoosh, a smiley face, a peace sign, etc. Perhaps the best example is the U2 slogan **Coexist** .

Here, you are working with symbolism to communicate without words, allowing God's Spirit (and social convention) to fill in the blanks.

When **you are the agent and the tokens are the patients**, we are asking you to make the invisible visible. This might include creating personifications, fantastical renderings, or manifestations that you either create or perform. This would include anything "imaginary," like drawing a picture of a unicorn, for example, or an angel; diagramming the relationship of the Trinity; depicting the Four Horsemen of the Apocalypse, or the Seven Deadly Sins.

Once, we had everyone in our congregation copy down key points to our teaching in Egyptian hieroglyphics,[250] mimicking the process behind the earliest historians recording the events of the Old Testament. Another time we showed people different representations of tetramorphs,[251] and still another time we invited a tattoo artist to ink on stage.

When **you are the agent and they are the patients**, we supply a platform to showcase your unique offerings and creativity to an audience. Outside of the liturgy, this is the "normal" mode of art, wherein artists perform and people

---

[250] An Egyptian refugee and trained hieroglyphologist modeled the symbols with a white board on stage.
[251] Strange, composite angels from Ezekiel's vision in Ezekiel 1 and John's vision in Revelation 4.

spectate; indeed, this is even the norm within the liturgy, as people most frequently spectate during worship and the teaching. But to design interactives where we subvert this convention, allowing every person to "preach," supplies great fodder for the priesthood of all believers.

For example we once redesigned our auditorium according to a bed & breakfast-style dining room. Every congregant was seated at a four-person table and the entire liturgy was scripted in such a way that foursomes served one another communion, read scripture, prayed, and sang. At first, of course, this was awkward; but after a few moments people relaxed and began to enjoy a new kind of table fellowship, one which felt both biblical and spiritual simultaneously.

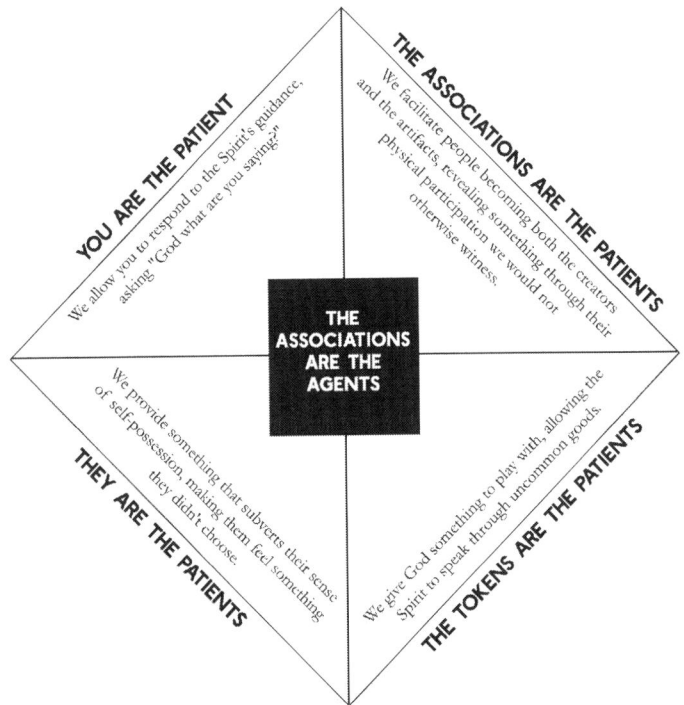

When **the associations are the agents and you are the patient**, we provide you opportunities to offer something in response to the Spirit's guidance. We want you to react personally when "God tells you" to make this, or do this, or say this. We prompt you to offer apologies, words of affirmation and encouragement, or vows for new effort and development. For example, a group of abused women recently wrote a goodbye letter to their old selves as part of their therapeutic healing. They wrote in response to God's promises for a better future, and these letters were read (anonymously) so our community could participate in their restoration.

Another of my favorite examples involved our three-month exploration of happiness. Each week we passed out wooden "menus" to our people and instructed them to take notes on the teaching. The menus were collected at the end of every service, and passed out again weekly to other parishioners at random. Initially, the menus were blank, but over the course of twelve weeks they became filled with people's observations, comments, and prayers. At the end of the season, we invited our people to search through their menu and highlight three things they believed God might be saying to them; then highlight three things they believed God might be saying to someone next to them, and share it.

When **the associations are both agents and patients** we are inviting our people to become both the creators and the artifacts. Ash Wednesday is a good example, wherein you receive the sign of the cross and then display it as you move through life. We did something similar on Good Friday last year, when we invited people to draw red circles on their wrists in emulation of Christ's wounds.

But there are many other ways you could do this. You could make shadow puppets, or a human pyramid, or create a sketch on a card that began with a coffee stain. In these examples, you are not only creating artifacts but refining them to better purpose. *Daily Monster*[252] evolved this way, as artist Stefan G. Bucher began each morning with an ink blot he subsequently drew into a monster. *Mad Magazine* also gave us countless experiences like this with their fold-in features,[253] and similar experiences are curated through things like connecting the dots.[254] The point is that something is already there, but will not fully be revealed until you participate.

---

[252]   http://www.dailymonster.ink/.
[253]   https://en.wikipedia.org/wiki/Mad_Fold-in.
[254]   https://en.wikipedia.org/wiki/Connect_the_dots.

When **the associations are the agents and the tokens are the patients**, we are attaching extraordinary significance to ordinary objects, in essence giving God something to play with. Since we believe God can, and does, speak through anything, we invite our people to wonder what God might be saying to them as they stare at an icon or play with prayer beads. One great example involved our *Glimpse* cards,[255] a game we designed where each card was decorated with a scripture and provided a key question for people to consider. Players would draw several cards at a time and posit how the scripture relates to their lives, asking tough questions about what God might be directing them to change, adopt, or discontinue in order to please him.

The point in all these examples is to recognize that God might speak to you through something that doesn't speak on its own. By allowing God to speak *through* an object, rather than just relying on the pastor or worship leader to tell us what God is saying, we give God the courtesy of having a unique conversation with every congregant. In this way, the token becomes something that adds focus to the voice of the Spirit, like a listening horn.

When **the associations are the agents and "they" are the patients**, we are creating something that subverts the audience's sense of self-possession, making them feel something they didn't choose. What first comes to mind is the old evangelistic tactic of placing an open coffin on display in a public place (like a shopping center). When people peer into the casket, they see their own reflection on a mirror, reminding them of their mortality. Stunts like these employ passive spectatorship, but with the caveat that we are deliberately leading people toward a surprise. Guided meditations are also

---

[255]   https://youtu.be/MvRal8DJn1M.

a good example, as well as any moment that gives people the opportunity to consider whether or not they might be blind, immoveable, or obtuse.

During a series on the earthly life of Christ we passed out MOO cards[256] to every congregant, each with a different portrayal of Jesus. These cards were curated from among non-western cultural depictions of Christ as a reminder that we are the immigrants to the Christian story rather than Christianity being a "white" or "American" religion.

Another of my favorite experiences in this regard involved a prayer labyrinth we created inside the church, leading participants through exercises at 15 different stations corresponding to Christ's journey of crucifixion. At the eleventh station,[257] participants were instructed to read Psalm 22 into a microphone ("my God, my God, why have you forsaken me"); and, at station fourteen,[258] they were instructed to pick up a pair of headphones and listen, only to discover the voice of another participant reading Psalm 22 over them prophetically ("Yet I will praise you, oh Lord").

---

[256] https://www.moo.com/us/.
[257] When Jesus is nailed to the cross.
[258] When Christ is buried in the tomb.

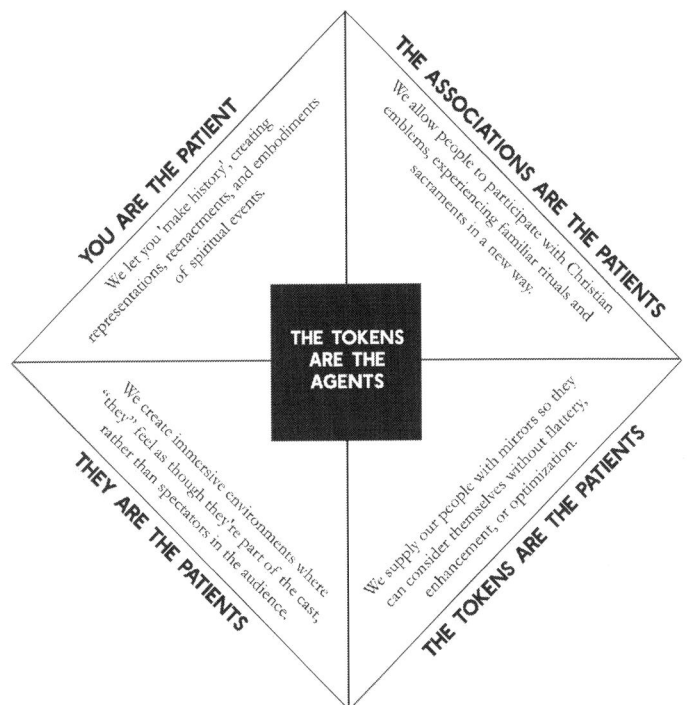

When **the tokens are the agents and you are the patient**, we provide opportunities for you to create representations, reenactments, and embodiments of significant spiritual events and personages. Here, we let you "make history." That is, we give you something historical (i.e. scenes from the Bible; great moments you must "see" or "create") and allow you to bring it to life at that instant, with those around you, in the space provided, using the materials at hand.

Communion is the most obvious example, wherein we invite people to partake of an ancient ritual in which they re-live the life of Christ, simultaneously bringing Christ into themselves. "Culinary Communion" was my favorite, where we replaced the traditional emblems with fresh *hors d'oeuvres*[259] prepared on stage by a selection of chefs.

The Orthodox Church accomplishes something similar through their many means of divinization; meaning, prayers and rituals that give people the opportunity for Christ to grow in them.

We once set up triclinium tables[260] and invited people to perceive Christ "in their midst" as their tutor, server, and entertainer (all people who would stand in the middle of the triclinium at a Roman home) which altered the experience of the Eucharist profoundly. Other examples of allowing people to "make history" include those times we've invited artists to scribe the scriptures. Randy Sottovia, a local engineer, created realistic portraits of characters from the book of John in charcoal. He performed this live, sketching over the entire book of John which we had fixed to the wall as a canvas.

When **the tokens are the agents and the associations are the patients,** we are dealing with scenarios that invite people to participate with classic Christian emblems,[261] albeit in a

---

[259] Including watermelon-mint feta skewers, orange-scented cream cheese stuffed dates, and tomato-basil bruschetta.

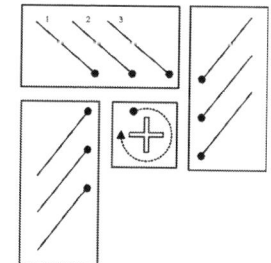

[260] https://en.wikipedia.org/wiki/Triclinium.

[261] The classical Christian emblems are wine, bread, fire, ash, water, and the cross.

new way. Writing specific sins of which we are guilty, then nailing them to a cross is a good example of how we re-live the necessity of the Atonement. Or, as we did one year during Holy Week, writing our sins on edible paper and then eating that paper during communion in place of the bread. Once, on Good Friday, we invited our people to do as Pilate and "wash their hands of Christ's blood," only we had added a chemical to the water so that when they dipped their hands into it, they were stained red.

The point is that this manner of interactivity deals with obvious meaning. In much the same way a portrait of George Washington "means" American patriotism, scenarios like this allow us to participate in something familiar in a new way.

When **the tokens are both the patients and the agents**, we are supplying participants with mirrors to ruminate without flattery, enhancement, or optimization. In these self-reflexive scenarios, "you" are the "thing" you must consider.

Our video confessional is a good example, where people sit in the booth and stare at an iPad. They have to watch themselves as they consider what they've done, what it means, and what they'd like to do in order to make things right. They film these short confessionals and email them to our elders, as both a declaration that they're ready to progress spiritually and that they would like us to pray.

Another time we had our people write six word testimonies,[262] where they had to craft their narratives, edit them, and record them for display during public worship.

---

[262] Examples: *Unselfishly loved through His love. Keep me where the light is. Distraught distractions exist. Love does too.*

When **the tokens are the agent and "they" are the patients**, we create immersive environments where participants feel as though they're part of the cast, rather than spectators in the audience. However, in these scenarios no one is the star; instead, each person feels like one of the supporting characters, extras, or members in the affair.

Liturgical readings are a good instance of this category of interactivity, and this sense of immersion governs our aesthetic at Westwinds overall—we design the room as a 360° environment, not just the stage at the front. We have sometimes even included our aesthetic into the parking lot, graffitiing the entire property with images from the teaching and inviting our people to contribute.

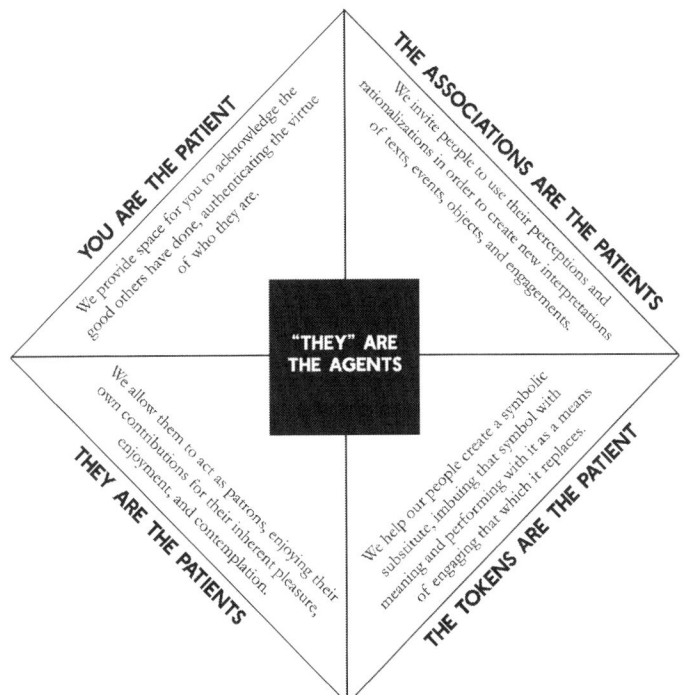

When **they are the agents and you are the patient**, we provide space for you to acknowledge the good others have performed. Here, the past actions of someone else are the driving force behind what you are required to do. If a favored basketball coach is present, a former player may seek out her coach in order to thank them for their investment.

Several weeks ago, I spoke of the importance of acknowledging our mentors, protégés, and peers[263] and tossed a ball of colored string into the audience. I invited the audience

---

[263]   I was explaining the brilliant research of my student, Scott Ness, and his concept of The Faith Web. See http://thefaithweb.org/.

to consider who had been meaningful to them, and then toss the string to that person as a show of appreciation.[264]

Another useful example involves giving people an artifact that identifies them (by having them write their name on the artifact or inviting them to draw a simple, representative shape), then encouraging them to give that artifact to someone else in the room, inviting the recipient to pray for them. This allows the recipient to feel valued, creates anticipation, and also allows the person who gave their artifact to receive prayer from someone they respect. Much the same effect is achieved in Charismatic settings, where congregants will line up in front of particular deacons to await prayer during the altar call.

When **they are the agents and the associations are the patients**, we are inviting them to use their perceptions, interpretations, and rationalizations in order to create meaning. This can happen exegetically, like when we displayed the book of Mark all over our auditorium and allowed people to scribble their thoughts in the margins; and this can happen semiotically, like when we created origami birds and asked people to write something on it they would like to "set free."

Here, we're giving guide lines as to what can be contributed, enjoyed, or received. In our cross garden, for example, we limit installations to only crucifixes. Likewise, when we commissioned artistic films about Holy Week, we required they fit the theme for each day. Also, when we projected the 21 "We see a church …" statements from this book onto scrims, we mandated people sign each statement with an accompanying vision for how they would participate in our ongoing metamorphosis as a church.

---

[264] This idea originated from Len Sweet, who shared a similar experience online for Portland Seminary.

When **they are the agents and the tokens are the patients**, we invite you to create a symbolic substitute for a person, place, or thing. We imbue that symbol with meaning, performing actions upon it as a means of engaging the assigned value, virtue, or significance. Youth groups were once fond of these interactives, requiring teens to burn their music as a demonstration of leaving their old lives behind. Similar interactives have occurred when people discarded cigarettes, pornography, or drug paraphernalia. Likewise, when people deface a portrait or venerate an icon, they are doing something to a thing as a demonstration of what they wish they could do to the "real thing." Performing Random Acts of Kindness serves as a "substitute" in the sense that we love our (unknown) neighbor because we are in love with our (unseen) God.

My favorite example of these substitutionary interactives was the tchotchke Rooakh.[265] This was a desk sculpture which included 9 triangular blocks that rotated along a copper rod. Each triangle represented a fruit of the Spirit, and each side of the block was labelled "demonstration", "ambition", or "receipt." We invited our people to keep this 12 inch ornament on their desk, rotating the blocks according to their interactions with others; so, if someone was kind to them, they would rotate the kindness triangle so the "receipt" side was showing; if they desired to show more kindness to others, they would rotate to "ambition." If they succeeded in exhibiting kindness, they would rotate to "demonstration."

Again, the purpose of these interactives is to employ placeholders, stand-ins, and representations so our people can manifest their noble ambitions in real time. Inversely, we're

---

[265] https://youtu.be/morWVTn8s24.

supplying opportunity for our people to act as ambassadors, doing to others what God has already done for us.

When **they are both the patients and agents**, we allow people to act as patrons, enjoying their contributions intrinsically. This might include people creating their own souvenirs, takeaways, or tchotchkes; or we might invite them to play with art supplies or musical instruments, almost as though they are in a grown-up playroom; or it might involve giving them the opportunity to bask in their contributions to their children during, say, a kids' choir concert.

iCreate[266] was our best success here—a poetry contest we ran in local elementary schools. Winners from each grade had their poems transformed into songs and performed by our musicians at a gala. This was edifying for the kids, their families, and our musicians as everyone enjoyed the way the kids were celebrated as much as the talent of the performers who arranged those poems into hip hop, rock and roll, and blues features.

Other examples include any time we give our people a hands-on experience similar to what they might encounter at a children's museum. On Christmas Eve one year we transformed our lobby into Santa's Workshop, giving parents and children the opportunity to meet the elves, write a letter to Santa, or even create a one-of-a-kind wooden toy. The point is that we're giving them something to do for their own pleasure, enjoyment, or contemplation.

---

[266] http://www.mlive.com/news/jackson/index.ssf/2013/03/young_po-ets_honored_at_the_thi.html.

CONCLUSION

I realize this may seem overwhelming, and you might be wondering where to begin. My advice is to skip over all the confusing terminology. Just read the sentence-length descriptor of each category and ask yourself, "How can we (*provide space for our people to acknowledge the good others have done*)?" This will work better in a group of 2-3 trusted friends, and you'll be surprised by how quickly and easily new ideas begin to flow.

But they must flow, for the church of the future will concern herself far more with what happens among the congregation than what happens upon the platform. She will realize and envision what it means for every person to be a minister, a missionary, and a maestro in concert with the Spirit.

How can you invite others to join in worship, connection, and prayer?

SEVENTEEN.FOUR

LITURGY

MAKING CHURCH UP

> Give praise to the Lord, proclaim his name; make
> known among the nations what he has done.
> - 1 Chronicles 16.8, NIV

> *There are no correct ways to plan church services, but some processes are*
> *more enjoyable than others.*

Typically, churches fall into one of three approaches to planning weekend worship:

- the Liturgical approach, where most everything is scripted through the tradition, the calendar, and the denomination;
- the Traditional Evangelical approach, where things are divvied up neatly between pastor and worship leader;
- and the Contemporary Mega Church approach, where the pastor entrusts creative elements to a director who will lead teams to execute his or her vision.

Westwinds' approach is a hybrid. We use a creative team, but they don't receive tasks and assignments. Instead, we design the entire service, series, and calendar together. All of it.

Together with my team, we decide what we want to experience as a church. I bounce these ideas also off of my elders and Ben Redmond, the other pastor who does a large portion of our teaching on the weekends. We plan out 12-18 months in advance, balancing the need for good biblical content with felt needs,[267] interesting doctrines,[268] and cultural concerns.[269] Sometimes, like in our three-month exploration of the theology, science, and sociology of happiness, these overlap. Other times, like when we blasted through the book of Titus line-by-line for seven weeks, things are more siloed.

But, again, the decision concerning where and what we tackle is handled as a group. Then I begin researching like a madman. I take this research to our team before my own conclusions have begun forming. I separate the research I submit, so that each team member has unique material, and that they and I are having a different conversation from those I have with their teammates. We bicker and laugh, suggest ideas and

---

[267] Financial and relational issues, for instance.

[268] For example, *Christus Victor* and the *Imago Dei*.

[269] Like human sexuality or social justice.

applications, reference other events and experiences, and talk about how we might adopt and adapt these concepts into our church. Then each of the team members begins generating ideas in an online forum, commenting on one another's suggestions.

At this point, I still have not decided what I will teach. Before I ever write anything, the designers are creating and dreaming and innovating ideas I'm still not sure apply. As I listen to them, I poke and prod, trying to provoke better application and deeper reflection. The team is eager to create something I've never heard before. Or done before. Or seen before. Conversely, I'm trying to articulate things that don't bore them. As any good pastor will know, the hardest people to inspire are your family and your staff. Those are the people who are most deaf to your voice, most immune to your charms, and most easily guess your approach before you've even figured it out yourself. They roll their eyes, politely disengage, then smile and nod before writing you off.

But this isn't disrespect. This is education. If I can't engage them, how will I ever interest an audience of people who may not know me, likely don't trust me, and aren't sure I have the credibility to make effective claims about an invisible world governed by an immaterial King? And this isn't to suggest that my ideas always have to be more complex or more theologically speculative; no, this is much more about finding fresh ways to express the eternality of orthodoxy. I'm asking: How can I make the familiar seem new? How can I de-familiarize the old, old story so our people can receive new wisdom from God?

So when my team begins to lose interest, I become increasingly driven to earn it back. I study harder. I spend more time looking for the real-life promise of my research. I play with the wording and phrasing of my key ideas, testing out different parsings until I see which combination puts a spark back in someone's eyes. It's difficult. I get depressed and wonder if anything I say will ever make a difference. But I know these episodes of melancholy are how God is growing both my capacity to teach and my character as a follower of Jesus.

As the team generates ideas, I'm looking for the crossover point between the ongoing sanctification of our congregation and the restless pursuit of creative expression among my staff, asking: How has the Lord equipped us to bridge our growth with that of our people?'

Ultimately, the team decides what we should help our people experience. From there we generate initiatives and interactives to provoke new thoughts, dreams, and behaviors in our people. And, of course, it is not only the people who benefit, but us as well as we play with new ideas and allow the Lord to speak to us and with us and through us. There is always a kind of spiritual triangulation between what God is doing in us, what God is doing in the Church, and what God is doing in our local congregation.

> Throughout the creative process, you're struggling and searching, and, at a certain point, you open a door, invent a scene, a movement, an image. Sometimes it's beautiful, but then it remains on the surface, a pretty invention, nothing more. Sometimes, without realizing it, you find something that touches the audience, and even something that might transform the audience. But no one has control over that. Picasso said that an artist's task is to discover things and then to find out what they are. That's absolutely true. There can be a huge gap between intention and result. Often poets will write up a rhyme, a pretty phrase, or a new

expression, and only afterwards will they search for what's hidden behind it. We have to learn to accept that meaning comes to us after the fact.
- Robert LePage[270]

As a preacher, I can often attest to the fact that people will tell me they were "blown away" by the message, then go on to repeat things I never said and never intended them to hear. I used to try and correct their misunderstandings, but now I take this as evidence the Spirit is speaking directly to them through my words, though not necessarily using my words. The church of the future will understand that ministry more widely opens the door for people to hear from God, and that God can bring them into a deeper understanding of himself regardless of what the preacher, singer, or teacher might be doing at the time.

> *If you were designing your own church service, how would you go about it and what might it include?*

---

[270] LePage, Robert, *Connecting Flights*, 28.

PHYSICALITY

CELEBRATING OUR BODIES

Do you not know that your bodies are temples of the Holy Spirit, who is in you, whom you have received from God? You are not your own; you were bought at a price. Therefore honor God with your bodies.
- 1 Corinthians 6.19-20, NIV

> *Our bodies are not to be disdained, but developed in worship and physicality for God's employ.*

If we are to look far into the future of the church, one trend
we'll see is the reclamation of our bodies and the celebration
of our physicality. Of course there are many ready-made
objections to "the flesh," but I do not think this growing
cultural concern is primarily focused on sexuality. Rather,
I think our culture is becoming increasingly aware that our
corporeality matters—that we must take care of our health, pay
attention to the circadian rhythms of our bodies, drink water,
and be aware of how we feel.

And with this renewed appreciation for the fact that 'our
matter matters', we will see new arenas of spiritual expression.
Yoga, for instance, has an inherently metaphysical component
even once the Hindu-Buddhist roots have been vacuumed off
the surface. And it isn't only the meditative component of yoga
that makes it meaningful, but the stretching and reaching of
our bodies in connection with our intention to become better,
more holistic human beings. We see this same soft-metaphysic
expressed in less-obvious ways in RomWod,[271] Cosmic Kids,[272]
and the tradition of bodily prayer.[273]

Inspired to create along these lines, I remember waking up
one night consumed with a combination of Tai Chi with
Breakdancing, performed in the contemplative tradition of
Orthodox Monastics, to create a kind of spiritual CrossFit. I
developed progressions, in which each pose was accompanied
by a meditation and a mantra, releasing the body from form to
form into a new manifestation of prayer. This experiment is
ongoing, but I've secured another theologian and two yogis to
help me continue developing the routines.

---

[271] *RomWod*, https://romwod.com.

[272] *Cosmic Kids*, http://www.cosmickids.com.

[273] "What is the significance of using different postures in prayer? *Institute in Basic Life Principles,* http://iblp.org/questions/what-significance-using-different-postures-prayer, accessed August 17, 2017.

Why?

Because the church of the future will celebrate physicality. Bodily prayer is one example, but I also think we'll see more and more shared experiences designed for public spaces. One good example of these bodily-operated moments is the now-famous video of the women in a city square riding pink bicycles, each connected to an LED strip show. The faster the women peddle, the faster the stick-figure projected onto the wall of the building takes off his pants.[274] Though silly, the experiment was staged to remind audiences of the importance and the enjoyment of burning calories through aerobic exercise.

And exercise is at the core of what we're discussing. We already know there are massive benefits to our mood, longevity, and sense of optimism when we exercise regularly,[275] and an increasing number of people are aware of the spiritual benefits associated with kinesthesia.[276]

All this to say, one under-explored manifestation of our body-obsessed culture is how we will sanctify movement, touch, sensuality, and poise without our shared experiences feeling strained, ridiculous, or inappropriate. Of course, in some ways we do this already through lifting our hands, dancing, passing the peace, and embracing one another in the lobby. But I'm suggesting bodily-kinesthetic worship, designed by liturgists

---

[274] Ibid.

[275] Mayo Clinic Staff, "Exercise: 7 benefits of regular physical activity," *Mayo Clinic,* http://www.mayoclinic.org/healthy-lifestyle/fitness/in-depth/exercise/art-20048389, accessed August 17, 2017.

[276] Edmondson, Ron, "5 Ways Physical Training Helps With Spiritual Training," *LifeWay Pastors,* http://www.lifeway.com/pastors/2014/01/07/5-ways-physical-training-helps-with-my-spiritual-training/, accessed August 17, 2017.

with the same level of intentionality as the sacraments, and received by participants as normative expressions of praise.

One bodily exercise at Westwinds involved rosary beads. During a teaching on prayer, I told our church about purchasing my first rosary on Orcas Island. Rosary beads get their names from rose petals. In the early days, people would ball up petals in their hands while praying the Lord's Prayer,[277] slowly hardening the petals into beads with the oils from their skin. The beads, then, were both meditative tools during prayer and evidence of past prayers prayed. As I taught, we invited our people to pray and make their own prayer-bead bracelets and necklaces, which solidified the teaching experientially and allowed participants to retain a keepsake associated with their experience that morning. The combination of making something they could later use to experience something they were previously taught was a good example of how movement and tactile experiences can enhance spiritual teaching.

The church of the future will find more ways to help her people use their bodies in worship, as worship, and for the purpose of worshipping God in all things.

In what ways do you use your body at church?

---

[277] "Rosary," *The Free Dictionary,* http://encyclopedia2.thefreedictionary. com/Rose+petal+rosaries, accessed August 17, 2017.

SEVENTEEN.SIX

COLLABORATION

COMING TOGETHER WITH GOD

Do two walk together unless they have agreed to do so?
-Amos 3.3, NIV

> *When inviting others into the creative process, make sure you both set expectations and prioritize outcomes.*

Collaboration is touted to be a generator of true creativity, and yet the most creative people often resist group brainstorming sessions and team meetings. Ernie Schenck, one of my favorite contributors to *Communication Arts*, claims most creatives are more like lone wolfs than bees, and find the increased number of participants to generate "a lot of crap that fertilizes the process."[278] Schenck goes on to describe the unhealthy focus on consensus and the frustrations that result among genuine creators as they are surrounded with those who 'play-it-safe' and 'saw this once.' "The secret," he says, "is that each participant needs to be creative on their own time and in his or her own ways, [that way] everyone can build upon each other's ideas [when they come together."[279]

If any collaboration is going to be successful, participants agree to having a point-person in charge of managing both the meeting's flow and intended outcomes. Ed Catmull, CEO of Pixar, claims this is the primary responsibility of the leader, and the most important function of anyone in the room:

> When someone hatches an original idea, it may be ungainly and poorly defined, but it is also the opposite of established and entrenched—and that is precisely what is most exciting about it. If, while in this vulnerable state, it is exposed to naysayers who fail to see its potential or lack the patience to let it evolve, it could be destroyed. Part of our job is to protect the new from the people who don't understand that in order for greatness to emerge, there must be phases of not-so-greatness. Think of a caterpillar morphing into a butterfly—it only survives because it is encased in a cocoon. It survives, in other words, because it

---

[278] Schenck, Ernie, "A Wolf Among the Bees," *Communication Arts Advertising Annual*, 2012, 18.
[279] Ibid.

> is protected from that which would damage it. It is
> protected from the Beast.
> - Ed Catmull[280]

The church of the future will maintain her commitment to bringing more and more people into the processes of liturgical design, spiritual formation, and church government. She will, however, avoid the pitfalls of groupthink and the quest to play it safe.

Here are some questions to ask before deciding if collaboration is needed for a project:

First, **In what areas would we benefit from collaboration?** The benefits of collaboration come with maximization, not ideation, meaning it's not always helpful for a group to brainstorm as many ideas as possible. If, however, a team leader can bring one malleable idea to the meeting, collaboration can become much more effective. "You make it, we help make it better" is a healthy way to proceed.

Secondly, it's important to ask **Who should be in the meeting?** Pixar's Braintrust has been famously effective in churning out number 1 box office hits. "The Braintrust [are] proven problem-solvers who work magnificently together to dissect scenes that were falling flat."[281] The types of people who need to be present vary from project to project. For a missional project—something the church wants to do to reach out to the community—it's most beneficial to have an artist, a business person, and a community leader present. A presentational project, like a concert or a show of any sort, calls for a musician, a visual artist, and a performance artist. And a teaching project—a class or a sermon series—needs the

---

[280] Catmull, Ed, *Creativity Inc*, 132.
[281] Ibid, 70.

input of at least one theologian, an educator, and a graphic artist. But beware social loafers, production blockers, and anyone afraid of looking stupid! These people contaminate generativity almost as much as a devil's advocate will kill it.[282]

Once the first two questions have been answered, we should also ask **Who will feel valued by being brought into the collaborative process?** Sometimes the collaborative process can be a good way to grow people who aren't equipped to contribute, but who will feel valued and blessed by being included in the meeting. We should be cautious, though, about setting expectations for those we include developmentally, so they know their involvement isn't a guarantee moving forward. They may prove to be an obstacle to healthy collaboration. Nevertheless, in the great majority of instances those with a glimmer of potential blossom when provided such opportunity.

The final question to keep in mind is **Who will continue to grow as a leader because of this collaboration?** Or, who will go from being a leader-in-training to being a competent leader through this process?
Such collaboration will require a higher degree of flexibility and mastery from preachers and leaders as they welcome artists, musicians, and designers into the early stages of planning. Even with careful and intelligent design, the church of the future will still wrestle with the preference of congregants to spectate rather than engage. But the goal is 100% opportunity, not 100% activity, since there are times when observation, reflection, and meditation are more highly prized than their counterparts. Ultimately, the church of the future will create environments where both ends of the spectrum are afforded equal dignity and opportunity.

---

[282] See *Quiet*, 89-90.

With all these caveats and cautions, we might do well to remember why collaboration is so important in the first place. It's simple, really: diversity.

Collaboration results in diverse suggestions, opinions, ideas, and meanings to a much wider swathe of people. And, diversity is an effective barrier against dis-ease. Consider the example of agriculture: "Plant one thing over a single field—corn, soy, whatever—and it becomes vulnerable to disease and pests. Diversity planting across a single field, however, and resistance to disease and pests rises sharply … survival means embracing diversity from the beginning."[283] But diversity isn't a magic bullet, either. After all, just because everyone has an opinion doesn't mean everyone's opinion is equally valid. This is why leadership is so critical during the collaborative process. There has to be someone with the authority to both keep the desired outcomes in front of the group and eliminate obstinate people and persistent problems from the process.

The *Cirque du Soleil* is a good example of how such diversity benefits both the creative process and the team members involved. *Cirque* brings different artists, mediums, nationalities, and features together to create a powerhouse presentation. *O*, for example, employs as many technical scuba divers as musicians, and many more lighting experts and stage designers, besides. It is "a melting pot of talents, backgrounds, and cultures, which brings challenges as well as rewards."[284]

But this isn't always (or even ever) easy. Some groups of people will respond differently to critique than discipleship, and individuals within the group may be resistant to church leadership being involved in their efforts at any

---

[283] Wendig, Chuck, "Best of Both Worlds," *Writer's Digest*, February 2014, 26.

[284] Soncini, Robert, "Empowering a Spectacle," *Alert Diver*, Spring 2016, 44.

level. "Sometimes cultural diversity can cause inefficiency and confusion," warns consultant Erin Meyer, "But if the team leader clearly understands how people from varied backgrounds behave, he or she can turn differences into the team's greatest assets."[285]

> Great artists die to self in their work, collaborate with their work, know it and are known by it as Adam knew Eve, and so share in the mighty act of creation.
> - Madeleine L'Engle

The church of the future will bring together different kinds of people from different backgrounds, all of whom are qualified and excited about the Kingdom, and will help us ensure the highest number of people enjoy the best possible experience in Christ.

What are the hallmarks of healthy collaboration?

---

[285] Meyer, Erin, "Navigating the cultural minefield," *Harvard Business Review*, May 2014, 123.

SEVENTEEN.SEVEN

PARTICIPATION

ENJOYING REAL-TIME ENGAGEMENT BETWEEN THE PRESENTERS AND THE PEOPLE

Each of us will give an account of ourselves to God ...
- Romans 14.12, NIV

The church of the future will respond in real time to decisions during worship.

There ought to be a dialectic between those on stage and those in the congregation, where the energy shifts back and forth between them. Like the moment when a tide comes through a narrow channel and all of the plants and fishes rock together, there ought to be more power given to the decisions of the people during worship. We want their choices to affect what happens on stage and during church.

Such interactivity occurs frequently in Pentecostal and Charismatic services. When the people are responding well to a particular song, for example, the band will often extend the song long after its originally intended conclusion. This may result in extemporaneous praise, the offer of prayer, words of exhortation or knowledge, and possibly an altar call. Many African American churches experience this, also. Baptist churches in the southern United States will often experience the phenomenon of "hooping" when their preacher gets excited.[286] Hooping is a kind of improvisational ending to a sermon, wherein the preacher begins to sing their conclusion, playfully bantering with the congregation, reiterating their main points in a lyrical style, and responding to the ad-lib accompaniment of their organist. My point is not that more people should adopt this particular style, but that there ought to be more styles that accomplish the good done by hooping.

At Westwinds we have experimented with a wide variety of tools used to garner real time feedback and interaction, most famously when we projected Twitter[287] onto several of our screens and engaged the content both via our Internet team and through the teaching onstage. We took questions, fielded

---

[286] See https://www.youtube.com/watch?v=a5DQJ1HQlxA for an example and explanation.
[287] Rochman, Bonnie, "Twittering in Church, With the Pastor's OK," *Time Magazine,* May 3, 2009, http://content.time.com/time/magazine/article/0,9171,1900265,00.html, accessed August 17, 2017.

responses, and sometimes broke off from the message to engage comments that appeared in real time.

But Twitter isn't the only tool we've used live, on display, in our services. We've surveyed our people using tools like Poll Everywhere, and invited our people to text their responses to secret numbers and join into public projects using Pinterest boards and scripted prayers. We've invited our congregation to vote on which songs they'd like to sing that morning, during

that morning, and even employed some basic holograms to animate our teaching.

> Designers will always have to stay abreast of the newest tools creatives employ as well as the devices consumers use. Having playtime set aside to investigate software, hardware, and user experience is paramount to an experiments' success. It's important that designers find pleasure in the projects they do, but remaining goal-oriented during the process assures your boss that play is also work.
> - Jason Tselentis[288]

We're always aiming for a sense among our congregants that "what I do matters." We want them to know they're involved, invested, and at least partially in charge. We want our services to ultimately feel like a Choose Your Own Adventure story, which we have sometimes facilitated through things like prayer Madlibs.

A prayer Madlib involves supplying most of the text in a piece of scripture like the Lord's Prayer, and then inviting people to fill in the blanks with words and images born of their own experience. For example, Matthew 6 might be rendered:

---

[288]   Tselentis, Jason, "The Power of Play," *HOW Magazine*, March 2014, 28.

Our _____, who is in _____, your name is _____.
May your _____ come, and may your _____ be done on earth as it
is in heaven.
Give us this day our _____, and forgive us _____ as we
_____ others.
Lead us not into _____ but deliver us from _____.
Amen.

During a recent experiment with this at Westwinds, we not
only invited people to rewrite the Lord's Prayer, but then
had them text their fill-in-the-blank answers to a direct
number; then, our tech team displayed those responses on our
auditorium screens live. This, again, is an example of letting
ordinary people make simple decisions that elevate corporate
worship beyond a "presentation" and into the community of
saints.

Of course, sometimes people want to just sit back and absorb
what's going on. Sometimes people just want to spectate. And
that's okay. The important point is to create an environment
where participation is normalized, expected, and modeled.
Because the medium is the message. And our message is that
you matter to God, and to us. How you think matters. The
choices you make and the preferences to which you cling
matter. And even if the only choice you're willing to make on a
particular day is to opt out of the experience and view it from
the dark corner at the back of the room, that's a choice that
can help form you into the person God has designed you to
become. And though it is common for churches to pressure
their people into participation, I think there may be seasons
where just watching is enough. When we're tired, when we're
vulnerable, when we're cynical, sometimes the Lord speaks to
our eyes as much as our ears; sometimes our inability to engage
allows us to bear witness.

The church of the future will be less of a spectacle and more of a carnival, where participants are called forth from the audience into the exhibition of grace.

What is the most meaningful experience in which you have participated at church?

PATRONAGE

HOW ARTISTS AND LEADERS WORK TOGETHER

These people come near to me with their mouth and honor me with their lips, but their hearts are far from me.
- Isaiah 29.13, NIV

Leaders should surrender art to the artists rather than trying to control or subdue them, recognizing those in scripture who ignored the prophets because of their strangeness suffered for it.

Over the years, my former co-pastor and I worked in tandem to create and to cheerlead, to explore and explain, our artistic endeavors. For example, when John would launch a massive community project, I would play the role of champion and leader—helping our people understand why these events embodied the gospel and how we might best contribute to these works as a church. Conversely, when I would write or mount a theatrical presentation, John would remind our people this wasn't something they should watch, but an opportunity for them to engage their friends and family, neighbors and coworkers with the Story of God. John and Charles Wesley enjoyed a similar relationship, as have Brian Houston and his son, Joel, from Hillsong Church; and, arguably, as did folk artist Howard Finster with his wife, Pauline Freeman.

Artists need leaders and pastors to shepherd their process, such that an artist won't, say, release a painting depicting a greedy-whoring preacher syphoning widows' wallets on the same day as the launch of a capital campaign. Of course, most artists I know would want to do precisely that, because it would garner the greatest reaction. And there's lots we might say about capital campaigns in and of themselves (and more besides about the proliferation of greedy preachers). But this is precisely my point. The church of the future will see artists and leaders working together, rather than at cross-purposes.

If art is to have a seat at the table and be considered a fully-fledged contributor to the future of the church, then artists cannot only and ever throw trash on everything else. There has to be more to art than insult, and what provocation there is has to be holy.

Pastors are typically concerned about what "works." We want to know what will get the people to respond to our messages—fill out the card, come to the altar, pledge to donate, sign up for the seminar, buy the book, launch the new campus, etc. Artists are always concerned about what "speaks." We want to know what will stay with the people—disturbing them, making them rethink their allegiances, helping them look critically at the world, rising up to the challenges of life with spit in their eye, etc.

This doesn't mean leaders are never artists, but in the great majority of cases among leaders, pastoral creativity is better applied to missional initiatives or theological connection than to art and aesthetics. But the reverse is also true. Most artists have little understanding of whether their art will create momentum or in some way subvert the ongoing transformation of the Spirit. Contemporary artists seem to have mainly given up on inspiring their audience, and grown content with provoking them. Provocation is often useful, meaningful, and even necessary, as it catalyzes growth and metamorphosis; however, there will always be the temptation for an artist to poke their audience in the eye, and to misuse their power because they are unaccustomed to the gross responsibilities of having power in the first place.

The goal is for art to work with the church as patron. Let the leaders commission the work and get the artist heading in the general direction, knowing that some course correction may need to occur along the way on both the part of the artist and the leadership. The church of the future will open dialogue between the experiential and the homiletical, between that which can be clearly articulated and that which must only be felt, knowing it's in the space between the two that the greatest truths are experienced by the highest number.

Can you think of a great partnership between a leader and an artist?

EIGHTEEN

WE
SEE
A
CHURCH

that **CELEBRATES** CULTURAL EVENTS *as* TEACHABLE MOMENTS;

that **ENJOYS** THE ORIGIN *and* RITUAL OF HOLIDAYS, **PERCEIVING** GOSPEL RESONANCE *in* FESTIVAL, SEASON, *and* TRADITION.

EIGHTEEN.ONE

AWARENESS

TRUSTING GOD TO WORK THROUGH THE CALENDAR

> You do not even know what will happen tomorrow. What is your life? You are a mist that appears for a little while and then vanishes.
> - James 4.14, NIV

> *We often fail to appreciate God's activity around us because we're too busy to pay attention.*

Paula d'Arcy is a well-regarded teacher and lecturer with a background in psychotherapy. Among her many wonderful insights is the oft-repeated maxim that "God comes to you disguised as your life."[289] And it's true: life is ever-changing, always unknown and unknowable, always in flux, never certain, never clear. And the only means of navigating this craziness is to stay in step with the Spirit.

> Merely believing doctrines and practicing rituals is very often a clever diversionary tactic to avoid my actual life.
> -Richard Rohr[290]

Every moment of every day has preloaded meaning, significance, and expectations—from episodes on TV to posts on our Facebook walls. But there are no more immediately significant occasions than holidays and cultural milestones.

Whether back-to-school or Christmas, the Stanley Cup Finals or St. Valentine's Day, our cultural calendar is laden with metaphorical observation, spiritual opportunity, and community interest. Don't waste these. Authenticate them. Explore them. Invite the Spirit into these moments to change and transform all you do.

> Life is what happens to you while you are busy making other plans.
> -John Lennon

Eventually, you'll realize that life is an endless parade of possibilities once you learn to trust the calendar. September

---

[289] d'Arcy, Paula, *Goodreads,* https://www.goodreads.com/quotes/385709-god-comes-to-you-disguised-as-your-life, accessed August 17, 2017.

[290] Niequist, Aaron, "God comes to us disguised as our life," *AaronNiequist. com*, May 24, 2011, http://www.aaronniequist.com/blog/gods-movement/god-comes-to-us-disguised-as-our-life/, accessed August 17, 2017.

11th, for example, will elicit different emotions, expectations, and needs than other days. Sadly, most people will minimize the significance of the calendar in favor of their planning. 9/11 will be acknowledged with a throwaway comment. Halloween will be renamed and celebrated on October 28. Valentine's Day will get a post on Facebook. But anytime we prioritize pre-prepared material rather than prayerfully considering what comes next, we miss the low-hanging fruit God has provided to nourish our people, our family, and ourselves.

Parents, pastors, and promoters are smart to acknowledge how God moves through rituals already established within our culture, and the church of the future will cooperate with the calendar rather than competing against it.

> *How do you imagine God working through the next significant cultural event this year?*

EIGHTEEN.TWO

ATTENTIVENESS

LEARNING THAT LIFE IS GOD'S CURRICULUM

...[make] the most of every opportunity, because the days are evil.
- Ephesians 5.16, NIV

We can learn from God how to be like God through ordinary encounters, experiences, and events.

What is a teachable moment?

I don't know where I first heard this phrase, but it certainly feels like it should have been at an introductory parenting class. Good parents are ever watchful for those accidental events loaded with more-than-the-intended meaning, or the bizarre encounter that reveals why we should be wary of strangers.

We look for these moments because our children's defenses are down and, for once, it feels like they will listen. *Now* they get it. *Now* they understand. *Now* they know why something matters, so we pounce on the moment in order to demonstrate how they ought to respond.

We get a lot further, a lot faster, when we cooperate with life to mature.

There are teachable moments in church, also. I remember one auspicious Sunday when my sermon was interrupted by a man accusing his wife of adultery. He caused a scene, humiliating her, and then stormed out. As he left the auditorium, our church was stunned into silence. We all felt brokenhearted, mourning whatever had deteriorated their marriage into this level of dysfunction. In the silence, I invited our church to join me in prayer. I asked God to minister to her, and to him. We asked God for wisdom in our church, that we would better understand how to help one another. We asked for guidance, that we might value our marriages and our friendships in order to inoculate ourselves against such devastation. And we asked for grace.

That was a teachable moment.

At the time, I didn't feel as though I handled the situation very well. I was overcome with sadness for the woman, and anger at the husband. But over the years that day has come back to me again and again, usually as someone else remembers that I prayed. Not what words I used, but simply that this was a moment when we learned prayer could heal. We learned that our church was made up of people, and that what happens in the life of one couple actually does affect the entire community. We learned about togetherness, and shared grief, and shared healing.

The church of the future will stay attentive to the movement of the Spirit in ordinary life, capitalizing on opportunities as they occur naturally and treating life as our curriculum.

What teachable moments have occurred in your life this week?

EIGHTEEN.THREE

FESTIVALS

CONTEMPORIZING ANCIENT SPIRITUAL PRACTICES FOR TODAY

Besides this you know the time, that the hour has come for you to wake from sleep. For salvation is nearer to us now than when we first believed.
- Romans 13.11, ESV

We must invest ourselves fully in the mundane so we can experience the infinite amid the ordinary.

The Jewish feasts outlined in the Old Testament remind us that God works with seasons and significant events, using ordinary time to remind God's people of his involvement in their lives.

The Bible is full of great meals and exuberant celebrations. Such times brought families together to worship, to laugh, and to enjoy one another's company in the presence of God and the certainty of his pleasure. Why? Because there is more to feasts and festivals than gluttony and frivolity, which is why Jesus sacralized ordinary moments, objects, and people with eternal significance.

Biblical scholars have enjoyed drawing parallels between these holy days and Christ himself, platforming off the pronouncement in Leviticus that "these holy convocations are my feasts."[291]

Passover, for example, commemorates the liberation of Israel from Egypt, during which time God's angel passed over the homes of his people and afflicted only their oppressors. The angel was warded off by the smearing of lamb's blood across the doorpost, a sign which my friend Jim Mueller noted is similar to the shape of the cross. "When you apply blood to the top of the doorframe using a hyssop branch, the blood slides down the front of the door. Then, when you paint the sides of the frame, your eye immediately sees the connection between top and bottom, side to side. It's clearly a crucifix." Additionally, the Last Supper Jesus enjoyed with his closest friends was a Passover meal, and the Apostle Paul went on to even refer to Jesus as "our Passover."[292]

Like our spiritual ancestors, the church of the future will find times to remember God's grace and deliverance in our lives.

---

[291] Leviticus 23.2.
[292] 1 Corinthians 5.7.

We will need to design moments for our families and friends to recall how God saved us from our own lesser Egypts, and so reinforce our belief that God still delivers those who call out to him.

The **Feast of Unleavened Bread** was also meant to commemorate the Exodus, since God's people were rushed toward deliverance and could not wait for their bread to rise before packing for their journey. Leaven was often used as a metaphor for spiritual contamination, and the Apostle Paul explains that Christians ought to remove the "leaven of malice and wickedness, [and proceed] with the leaven of sincerity and truth."[293]

Here, too, the church of the future will need rituals and routines that remind her people sin contaminates and we must rush to be cleansed. Some things are too important to wait— like penitence—so we will make the time immediately to get right with God.

The **Feast of Firstfruits** was designed to honor God for the fertility of the land he had given his people by bringing the very first of their spring crops to the Temple.[294] Jesus' resurrection was called the "firstfruits" of God's New Creation, evidence of his power over death and down payment on his plan to heal the world.

In many ways, praying before meals is a micro-practice of the Firstfruits in that we acknowledge God's "ordinary" provision. But we must also look for opportunities to authenticate God's provision in other ways. For example, I make a habit of leading our family in thanks every time we're in the car or speaking about work. Carmel and I do this to model for our kids that God is involved, benevolently, in everything. We celebrate the

[293] 1 Corinthians 5.8.
[294] Leviticus 23.10-11.

freedom we have to go on adventures and the joy of loving our jobs.

The **Feast of Pentecost** was celebrated fifty days after the Feast of Unleavened Bread and was meant to celebrate the harvest. In Acts 2, the Day of Pentecost was the day the Holy Spirit baptized Jesus' followers with fire in the upper room, signifying the Spirit-empowered life now available to all Christians.

The Holy Spirit remains the great unopened gift of the church, but the church of the future will rely on the Spirit's guidance and power to determine every aspect of her vitality. She will teach on the Spirit, design environments where people can experience greater openness to the Spirit, and remind her people that the Spirit is the energy source of the Christian life. My father's church used to host something they called "Spirit Convocations," which I think is the right idea. The church of the future will press more deeply, through season and calendar and event and time, into the life of the Spirit.

The **Feast of Trumpets** was a holy gathering commemorated with horns[295] in honor of God's wartime deliverance. Trumpets signified victory, so this Feast bore some connection to the promise of Christ's return, when he promises to fully and finally vanquish evil.[296]

We have all endured spiritual warfare, and if you're reading this you know what it's like to be in a battle and come out the other side bruised, bloodied, but alive. We need to tell these stories, reminding each other that the battle we're currently fighting is neither the last nor the fiercest. We need to be emboldened, strengthened, and encouraged.

---

[295] Leviticus 23.24.
[296] 1 Thessalonians 4.16; Revelation 11.15.

The **Day of Atonement** was when the High Priest expiated the sins of Israel. This was accomplished when the priest lay his hands on a goat, symbolically placing Israel's collective sins on the animal, and then drove it into the wilderness. Another goat was then offered as a sacrifice to God to remove the stain of sin from God's people. Christ is referred to as both our sacrifice and our high priest throughout the latter New Testament,[297] and we honor him as a priest sacrificed on his own altar.

The church of the future will create more rituals of repentance, times and opportunities for those who have grown cold or callous to stoke the fires and become red-hot once more. We have such events in our recent history—Camp Meetings, Revivals, altar calls—but they have fallen out of fashion. We may not revitalize these methods, but we will provide new opportunities for the same metamorphosing encounters, knowing that such moments are tremendously powerful for the will of a believer.

The **Feast of Tabernacles** involved setting up temporary shelters to assist God's people in their remembrance of wandering in the wilderness for 40 years, constantly roving and never settling. Christ is said to 'tabernacle among us'[298] in the Incarnation, and we are meant to understand that our present circumstances are neither permanent nor defining for the People of God.

The church of the future will provide temporary times and places for seasons of sustained prayer. Whether it be like Westwinds' Garden Path,[299] or the prayer closets and War Rooms of contemporary church culture, we will intentionally

---

[297] Hebrews 13.11-12.
[298] John 1.14, translated literally.
[299] https://www.facebook.com/WestwindsGardenPath/.

design and mediate expressions of prayer that capitalize on space and time.

The church of the future will not depart from her past, but continue the trajectory of faith. She will shape both her learning and her activity by understanding the movement of God's Spirit through history.

How can we adapt or adopt festivals like these today?

EIGHTEEN.FOUR

TRADITION

LIVING THE LIFE OF CHRIST UNTIL IT BECOMES OUR OWN

> He has made everything beautiful in its time. Also, he has put eternity into man's heart, yet so that he cannot find out what God has done from the beginning to the end.
> - Ecclesiastes 3.11, ESV

The liturgical calendar is the Christian method for re-living the life of Christ, authenticating God's movement in and around us as we remember his Son.

When I began exploring the liturgical calendar, I learned about Holy Week. I imagine that seems strange if you come from a more traditional background, but I'd never considered that the events of Easter should begin observance with Palm Sunday. Once I learned how "everyone else" does it, I realized there was plenty of meaningful material available to our church for both reflection and worship. Whether with film series, print publications, on-location services, or social media campaigns, we have observed Holy Week for the last several years, building on the cultural awareness of Easter and re-infusing this cultural holiday with spiritual DNA.

The liturgical calendar also taught me about Advent, the season leading up to Christmas. Since learning more about it, we have taken the entire month of December each year to explore the Nativity. And, because we do not repeat ideas or sermons, that means we've had quite a journey exploring more and more avenues of Christmas. From the origins of Christmas Carols to the hidden spirituality of television specials; from the Holy Family to Herod; from legends to legacies; from famous Christmas-day historical events to the history of the census in Rome. Advent has fostered a growing appreciation for the Incarnation in our nontraditional church, and it began because of a calendrical awareness rather than a theological conviction.

Unlike Easter of Advent, some of the holidays in our calendar do not—at first—appear spiritual, but once we recognize that God saturates every event into which he is welcomed, then everything becomes sanctified, sacralized, and holy.

I love Halloween, for example, and don't ascribe to the belief that it's the devil's holiday, nor do I hold that its pagan origins affect its present-day manifestation any more than those of Saturnalia affect Christmas. Halloween is just a fun dress-up holiday for kids during which time their parents get to spoil them with sugar.

One of my favorite events every year at Westwinds is our Halloween Party. We decorate the entire building with good ole fashioned spookiness and invite the community inside for buckets and buckets and buckets of sweets. There are dancers and musicians, costumed weirdos and energetic hucksters galore.

It's amazing.

But it still startles me that the church at large has such an issue with Halloween. Especially among kids' ministries. If you're thinking like an evangelist, then the earliest process of your cultural exegesis has to be anthropological. You've gotta ask: What do children love? Where do children go? When are the optimal times to get droves of children together with their families?

There is no better answer to any of these questions than Halloween.

The next step is to consider: Is there any gospel resonance in this occasion? Any way to bring good news without feeling contrived? Are there any felt needs or points of overlap which might create space for spiritual conversation?

Again, consider that Halloween is one of the few family-centric events on the calendar and one of even fewer child-centric events; that Halloween deals with community, family, imagination, and play; that Halloween also raises issues about safety, fear, and protection.

Which part of this doesn't sound like ripe gospel opportunity?

I know Christians are leery of thoughtlessly participating in something that might be subversively sinister, but I'm not sure I've even met anyone who stumbled onto something witchy on October 31st. If we would look for ourselves, rather than listening to the fear-mongering or alarmist rhetoric, I think we'd see opportunity to love and serve our neighborhoods rather than a requirement for us to shut our doors and hide.

Halloween may be the most obvious example of a significant cultural holiday, but there are plenty of others—Thanksgiving and Independence Day, for example. The church of the future will find gospel resonance in the special events of our cultural calendar, teaching her people to engage the culture with the gospel rather than run from the culture for fear of perverting the gospel.

What is your favorite holiday?

EIGHTEEN.FIVE

INCULTURATION

EXPLORING NEW CROSSOVERS BETWEEN OUR CULTURE AND GOD'S HISTORY

How then will they call on him in whom they have not believed? And how are they to believe in him of whom they have never heard? And how are they to hear without someone preaching?
- Romans 10.14, ESV

There are more intersections between our story and God's Story than we have yet explored.

The United States has a special relationship with Christian spirituality. We are not the most Christian nation on the world, nor the most zealous, but we still generate the most content, finance the highest number of charitable works worldwide, and consider ourselves primarily a Christian nation.

There is much we might say about the myth of a Christian nation, and there are many appropriate critiques of cultural Christianity; but that's not my interest here. I mention this special relationship because I think there's opportunity to explore the gospel in, and for, America.

Allow me to explain.

When missionaries travel to new places, their first endeavors are anthropological. They want to know what the people are like, how they find meaning, how they determine things like authority, law, and morality. Once the missionaries know more about the people, they begin with the natural crossover points from the biblical story that illuminate God, then Jesus Christ. This leads to many wonderful cultural renditions of the gospel. For instance, Dr. Joanne Pepper once wrote about a Peruvian tribe that referred to Christ as the "Jaguar of the Tribe of Judah" since they had no lions in Peru.[300]

Given the strong convictions of the Founding Fathers concerning Christianity, and the oft-ignored apocalyptic fantasies of Christopher Columbus, I think there's a way to tell the story of the United States through the lens of anthropological missiology that's never been done before. Without falling into the slippery slope of American exceptionalism, I believe there is nevertheless a way to bring the gospel to the United States as though it were for the very

---

[300] Joanne Pepper, Ph.D., *Trinity Western University,* https://www.twu.ca/profile/joanne-pepper, accessed August 17, 2017.

first time, tracing the movement of God through the pioneers, lawmakers, and peacemakers of America.

I'm not ready yet, but sometime within the next decade I imagine I'll be publishing this juicy gem on the 4th of July. More importantly, I think clever individuals will follow suit in South Africa, Canada, and the UK. Of course there may be many more besides, but my point is that we can do this with any culture. And should. The church of the future will teach her people to think like missionaries, bringing the gospel in fresh new ways to our people again and again and again.

What would a uniquely American (or Pakistani? Or Taiwanese? Or Swahili?) gospel include?

EIGHTEEN.SIX

GOSPEL

BEING SAVED FOR ALL THINGS

Beloved, I pray that you may prosper in all things and
be in health, just as your soul prospers.
- 3 John 1.2, NKJV

Perceiving God in everyday events requires an expansive understanding
of the good news.

The Bible doesn't neatly divide salvation into purely spiritual terms about heaven and hell, nor is the Scripture solely concerned with people. Rather, salvation is about life. Salvation is about life on earth *now*.

The Law and the Prophets, the Gospels and the Epistles, the History books and Revelation and everything in between, are focused on how we live. Who are we in relationship to God? To one another? To Creation? How do we see ourselves? Why are we here? How are we meant to progress? How do we please God?

These issues are inescapably prevalent now, not later. There is precious little in the Scripture about heaven, and even less that is specific, concrete, or clear. Jesus hardly addresses the topic of the afterlife, and almost never even mentions hell. Most of what Jesus taught concerns obedience to God in this life— not so that we gain entrance into the next, but so that God will be pleased with our character, our relationships, and our cooperation as we work to heal the world.

Don't get me wrong: I think the issue of what happens when we die is important. Scripture is clear that there is another life after this one (and one more after that—*life after life*-after-death in God's New Creation). But God emphasizes this side of eternity far more than the other. God's focus is on what we do now. In this moment. To live well with him and others.

Our frame of reference for what it means to be human begins in Eden, and to Eden we are often invited to return. God has never rescinded his commission that we are stewards of the earth. He never changed who we are or what we're for. From Adam to Noah to Abraham to David to Jesus, we have been made by God to cooperate with God, to walk with our

Creator as he ennobles us to be a royal priesthood unto whom administration of the world has been eternally entrusted.

If I went out of town and asked you to house sit, would you neglect to feed my pets? Water my lawn? Vacuum my living room after you hosted a party? Check my mail?

Of course not. When you housesit, you know that every detail of that home falls under your care. You know that, when I return, I will ask questions about unexpected visitors, encounters with my neighbors, and any issues pertaining to the wellbeing of my property and my possessions. In short, you know that I care about everything—that's why I hired a housesitter.

We are house sitters over Creation, God's stewards entrusted with care for everything he made and everything to which he lays claim. Which means ... *everything*. The environment. The animals. The oceans. The cultures and economies and neighborhoods and histories. Of course every metaphor breaks down eventually, and here it's worth mentioning that God has not abandoned us to so he might enjoy a cosmic vacation; but the house sitter metaphor is designed to elucidate both the authority and the responsibility we have as God's agents in God's Creation.

And when the scripture talks about salvation, the Greek word *soteria* is used, which means health, wellbeing, and overall flourishing of each person. It is closely linked to the Aristotelian concept of *eudemonia*, commonly translated as "human flourishing." Which is why we are instructed to prosper, even as our soul prospers. Because God cares about every part of who we are, not just whether or not we go to heaven when we die. God is concerned with our health, our hearts, our friendships, our homes, our jobs, our hobbies.

The church of the future will understand the gospel concerns life. Christ brings life. And often the easiest and most approachable means of gospel-sharing are the events and holidays that already have Christ within them, waiting for you and I to make him known.

What does God intend to save?

NINETEEN | WE
SEE
A
CHURCH

ENNOBLED *in* CREATIVITY *and* THE ARTS, *not* **EMULATING** PRESENT FASHIONS *but* SURPASSING THEM *in* STYLE, ABILITY, *and* VERVE.

NINETEEN.ONE

CREATION

HOW GOD WORKS THROUGH US

Now the Lord God had formed out of the ground all the wild animals and all the birds in the sky. He brought them to the man to see what he would name them; and whatever the man called each living creature, that was its name. So the man gave names to all the livestock, the birds in the sky and all the wild animals.

 - Genesis 2.19-20, NIV

God's creations mirror their Creator through creativity.

In biblical times, ancient temples housed at least one priest and many idols. Yahweh, however, required something different. God's temple is the whole earth and *we* are his idols.[301] But we are also more than idols, for every one of us responds to the Presence of God, minding his cares, and mending his world; which means we function like priests.

God doesn't have little stone men protecting little stone churches. Instead, God created his idols to patrol the world, governing Creation in his stead. The earliest, specific, task in this regard was to name the animals.

Naming something connotes some kind of power over that which is named. The root word of 'authority' is 'author', and with his divinely-granted authority Adam defined how those animals would be known by the rest of the world. Thus, there is a special quality to Adam, superior to the nonhuman inhabitants of the world, but also responsible for them.

Notice, also, that Adam was permitted to craft the names themselves. His task was not simply to label them with pre-existing terms, but to name the essence of those creatures from within the witness of his God-bearing self. As an image-bearer of God, Adam was invited to create alongside God – doing his own creating, not simply copying the creative choices of God.

God's first activity in our world was a creative act, and humanity's first activity in our world was a creative act, also.

This connection between God's creativity and ours has been fodder for thinkers even outside of the boundaries of religion.

---

[301] Strong's H6754, *tseh'-lem*; from an unused root meaning to shade; a phantom, i.e. (figuratively) illusion, resemblance; hence, a representative figure, especially an idol:—image, vain shew. http://www.bibletools.org/index.cfm/fuseaction/Lexicon.show/ID/H6754/tselem.htm, accessed August 17, 2017.

Consider that theta waves, the slowest conscious brain waves, are essential in the exercise and development of creativity.[302] Of the five brain states, theta waves retain memories and feelings, adjudicate belief and behavior, and are the active state of meditation and REM sleep.[303] These waves run through each of us, and are so named after the Greek word *Theos*, which means God. The power to create is representative of the ability to imitate God.

Notice, also, that in Genesis 2 the all-knowing God who can see all possible futures, is *curious* about Adam's creative thoughts. God is present in our creativity with a special interest. To express ourselves in creative acts is to more fully experience the richness of being human, of being a God-bearer. Our desire to create and our pleasure in doing so are all part of God's original enjoyment in creating the world.

I have always been enamored with the similarities between priests and artists, perhaps largely because of Madeleine L'Engle's assertion that "Almost every definition I've ever heard of being an Artist is also a definition of being a Christian." Both priests and artists carry a message, a heavy burden, given to them by God for the world.

A priest experiences joy and suffering with (and on behalf of) others. A priest understands the reality of the nonmaterial world. A priest challenges the world to be different. A priest causes us to pay attention. Artists do this, also. They express their deepest wounds and their most ecstatic joys, goading the

---

[302] "Theta Waves—Meditation and Creativity," *Binaural Beats Freak,* https://www.binauralbeatsfreak.com/brainwave-entrainment/theta-waves, accessed August 17, 2017.
[303] "ThetaHealing® Theta Brain State," *Theta Healing,* https://www.thetahealing.com/about-thetahealing/thetahealing-theta-state.html, accessed August 17, 2017.

world into a better iteration and demanding we pay attention to that which is invisible.

> In some mysterious sense, all art aspires to be worship.
> - William A. Dyrness

As priests and artists, we try to help one another make sense of the raw material of our lives. We invite each other to help us build on what we have, sharing stories of glimpsed beauty and true goodness. We invite the Spirit of God to play and create with us, in us. We paint ourselves with the brushes of repentance, love, and trust. We sculpt our souls in the gentle hands of God. We edit the text of our lives with the ruthless verve to be more precise.

You may not consider yourself artistic, creative, or concerned with the outward appearance of things but in this regard you are a true Artist.

You make yourself for God, your Patron.

> The transcendental face of art is always a form of prayer.
> - John Berger

How would you describe the relationship between Creator, Creation, and Created?

NINETEEN.TWO

AESTHETICS

REFINING OUR DIVINE SENSE OF BEAUTY

Day and night the creatures never stop saying: "Holy, holy, holy is the Lord God Almighty, who was, and is, and is to come."
- Revelation 4.8, NIV

The church of the future will take aesthetics seriously, recognizing that our taste is a language of prayer all its own.

The Hebrew people had no professional language for beauty. Something was beautiful if it was truly itself. Original. Faithful. Honest. Accurate. Beauty was never spoken of as being something isolated or morally neutral. Neither was beauty seen as particularly strange or out of the ordinary.

Quite the contrary—the beauty of someone or something largely resided in how true it was to its original design; for example, whenever there was a flower that looked just as a flower should, it was considered beautiful; whenever there was a building or tool that worked and stood just as it ought, it was considered beautiful. There was never any differentiation between the character of a thing and the thing itself–things that were beautiful were things that reflected the well-ordered meaning of God's good Creation.

That beauty came to its fullest expression in the Temple in Jerusalem, which was seen as the place where God's glory congealed. The Temple's construction was the first time where someone was given special gifts by God to do something "artsy," namely Bezalel, a craftsman, and Oholiab, a designer.[304] The language used to describe their work was the language of wisdom, knowledge, and skill, which indicates art is a manifestation of holiness.

It is common for us to focus on the bonds we share through our beliefs, and our history, and our worship; but there is an equally strong bond connecting Christians through our aesthetics. Famed sociologist Zygmunt Bauman alluded to this kind of bond in his book *Community*, claiming that a shared aesthetic even has power to steer us into the future together.[305] Certainly the community of Westwinds can attest to this truth: during our most painful period of transition, when the church was deeply fragmented, it was only primarily our experience

[304] Exodus 31.1-11.
[305] Bauman, Zygmunt, *Community: Seeking Safety in an Insecure World*, 71-72.

of Westwinds' architecture and liturgy that kept many coming back. My friend Bill, for example, told me he wanted to leave, "But we built that building, and there's nothing else like it, and so I kept coming back to the promise I'd made believing our church could be something special."

Christians have a shared aesthetic, and this will only deepen as the church progresses into the future. Christians already recoil from nihilistic conclusions, for example. We may explore the frustration of everything being "meaningless," but we will never allow our exploration to cease with emptiness. We know something more exists, and if we cannot yet find it we will keep searching until we do. Likewise, Christians will always celebrate redemption. Despite the fact that there are those who seem in endless need of new beginnings, cheapening grace while simultaneously flouting it, Christians will be drawn to the hope of genuine metamorphosis resulting from the power of God's Spirit alive and at work in God's people. So when we see hardened sinners accept forgiveness and make amends, we will always celebrate because we know such transfiguration is possible—promised, even!—through Christ. These are aesthetic preferences. And we do not merely shares these "tastes" with one another, but also with God.

Having read the Revelation of St. John many times, I cannot help but think that it is better understood as art than crystal ball gazing. In one sense, we might be better off to sing and dance the book of Revelation than to read it under our covers after Mom and Dad have gone to bed. Perhaps only through an artistic rendering of the text would we ever be able to get close to the kind of mystery God ordained for us to experience.

My friend John Voelz, now the curator at Lakeside Church in California, has often pointed out that in Revelation the angels "say," not sing. Only human beings "sing," and for all their preternatural power, there are some acts of worship that elevate human beings above angels.

Several years ago, we liturgized the entire Revelation of St. John on Good Friday. We sang and performed every line of the text, utilizing old hymns, modern choruses, and original compositions in between theatrical readings of the narrative. It was a very different experience from reading the book in isolation. For starters, it was much less esoteric—the storyline made better sense when you heard the whole book all together, rather than just reading a few verses at a time. It was also much more triumphant, on account of the songs we included ("Holy, Holy, Holy," "Hallelujah, What a Savior," "O Sacred Head"). These qualities diminished the effect of often frightening narratives, and allowed the overall experience to feel more celebratory.

The church of the future will recognize the creativity inherent in scripture, perceiving God as an artist, rather than casting God's creativity in purely utilitarian terms.

How much of our understanding has been limited by reducing the scripture to essay form?

NINETEEN.THREE

REFLECTION

ANGLING OUR EYES TOWARD HEAVEN

For now we see only a reflection as in a mirror; then we shall see face to face. Now I know in part; then I shall know fully, even as I am fully known.
- 1 Corinthians 13.12, NIV

We don't predict the future, but court it.

In scripture, the Levites served as mankind's representative to God. Prophets, on the other hand, were God's representatives to man. As God's mouthpiece, the Old Testament prophets were involved in two kinds of representation: communicating the mind of God for the present, and communicating the mind of God for the future.

Prophets were the teachers of true religion, divinely commissioned and inspired seers who were gifted for the exposition of truth. These days, however, too many are too fascinated with scrying the future and so miss the prophetic capabilities of art and aesthetics to shape the present. But the truest prophecy speaks to the present out of the matrix of eternity.

The prophetic quality of art has long been a favorite topic of coffee-house theologians and philosophers. Art is a window into a more just, egalitarian world where idealism is the *lingua pura* and hope is unnecessary. It is this quality of making the inaudible audible and the invisible visible that makes artists so crucial to the church. They explore the incongruity between the way things are and the way they should be.

As Walter Brueggemann put it, "knowing consists not in settled certitudes but in the actual work of imagination." St. Paul said something similar: "Look not to the things that are seen but to the things that are unseen; for the things that are seen are transient, but the things that are unseen are eternal."[306]

The church of the future will be led by seers, and it is the job of the seer to flesh out the unseen. Artists are seers, taking raw materials and transubstantiating them, infusing ordinary materials with divine meaning. Thus, artist's terms are spiritual terms like "inspiration" (literally "bringing in the spirit"), or "animation" (meaning "the imbuing with animus or soul").

---

[306] 2 Corinthians 4.18.

This spiritual vocabulary is more than just vernacular, though; it is representative of real connection between Heaven and Earth.

The New York DJ Danger Mouse made a name for himself by blending the rap lyrics of Jay-Z and the acoustically-driven pop of early Beatles' tunes, calling the project *The Grey Album*. *The Grey Album* is a brilliant example of the way in which art can pull apart the layers of reality in order to see what is at the root, the source, of each message and gesture. Prophets use this kind of vision to discern what is happening in churches and in individuals' lives and spiritual formation so they can better aid the purposes of God. As such, it is important to note that the "thing" itself – the art, the words, etc. – is not as important as the meaning behind it. Art is the vehicle. "It's not what you see that is art," says critic Marcel Duchamp, "Art is the gap." That gap is the space between God's purposes and vision and what we do with that purpose and vision.

We have to learn the difference between truth and falsehood, in ourselves and in our worship. Such discernment will require a way to see. Hence, the biblical image of a mirror.

Mirrors are scarcely referenced in the Bible, but they do serve as a fitting image for our employment of art within the church. Mirrors reflect beauty. In the time when the Bible was written, they were the exclusive property of the rich, hammered out of bronze, costly, heavy, and imperfect. Job referred to the heavens as God's mirror[307] and both the basin and the bronze stand in the temple were made from the mirrors of wealthy women who donated them to the Lord.[308] Mirrors show us a dim reflection of reality, and yet people stare at them for hours, appreciating the care and results of that care in their appearance.

[307] Job 37.18.
[308] Exodus 38.8.

But we can fall too much in love with our reflection and lose ourselves in ourselves. Or in our art. Or in our worship.

> The world is neither so full of evil that we can't enjoy it nor so full of goodness that we can abandon ourselves to it.
> - Steve Turner[309]

Our mirrors must always be angled toward heaven, so that it is the beauty of Christ we see reflected in us, around us, and through us. This, of course, is difficult. I've never met someone who perfectly reflects Christ all of the time. There's always a little ego in a catchy worship tune. There's always some vanity in the preacher, the poet, or the filmmaker. We know this. We're immeasurably intolerant of it in others, and so we fudge the truth in our estimation of ourselves. But I think we're better to acknowledge that we'll never be entirely free of our own sense of pride and accomplishment. Yet to acknowledge that we won't achieve complete success doesn't excuse our ambition for total honesty.

> Do not merely listen to the word, and so deceive yourselves. Do what it says. Anyone who listens to the word but does not do what it says is like someone who looks at his face in a mirror and, after looking at himself, goes away and immediately forgets what he looks like.
> -James 1.22-24

The church of the future will take her art more seriously. She will realize that, by gazing at a mirror, her people can actually see God. She will not try to shine her mirror sideways, copying and reflecting the image of others, but upwards, sharing her reflection with the Lord.

Whose reflection do you see most clearly in your life?

---

[309] Turner, Steve. *Imagine: a Vision for Christians in the Arts.*

NINETEEN.FOUR

ORIGINALITY

SUMMONING OUR ARTISTS TO THE FORE

Don't copy the behavior and customs of this world,
but let God transform you into a new person by
changing the way you think. Then you will learn to
know God's will for you, which is good and pleasing
and perfect.
- Romans 12.2, NLT

> *The church of the future will perceive artists as conversation partners,*
> *such that doxology and theology work together to reveal the mind of God.*

The church of the future will consider itself a patron of the arts, moving forward and gaining ground and bringing something new and true and beautiful into existence.

This will require church leaders to purposefully identify artists and cultivate their abilities. This will also require artists to step out in faith and offer their talents. Neither of these requirements will happen without frustration, dis-ease, or the determination to persist despite repeated failure. Yet our conviction is so strong that this must happen, the church of the future will aggressively make it so.

We can no longer allow our artists to languish. Neither can we allow those in charge of our aesthetics to be content with imitation, which Len Sweet describes as "just another word for dis-incarnation." The harder we work to imitate others, the further we travel from the purposes and plans of God for ourselves.

That doesn't mean we can't learn from one another. But the avenues for education and enrichment are the means, not the ends. We learn more by understanding Rick Warren's thought process than by simply copying Saddleback's church services. If we follow recklessly after God like they do, the manifestation of God's Spirit will be equally intense in us.

> "What made Tolkien's Middle Earth so wonderful—
> what made it feel so rich and full—is the fact
> that it was informed by the things that Tolkien
> was passionate about. He was a linguist, he loved
> mythology and history. He was a geek for them, in the
> truest sense of the word."
> - Rich Shivener[310]

---

[310] Shivener, Rich, "Patrick Rothfuss: Worldbuilder," *Writer's Digest*, July/August 2015, 43.

Don't look for replication, but innovation.

Don't try for implementation, but imagination.

Don't model procedures, but creativity.

This is what I love about the success of horror/fantasy writer Joe Hill, who also just happens to be the son of Stephen King. Yes—*that* Stephen King. Hill adopted the pseudonym because he didn't want to trade on his father's lucrative coattails, opting instead to earn his seat on the bestseller list rather than be exploited for a quick buck. The road wasn't easy (his first 8 novels were rejected out of hand), but he learned his lessons and now sits at the top of the charts. Why? Because he was committed to being the best possible version of himself, not a poor imitation of his father.[311]

God hasn't called us to copy others. God has called us to minister to our people with the gifts he's supplied. Don't take shortcuts. Don't cheat. Bleed your own blood.

> True originality comes from indifference to trend.
> - Jihan Zencirli, GeronimoBalloons.com

The church of the future will realize her artists have more to offer. She will move beyond the obvious and sentimental, demonstrating less anxiety about how "Christian" art appears.

What is most original at your church?

---

[311] Petit, Zachary, "The Once and Future King," *Writer's Digest*, July/August 2013.

NINETEEN.FIVE

INNOVATION

TRAVELING ALONG THE FRONTIER OF CREATIVE MINISTRY

The Lord said to Moses, "See, I have called by name Bezalel the son of Uri, son of Hur, of the tribe of Judah, and I have filled him with the Spirit of God, with ability and intelligence, with knowledge and all craftsmanship, to devise artistic designs, to work in gold, silver, and bronze, in cutting stones for setting, and in carving wood, to work in every craft.
-Exodus 31.1-5, ESV

> *The church of the future will delve into entirely new reservoirs of creativity.*

Was there ever a more extravagant experience of worship than the Temple in the First Testament? With the rituals, elements, personnel, and pageantry, it was a parade, preceding an immersive theatrical engagement, wrapped in smoke and baked with gold.

We may never experience the opulence of Solomon's Temple, but the church of the future will delve into entirely new reservoirs of creativity, including:

Financial creativity: giving away for free what we bought with blood, sweat, and tears; satisfying the triple bottom line of publicity, community development, and inter-business cooperation; using micro-lending to fund local missions.

Missional creativity: discerning the difference between mission and charity; prioritizing the Spirit over our polity, policy, and preference; finding favor with the media.

Relational creativity: moving beyond groups and clusters into spaces, environments, and opportunities; forming ad hoc relationships among adjuncts and addicts; exploring the different manifestations of *communitas* in social and evangelistic disciplines.

Formational creativity: acknowledging that different people connect best in different ways, many of which we need to help them invent; cultivating new spiritual disciplines that engage the technology, velocity, and convenience of our time; the realization that cyber-spirituality is not what you think; the miracle of non-local connectedness.

Pedagogical creativity: designing experiences and artifacts that "rhyme" with the weekend teaching; employing new taxonomies to help us better communicate gospel truth so it sticks; exploring multiple intelligence theory; multi-device, multi-disciplinary data-mining.

Homiletical creativity: learning oratory in the world of *Last Week Tonight*, *30 for 30*, and *Adventure Time;* making better use of digital appendices; supplying the audience breadcrumbs to follow after the weekend teaching.

Liturgical creativity: designing weekend services that neither disdain nor demand lights and lasers; kinesthetic expressions designed to help everyone experience God; moving past the digital-OR-physical debate and into the middle ground; coaching people beyond therapy and into holistic living without sounding like new age gurus.

The church of the future will press into new manifestations and new categories of creativity, eager to help her people experience God.

Of those listed, which manner of creativity most resonates with you?

TWENTY | WE
SEE
A
CHURCH

where **PENITENT SAINTS** *and*
REMORSEFUL SINNERS KNEEL
in **RECOGNITION** *of* THE
UNDESERVED GRACE *of* GOD;

that **BELIEVES** PRAYER IS LIKE OXYGEN
and that **WE** WILL NOT SURVIVE
UNLESS WE INHALE THE PRESENCE
OF CHRIST
PERSISTENTLY,
PATIENTLY
and WITH THE EXPECTATION
THAT HE RENEWS US
BOTH TOGETHER
and ALONE;

a **CHURCH** BORN AGAIN *and* AGAIN *and* AGAIN,
FINDING NEW LIFE *in* CHRIST
EVERY DAY;

a **CHURCH** THAT THIRSTS FOR THE HOLY
and INCORPORATES THE LONG MYSTERIES
of FAITH.

TWENTY.ONE

TARGET

ANSWERING THE QUESTION 'WHO IS CHURCH FOR?'

> You are the light of the world. A town built on a hill cannot be hidden. Neither do people light a lamp and put it under a bowl. Instead they put it on its stand, and it gives light to everyone in the house. In the same way, let your light shine before others, that they may see your good deeds and glorify your Father in heaven.
> -Matthew 5.14-16

We must consider all types of people as we plan our services.

Who is church for?

That's an important question, and one most of us don't answer. Ever. But I'd like you to consider it.

Is church designed for God—to satisfy his requirement that we worship him, elevate him, and congregate around the history of his movement and the promise of his redemption?

Is church designed for Christians—to gather us, so we can comfort and encourage one another, learning and growing in our faith, bolstering our sense of community and mission?

Is church designed for people who do not follow Jesus—as an invitation to begin journeying with Christ, as an introduction to Christian spirituality, or as an apologetic for why our faith is valid and powerful?

Or is church designed for the world—as a billboard announcing we are a significant cultural and social force, that we are too expansive to be ignored or taken for granted, that we are good and decent and vibrant?

If we forced ourselves to consider this issue, I'd wager most of us think church is meant for Christians and, to a lesser extent, God. But the New Testament gives repeated admonitions for the church to be a light to the world, for believers to let their light shine, and for the witness of the community to testify to the goodness of God.

So church is, biblically, for Christians and non-Christians, God and the world.

That affects how we think about church. How we plan our services. How we distribute our time. How we consider our rhetoric. We're not just in it for ourselves. We're not a supper club, but a missional outpost. We're not just a rescue station, but also an education center. We're not just a school; we're also a temple. We're not just a pilgrimage; we're also a headquarters.

The church of the future will train her people to constantly be thinking hospitably about us and God, the world and her people, looking for ways to welcome everyone into an environment of grace and peace.

> Offer hospitality to one another without grumbling.
> -1 Peter 4.9, NIV

Everyone gets to be a part of what God is doing free of charge, without restriction; however, we recognize that despite our willingness to welcome everyone, not everyone wants what we're offering. It took us a few years, but we finally woke up to the fact that Westwinds resonates best with four kinds of people. So, rather than identifying a "target market" we affectionately refer to these folks as our "market of resonance."

Those who are **spiritually curious** like Westwinds because of our preference for anonymity. We have a dark auditorium and never call attention to people in the crowd. We let them decide how much they want to be involved in the service and, afterwards, encourage people to come talk to us. We never make people feel stupid for not knowing the "right" answer, and we openly invite others to disagree or ask follow-up questions. As a result, Westwinds is a really safe place to explore Christian spirituality without feeling scrutinized for not being holy enough or judged for having incorrect doctrine. In this respect, we think of our church as a learning lab where truth-seekers are welcomed with open arms.

Those who are **disenfranchised** with organized religion enjoy Westwinds because we have tattoos and body piercings, we play rock music loudly, and cite popular movies. We dress like normal people and talk like normal people and have stripped away many of the outward trappings of the religious life. Don't be fooled—inside we're still 110% playing for Team Jesus— but on the outside, we look like athletes and business owners, musicians and teachers, retail clerks and students; which is to say we don't look like anything at all. We're a place for people who love Jesus but are tired of "church stuff."

Intellectuals like Westwinds because of the high value we place on teaching and theology. We mine the depths of Christian history and tradition in order to find outstanding work that speaks to our contemporary context. Thinkers can tell how much research we've invested so everyone can understand what we mean and why it matters.

Creatives like Westwinds because of our high aesthetic. Nothing happens at The Winds unless we're absolutely convinced it can be done with excellence and care. We always keep things fresh and never repeat an old idea. Everything gets reinvented in an effort to maintain our own creative edge and in response to the ever-complexifying movement of the Spirit.[312]

The church of the future will welcome more and more people into worship, community, and mission. She will open her doors more widely, and more hospitably, than ever before.

> *Who is God leading you to bring into your church?*

---

[312] The description of Westwinds' market of resonance was first published in *A Handbook for Hellfighters*, 34-35.

TWENTY.TWO

SACRAMENTS

ALIGNING THAT WHICH WE SAY, THAT WHICH WE INTEND, AND THAT WHICH WE DO

And he took bread, gave thanks and broke it, and gave it to them, saying, "This is my body given for you; do this in remembrance of me."
- Luke 22.19, NIV

> *One of the things we've tried to instill in our church is the need for new sacraments in order to interrupt the ordinary with the eternal, teaching our people to participate in the holiness of Christ.*

One of the most powerful sacramental experiences I've experienced at Westwinds took place at Grand River Brewery. We held services during open hours for two years at Grand River, and though they were controversial, the price was worth the reward. Those services helped us minister to a significant number of new people.

At the back of the brewery, there is a semi-circular wine bar from which we often served communion. People would stand in line and I would serve them one by one, pouring a small glass of wine and presenting a small portion of bread, praying over them as they partook. Those were holy moments. But my paradigm changed when we decided to anoint people with oil. Inviting them to the wine bar, I explained that Christians had been anointing one another with oil since the earliest episodes in scripture. Sometimes this was to ask for healing. Sometimes for commission into ministry. Sometimes for consecration. I taught them a simple symbol I had seen in Christian catacombs, a circle with a cross in it, and when they came to receive prayer I dipped my thumbs in oil, held their hands, and traced that symbol across the back of their hands.

The combination of the backstory, the expectation, the prayer, the symbol, the oil, and the human contact was potent. We prayed for well over an hour, and when I looked up to see whether or not we'd be asked to leave on account of how late our service was running, I was shocked to realize our people had begun anointing one another.

That's a sacrament—when what we say, and what we intend, and what we do align with the scripture in the power of the Spirit.

Here I think it's important to delineate the difference between Sacraments as instituted by Christ, for all people, and sacraments, which are emulations and imitations of the Timeless participation in Christ's body. But the basic idea is that a sacrament occurs when the signifier, the signified, and the sign become one.

Let me explain.

- A **signifier is a thing** (sound or image or gesture) that means something because we share the story with our people. So, if I fold my hands to pray it's just a gesture. But if I fold my hands to pray and tell our people this gesture has been common for thousands of years among Christian people earnestly seeking God, the gesture has enhanced meaning.
- The **signified is an idea** the signifier is meant to represent. In the case of folding hands, the concept it represents is earnestly seeking God in prayer.
- The **sign is an action** we invite our people to do, to give them agency and control over that which the signified represents. In this overly simplified example, our people would fold their hands as they begin to pray, earnestly seeking God. Because you've likely been folding your hands to pray since you were a child, this example is understandable but relatively meaningless. But if you change the variables, I think you'll begin to see how simple things can take on extraordinary significance. Lighting a candle, for example, or displaying an icon, or singing a prayer.

The church of the future will cultivate new sacraments in her pursuit of the transcendent as she elevates her people into the throne room of Christ.

Have you ever experienced a moment of sacramental worship?

TWENTY.THREE

REVITALIZATION

BEING BORN AGAIN, AGAIN

> When I was a child, I talked like a child, I thought like a child, I reasoned like a child. When I became a man, I put the ways of childhood behind me.
> -1 Corinthians 13.11, NIV

> *We need to be born again, again. We need to be renewed, refreshed, and revitalized.*

Perhaps you know what it means to have Christ bring newness into your spirit even after you've been following him for a long time. This, I think, is why Christians are sometimes compared to babies in the New Testament, and the life of the church compared to the gestation of a child.

Babies are made. A baby cannot make itself, neither can you or I make ourselves new. Christ renews us. So our hope is entirely in him. We invest ourselves in him, rather than in our passions or vocations or gratifications.

Babies require both fathers and mothers to be born. If God is our father, then the church is our mother. Our contact, our feeling, our development all happens within the construct of the church—not the building, but the community of saints. We grow together. We learn together. It takes a village to raise a child, and we are all villagers.

Babies share the DNA of their parents. You and I were made by God to be like God. Jesus Christ was the first idealized human being, and we are increasingly becoming like him. With his strength, his power, and his authority, we are growing up in our Christian perfection.

Babies are brought forth into the world as it is, not as we wish it might be. Sometimes, children are born in the backseat of a car, or in a remote wilderness, or without proper medical care. Likewise, we have been born into a world of violence and chaos. But the baby never gets to choose where or when she arrives; we must all endure what has been prepared for us.

Healthy babies have everything they need to grow, to survive, and to become parents themselves. That's you and I—capable, but immature. Even when we are born again and again, we still recognize perhaps for the first time—that there is much we need.

Babies desire their mother's breast. Having just been born, babies crave the closeness of their mother in order to retain some of the protection of the womb. So, too, after a fresh experience of God's grace we will want to stay with the church, to have that experience linger, and to bask in it just a little longer.

Babies grow quickly. After being born again (and especially after being born again, again) we sprout upward in our spiritual development. It's like we've been given a quick-growth hormone and we feel ourselves becoming strong, fast.

Babies are weak in knowledge and understanding. One of the least comprehensible parts of our faith concerns the experience of God. If you've ever had a remarkable time in prayer or worship, a "throne-room" experience in which you felt like you were transported directly into the presence of God, then you'll know your mind and your spirit are struggling for understanding. You want to know why that happened, why it happens so rarely, and you'll be eager for it to happen again. You'll rationalize it. You'll strategize for it. You'll describe it to others. But almost all our conclusions will be wrong. We won't know it yet, but after some time we'll be dumbfounded, realizing that God gave us this gift and our behaviors and actions and expectations had little to do with it.

The church of the future will enjoy her birthing and rebirthing experiences without neglecting the wisdom and maturity she learned in the past. She will seek the face of God, and crave the fresh experience of God, but also settle herself in the confidence of God's long-term plan to heal the world through her maturity, community, and love.

Can you think of a time when your spirit was renewed and you felt born-again again?

TWENTY.FOUR

PHENOMENA

DISTINGUISHING THE MARKS OF GOD'S SPIRIT

> Trust in the Lord with all your heart and lean not on your own understanding; in all your ways submit to him, and he will make your paths straight.
> - Proverbs 3.5-6, NIV

The more we experience with God the more we'll need to evaluate those experiences.

I've see no shortage of crazy, unexplainable, strangely spiritual phenomena in my short life. I've seen healings, heard prophecies, witnessed miracles, and watched as the impossible became actual right before my very eyes.

If it weren't for those experiences, there is no way anyone could ever convince me the supernatural is real. Of course, not everyone has had the experiences I have and many have developed a robust faith without any supernatural encounters; but I needed them. My mind is too set against the impossible. My education—perhaps especially in seminary—has led me to believe it's all superstitious nonsense.

But I can't deny what I've seen.

Others may scoff at my childlike faith, but at the end of the day, I was there. I saw. I experienced miracles. And nothing— no argument, no appeal to rationality, no suggestion that I hallucinated or was unknowingly drugged—will ever convince me otherwise.

I'm not the only one who has had dramatic experiences of the supernatural. I will admit I am often skeptical when others tell me about their experiences. Isn't that ironic? I suppose part of the blame lies with my upbringing. I was raised in a Pentecostal church, and it attracted some real kooks, which meant I've expended a lot of energy helping others adjudicate their experiences.

In college, I read Jonathan Edwards' famous text *The Distinguishing Marks of a Work of the Spirit of God*, which gives five ways to discern whether something we experience really is "from God." It's a complete de-kook-ifier, and I think we're smart to remember his advice.

1. Every true movement of the Spirit exalts Christ.

2. Every true movement of the Spirit opposes the devil and cultivates the Kingdom.

3. Every true movement of the Spirit leads people to value scripture.

4. Every true movement of the Spirit produces good fruit in the lives of its participants.

5. Every true movement of the Spirit cultivates love for God, ourselves, creation, and one another.

Edwards also cautions that some people will act like weirdos, while others will dismiss the whole business as delusional. Some people's imaginations will totally run away with them, and they'll begin describing their experiences in spooky ways. Some people will only copy what they see others doing. Some people will take too much authority for granted and act like jerks. Some people will actually be phonies. Some will start out genuine and become corrupted along the way. But none of these occurrences mean that the whole thing is a farce or that these people are not being truly affected by God's Spirit.

We tend to limit God's activity to that which we've already experienced for ourselves. But that's foolish! If the first followers of Jesus limited God to their own understanding, they would never have become apostles.

Just because 'we've never seen anything like this before' doesn't make it illegitimate, only new. But the church of the future will neither embrace nor disparage "the new" automatically. Instead, she will test all new things for the 'distinguishing marks of the Spirit of God.'

What's the craziest spiritual experience you've ever had?

TWENTY.FIVE

PRAYER

NOT GETTING WHAT WE WANT, BUT GETTING WHAT GOD WANTS IN US

And whatever you do, whether in word or deed, do
it all in the name of the Lord Jesus, giving thanks to
God the Father through him.
- Colossians 3.17, NIV

> *Prayer is the essential pathway for spiritual maturation.*

When we first crafted the 21 statements this book explores, there was nothing in it about prayer. My friend Rick Martoia, one of our elders, brought this to our attention. "We've gotta fix this," he said. "The church won't have a future if she doesn't pray."

Rick is correct.

The church of the future will not only continue to pray, but will recognize that she has persisted precisely because of her prayers. She will be filled with Christians who pray alone, together, in public, in groups, in private, and with the expectation that prayer heals the world. Prayer changes us. Prayer molds us. Prayer empowers us. Because prayer isn't concerned with itself. We don't pray to become better at praying. We pray to become unified with God.

> What we think about when we are free to think about whatever we will—that is what we are or will soon become.
> - A.W. Tozer[313]

Once we realize that prayer is the path to God, and we acknowledge that God is everywhere if we open up to his Presence, then we also realize that we can pray ceaselessly. At work. At school. On a date. While writing this paragraph.

> It may be very difficult for the average Christian to get hold of the idea that his daily labors can be performed as acts of worship acceptable to God by Jesus Christ.
> -A.W. Tozer[314]

---

[313] Tozer, A.W., *On Prayer*, 39.
[314] Ibid, 31.

Even our exercise can be prayer. For example, from Memorial Day to Independence Day, I prayed for a specific veteran or active duty serviceman while performing the Murph. Named in honor of Lt. Michael Murphy[315], the Murph is a CrossFit workout that consists of a one-mile run, 100 pullups, 200 pushups, 300 squats, and another one-mile run while wearing a 20 lb. tactical vest. I prayed while running and concluded by reciting Psalm 91. Most days I did this alone, miserably enduring my own stubborn commitment, but some days I had friends join with me. I came to love those people very, very much because nothing is so miserable as Murphing alone.

At first I was reluctant to discuss my daily Murph-prayers, and indeed I have often spoken of my discomfort with public prayer, leading to my reluctance to address the topic at all. When I released *How to be with God: a primer on Christian prayer* I was terrified of the blowback. Not because I was suggesting anything unbiblical, but because so many Christians have unbiblical notions about prayer, and I was going to address them with the honest sort of nitpickiness that usually gets me in trouble.

My main concern with how many Christians pray is that we treat prayer like magic.

Magic works on formulaic compulsion. Sorcerers, in fiction at least, cast spells and perform incantations; which is a fancy way of saying that they say the right things and do the right things, which results in the desired outcome, provided they have performed their parts perfectly.

Sadly, that's how many Christians perceive prayer. We think if we just believe the right things and pray the right ways

---

[315] KIA in Afghanistan; Michael Murphy's story is told in the movie *Lone Survivor*.

concerning issues we're certain we understand, God will answer our prayers in the precise manner of our request. For example, it is common for Christians to think that if they have purged their lives of any deliberate or unconfessed sin and maintain a standard of holy living consistent with scripture; and if they pray consistently, fervently, humbly, beseeching Jesus Christ by name both when they are alone and, more importantly, when they are gathered with two or three others; and if their request is consistent with the will of God, which includes financial self-sufficiency, physical healing, wisdom, the repentance of wayward loved ones, and the presence of joy rather than anxiety; then it is only a matter of time before God grants their request.

But this simply isn't true.[316]

There are innumerable times in the life of healthy, holy Christians when their prayers remain unanswered despite meeting the above criteria. Because the circumstances above, even though they can be proof-texted in scripture, betray a fundamental misunderstanding of the nature of God and his communication with us.

What I have described above is spellcasting, not prayer. Again, magic is the system of belief that maintains if our beliefs and our behaviors align perfectly with the powers of the invisible world, we will get what we want.

But prayer isn't about getting what we want. Prayer is about getting what God wants for us. From us. With us. In us. Consequently, when we pray and ask for things we often short-circuit the process, placing our desires ahead of God's. The

---

[316] Do you see now why I've had some reluctance to speak about prayer? The first and arguably most important thing I have to say is that prayer doesn't work. Not like that. Not at all.

confusion sets in when God, because he is a loving and gracious father who wants to bless his children, sometimes answers our prayers in the way we had hoped, thus setting us up for disappointment every other time he does not. And the simplest explanation as to why he does this is still the best: he can do whatever he wants, whenever he chooses.

Because he is God.

But insofar as we are concerned, we must consider prayer like mentoring. Prayer is how God teaches us to become like God. Prayer is how we become fascinated with God, since Christian prayer is primarily about empowerment and prayer is the means by which God gets bigger in us.

The church of the future will concern herself with God-centeredness, asking the Father for more of himself and trusting that more power and more resources will follow.

How would you describe the way you pray?

TWENTY.SIX

REINVENTION

TRIANGULATING BETWEEN CHRIST, COMMUNITY, AND CULTURE

For I know the plans I have for you, says the Lord,
plans to prosper you and not to harm you, plans to
give you a future and a hope.
- Jeremiah 29.11, NIV

> *Church ought to be spiritual, transcendent, and holy. It ought to provide*
> *an experience with God that cannot be counterfeited.*

Our church has had to reinvent herself a few times. We began as a Charismatic collection of Holy Rollers from Oral Roberts University, but after a few years realized that the only people drawn to our community were other hair-sprayed hallows looking to roll. So we morphed into a new kind of church, modeled after Willow Creek in Illinois.[317] We embraced the seeker-sensitive movement and began seeing more and more people surrender their lives to Christ. Our church grew rapidly. But after a time, we realized our culture had surpassed the model of ministry to which we had become accustomed. Our concern for reaching the world forced us to change yet again into a hands-on, experiential model of ministry known then as the Emerging Church. We experienced a change in leadership, and the emerging church movement at large derailed, so our church changed again to become a more orthodox, holistic congregation with an emphasis on imagination, participation, authenticity and community. A decade later, we've changed again and again, including redefining our mission from "leading all people in full life development" to "shadowing God, building the church, and healing the world."

One might think we had a problem picking a strategy and sticking with it; but the truth is that we have been responding to God and the world in much the same way as an athlete responds to the shifting play on the court. In basketball, for example, a good defender always creates a triangle between their check, the ball, and the basket so they can keep themselves in an optimum position to guard, to intercept, and to rebound. That's how we've approached ministry, with a triangular orientation considering God, the culture, and our community.

And let's be clear: church has to change. Not with one big change, accomplishing everything we'll ever need in one fell

---

[317] https://www.willowcreek.org.

swoop, but with a thousand incremental changes. We need to stay light on our feet. Responsive. Nimble. Because the world is not the same as it was even four years ago. Consider Moore's Law, which theorizes our computing ability will double every 18 months, perhaps indefinitely.[318] That means our capacity to process information, to plot trajectories, and to accurately predict and prepare for the future will dramatically alter our lives, and thus our churches.

The speed at which our world is changing is incomprehensible. We didn't have the Internet twenty years ago, and now we primarily access the web through our phones, not our computers. This has affected the ways we communicate, work, learn, travel, manage our finances, and organize our homes. And the inexpensiveness and accessibility afforded to impoverished peoples worldwide through the web have democratized commerce, education, and government. Everywhere, everything is being brought to the light— sometimes hastily, sometimes thoughtfully, and sometimes vengefully. We see everything, always, and can no longer live in ignorance.

The church of the future will take the shifting pace of culture in stride—she will meet the shifts with shifts of her own, not in belief but in behavior, maintaining her commitment to Jesus Christ while also maintaining her cooperation with God to heal the world.

How do you see your church adapting to the future?

---

[318] "Moore's Law," *Investopedia,* http://www.investopedia.com/terms/m/mooreslaw.asp, accessed August 17, 2017.

TWENTY
-ONE

WE
SEE
A
CHURCH

DESPERATELY IN LOVE *with* JESUS,
     CONSUMED *by* THE ENERGY *of* THE
     SPIRIT,
          and in **PERPETUAL** SUBMISSION *to*
          THE FATHER.

WE SEE A CHURCH NETWORKED BEYOND
THE GHETTOS *of* DENOMINATION *and* POLITICS,
     ELEVATING CHRIST *above all* COMPETING CONCERNS.

IT *is a* **CHURCH** WHERE THE MEANS *of*
EXPANDING *the* KINGDOM ALWAYS DEFER
     to the **END-GOAL** *of* KNOWING,
          and LOVING,
          and FOLLOWING,
               the KING.

TWENTY-ONE.ONE

KINGDOM

RECOGNIZING CHRIST IS GOD'S KINGDOM

[Christ] is the radiance of the glory of God and
the exact imprint of his nature, and he upholds the
universe by the word of his power.
- Hebrews 1.3a, ESV

> *Scripture is replete with metaphors that should not lightly be discarded.*

In my work with seminary students I am often confronted with a nonbiblical yet important term, kin-dom. It is a deliberate misspelling and reframing of Kingdom, meant to do two things simultaneously: remove patriarchy from our spiritual nomenclature and reinforce the importance of family in our ecclesiology. At first blush, I like the term. I appreciate the warmth and familiarity of kinship and think that emphasis is both missing and needed in our churches.

But I am uncomfortable with the idea of a kin-dom that has no King. I understand why there are those who want to remove the sting of male hegemony from our faith. After all, the church has been guilty of suppressing women over the years and of unduly elevating men; but it won't do to pretend the Bible says one thing when it really says another. Furthermore, the discipline of historical context reminds us that in biblical times there were certain things that only a man could provide, such that using male language was very helpful to Jesus' original audience. We must translate his intent, of course, but if we do so faithfully we cannot eliminate the central motif of his teaching—that the reason the kin-dom is welcoming and just and loving and good is precisely because the King embodies these traits, catalyzes them in us, and ensures their opposites never take root in his well-ordered New Creation.

You cannot have a Kingdom without a King, and in the Kingdom of God, King Jesus must reign. When we remove the King in favor of kin, we lose all the power and authority to ensure the kin-dom thrives in the first place. For even all of us working together as "the body of Christ" are no fit substitute for Christ himself.

Jesus is not an idea. He was a living human person, now Ascended and alive once more, and as Christian people we hold to the hope that one day he will return to fully and finally heal the world. We do not look forward to a New World Order of equality and justice for all, managed by all, and held mutually by all. We look forward to a New Creation where Christ is all in all. He is the source and substance of our salvation, not us. Him—a person—not an idea, ideal, principle, or religion.

I would rather live on an island alone, with Christ, than in a metropolitan utopia without him. Give me the King and I'll always have the Kingdom. Take Christ away, and the kin-dom will collapse under its own weight.

How will you ensure Christ is not reduced to an idea, ideal, or principle?

TWENTY-ONE.TWO

KINGSHIP

SERVING CHRIST, OUR KING

God, the blessed and only Ruler, the King of kings
and Lord of lords, who alone is immortal and who
lives in unapproachable light, whom no one has seen
or can see. To him be honor and might forever. Amen.
- 1 Timothy 6.14-15, NIV

God extends protection and obedience to his people.

There is tremendous value in exploring the kingly imagery in scripture. God chose to reveal himself as a king, and such revelation should be engaged rather than decried. However, before we explore "king", we need to explore "father" and, especially, any male-oriented language associated with God in the Bible.

Two things are important here: first, that the biblical term "father" is often shorthand for "father and mother." In fact, unless the context demands exclusive male emphasis, it is usually wise to presume an inclusive intention;[319] second, that "father" does not merely connote "parent of the children" but "one who oversees the welfare of his people."[320] There were rights and responsibilities afforded to males throughout the timeline of scripture that meant perceiving God's divine masculinity allowed God's people to experience a level of security and confidence they would otherwise have missed. Of course God is beyond gender, but the purpose of the gender-specific language was to reinforce God's power on behalf of God's people, rather than to highlight God's nature.

When we apply these basic insights to the King metaphor, we can more fully understand that the responsibilities of the King extend to the oversight and protection of his subjects; his provision and fecundity; and the assurance of justice and equity throughout his fiefdom.[321]

God's kingship is eternal,[322] but not yet fully visible on account of its future dimension.[323] And yet the ancient Israelites believed the coming Messiah would rule Yahweh's Kingdom.[324]

---

[319] Crossan, 36-44.
[320] Crossan, 40.
[321] cf. Numbers 33.21; Deuteronomy 33.5; 1 Kings 22.19.
[322] Exodus 15.18; 1 Samuel 12.12; Psalms 145.11ff.
[323] Isaiah 24.23; Zephaniah 3.15; Zechariah 14.16-17.
[324] 1 Chronicles 17.14; 28.5; 29.23; 2 Chronicles 9.8.

Concordantly, there were little glimmers of God's future Kingdom breaking through in the present, perhaps best expressed through the Coronation Psalms.[325]

In the earliest portions of the Bible, Yahweh was perceived to be the king of Israel, bringing peace to his chosen people. Later, he is called King of the World, enthroned in Jerusalem and magnified by all nations.[326] Similarly, the Messiah becomes the King of Kings[327] and the kings of the earth bring tribute into his holy city because they acknowledge his Lordship.[328]

The church of the future will acknowledge she is her truest and purest when honoring and worshipping Christ, her King.

How will you prioritize your fealty to King Jesus?

[325]   Psalm 47; 93; 96; 99.
[326]   Revelation 15.3.
[327]   Revelation 19.19.
[328]   Revelation 21.24.

TWENTY-ONE.THREE

FOCUS

MAINTAINING THE SUPREMACY OF CHRIST IN ALL THINGS

> But seek first his Kingdom and his righteousness, and
> all these things will be given to you as well.
> - Matthew 6.33, NIV

> *The church of the future will realize her hope is ultimately rooted in*
> *Christ and manifested most nobly in his passionate love for the world.*

My wife is a teacher. I love her, and she loves education. But how sad would it be if I began to love education so much I lost sight of my wife's role in teaching children. It would be uncomfortable to be stuck in a marriage where all I ever did was show up to her school and remind the children of the importance of learning, all the while ignoring their teacher standing embarrassed at the front of the class.

But too many churches, and far too many Christians, have lost their first love. They love Jesus' things, but fail to appreciate Christ himself. We've become obsessed with worship, and made an idol out of the very mechanism for avoiding idolatry; we've fallen in love with justice, and forgotten about Jesus; we've elevated the principles of organizational leadership to a higher status than our Savior.

But the church of the future will reclaim her first love. We will re-Jesus ourselves.

This will require not only a determination to keep our focus on Christ, and the discipline to follow through, but also equally a fresh encounter with Christ. We'll need to invest ourselves in the gospels, in prayer, and in the growing awareness that Christ is with us at all times and in all circumstances through the power of his Spirit. And in order for the Spirit's power and presence to move us, we will need to be in perpetual submission to the will of the Father.

This was John Wimber's great contribution to the spiritual thought of 20th century evangelicalism. Wimber, the founder of the Vineyard Association of churches, a radical charismatic group that originated in southern California, was insistent about asking, "What is the Father doing?" He maintained that any endeavor was shortsighted and egocentric unless Christians first began by asking what God was already doing and how we might help.

This is why I get frustrated with the many denominations that become increasingly committed to self-preservation. I don't mean to suggest that denominations in and of themselves are misguided, only that without proper stewardship it is inevitable that a declining denomination will allow anxiety about its future to distort the decisions made in the present. Buildings and ordinations supersede evangelism and discipleship, and increased efforts to legitimize the movement with higher education and additional certifications only remove the clergy and administration from the daily concerns of parishioners and the local problems in their neighborhoods. Issues like marital frustration and financial constraint are not worth studying in seminary, but those are often precisely the issues with which ordinary people struggle. Instead, denominations mount massive campaigns against injustice that only ever seem to result in more anger, more demonstration, and less metamorphosis. But the fight against injustice cannot save a dying church. The embittered cries from a palliative pulpit that whimper "not on my watch" will do nothing to galvanize the final few.

You can't save the church by fighting *against* anything. If you want to save a church you have to revitalize it. You must put life back into it. The fight *against* something takes energy dying churches do not have. Moreover, that energy is spent in death—the death of injustice, the death of a regime, the death of an adversary. But for churches to come back to life they must invest in the source of Life.

Jesus is that source. He is the vine and we are the branches. Apart from Christ we can do nothing but wither and die.[329]

---

[329] John 15.5.

This is why so many of our big campaigns feel desperate and lifeless. We have been cut off from the True Vine and are grafting ourselves to straw—straw causes, straw economics, straw politics. But our energy to fight these battles can only be renewed when we ourselves are renewed in and with Jesus Christ.

Christ first; the fight, second.

The church of the future will walk in step with the Spirit, who convicts us of our sin, not just the sins of others, and stay focused on Jesus, whose example and whose teaching will never allow us to feel as though we've arrived at such perfection we can now focus on larger concerns than his mission, his holiness, and his presence.

How do we best stay connected to the True Vine?

TWENTY-ONE.FOUR

MISSION

APPLYING THE KINGDOM QUOTIENT TO KEEP CHARITY "CHRISTIAN"

Walk with the wise and become wise, for a companion
of fools suffers harm.
-Proverbs 13.20, NIV

> *Sometimes we can become enamored with what we're doing to serve God*
> *at the expense of God himself.*

Westwinds used to have very little involvement in our community, and that was one of the things our staff set out to change in 2005. In just a few short years, we'd initiated a massive turnaround in this regard, most significantly with the Hub Teen Center[330] under the leadership and direction of Ben Redmond, a longtime staff pastor.

The Hub combines educational help, vocational training, and recreational opportunities for the youth of our community, providing care and support from a faith base without proselytization. Over the years, the Hub has hosted job fairs, launched for-profit businesses run by teens, and given countless opportunities for integration among groups that normally would neither cooperate nor socialize. It's a great model of how Kingdom ministry crosses racial, economic, and sociological boundaries, bringing people together for the good of the world, born out of the love of the Lord.

But between the large-scale initiative of the Hub and the hundreds of smaller projects in our community, we soon realized our people were much more comfortable doing favors for our city than they were ascribing their good deeds to God. Consequently, we had to coach our people on how to talk about God while cooperating with God, so that our church was more than just a charitable organization—we were charitable because of Jesus Christ, not because we were inherently kind.

Our Kingdom Quotient contains four little ideas that are rooted in everything we do to ensure our work is "Christian."

1. We want to ensure our people **understand the biblical foundation** for why we're doing what we're doing. This doesn't

---

[330] https://hubjackson.org.

have to be a deep theological treatise, just a short biblical reference to help anchor the day's work in God's Word.

2. We want our people to **invite the Spirit** to change them from the inside out as they do good work. Without the rejuvenating energy of the Holy Spirit, our community efforts can begin to feel like God-chores, and we tire of our obligation to serve. But once we invite the Spirit to change us as we work, all our work becomes prayer. We lay sod and mow lawns, but our hearts are attuned to God and under constant renovation. It is this personal development in the midst of societal contribution that separates what we do from the noble work of secular agencies.

3. We want to **include our church** as part of the Story because we used to have a very negative reputation in our city. While we aren't interested in celebrating ourselves, we believe it's important that our people know we repent of our former disengagement. We want them to know we are actively working to be a more faithful representation of Christ. That's significant, since we are modeling corporately the same process we advocate personally.

4. We want to **elevate Jesus** over all competing concerns. We want others to speak more about Christ than our kindness; more about Jesus than our commitment to justice; and more about our Lord than even our love.

The church of the future will persist in charity, justice, evangelism, and good will, but never at the expense of her first mission, her first calling, or her first love.

Have you ever invited the Spirit to speak as you work?

TWENTY-ONE.FIVE

REFORMATION

ABOLISHING THE DIFFERENCE BETWEEN THE CHURCH AND THE WORLD

There will always be poor people in the land.
Therefore I command you to be openhanded toward
your fellow Israelites who are poor and needy in your
land.
- Deuteronomy 15.11, NIV

> *The church of the future will understand that our commitment to Jesus*
> *Christ must always result in a commitment to the world.*

This October, I will be in Wittenburg, Germany, for the 500th anniversary of the Protestant Reformation, teaching on the spot where Martin Luther nailed his 95 Theses and started an ideological revolution. It's an exciting opportunity, especially given that many hypothesize our faith is in need of another reformation.

But I think something different is about to occur.

We are in need of another reformation, but it's unlikely to come from within the church. The first reformation called into question the difference between clergy and laity, celebrating the priesthood of all believers. Luther maintained that every single follower of Jesus was equipped and set apart for the work of the ministry.

But the next reformation will abolish the difference between the church and the world. I don't mean the church will become more worldly, but that the world will become more charitable, more hospitable, and more social. Whereas the church used to be the only institution wading selflessly into the murky waters of poverty, sickness, and corruption, nowadays we see businesses with social and ecological agendas performing the very same activities once espoused by the people of God. It is common to celebrate a triple bottom line of people, profit, and planet as a reminder to businesses to uphold their responsibility to their fellow citizens and sojourners on the earth.

> Humanity is now stuck with a planetary stewardship role...we are as gods and have to get good at it.
> - Stewart Brand[331]

---

[331] Brand, Stewart, *Whole Earth Discipline.*

Reebok has begun a campaign using the hashtag #bemorehuman to describe this sort of activity. It's become especially common among fitness enthusiasts who help others in need. The campaign celebrates charitable service, altruism, and practical acts of goodness.

The problem is that our humanity, while a good goal, is still a goal in need of ongoing reformation.

Sin is the energy that works against our noble efforts toward the renewal of all things. The longer we ignore sin, pretending that the only real changes that matter are social and political change, the longer we commit to an ultimately incompetent strategy for global transformation. That's not to say politics and legislation are unimportant, only to remind us that the business of the church is human metamorphosis. We begin with individuals, moving outwards to society because God intends to heal the world through people. There will never be a law that helps you fall in love with your spouse a second time, or teaches you to forgive your father, or awakes in you a desire to become a better neighbor. The only law with that power is love.[332]

> We know God less by contemplation than by emulation.
> – Jonathan Sacks, Chief Rabbi of the United Hebrew Congregations of the Commonwealth

Our world is sick, and we have forgotten what it means to be human. As a species, we are rarely noble and even less frequently humane. That's a word we use to refer to benevolent action. To be "humane" literally means "to have qualities benefitting human beings."

---

[332] Matthew 22.36-40.

The Humane Society, for example, was founded as a chapter of lifeguards in Britain. Over time, they became more concerned with animal rescue than drowning swimmers, but the fact remains that they are caretakers. They are rescuers. They are heroes.

And our world is desperately short of heroes. In Africa I watched as dozens of unfortunates were willfully ignored by those with ample means to help. I have seen similar behavior in Canada, in Germany, and in Michigan, as indigents were derided as "useless" and "unworthy."

But that's not the worst of it.

Yesterday I listened as a friend told me about the rape of a nine-year-old. Two days ago I read an article about parents in the southern states who kept their children in a cage in the basement. I used to think that the world would make better sense once I got older. But now I'm older, and the world keeps deteriorating. I'm more aware of the brokenness, and the severity of fragmentation is much worse than I imagined.

Some might contend that humanity is better off than we were two hundred years ago. After all, there have been considerable advances in medical science, communication, and information technology. But I'm not sure that our root problem has been addressed. If a husband beats his wife, does she care about their new computer? If we keep fighting wars, at what point does our ability to heal wounds enable us to continue causing them?

And yet, we're aware that our existence is impoverished. We know we're meant to find meaning and purpose in this life. We want it. We wonder who can tell us what it is.

A few years back I purchased a new piece of hardware equipment to interface my computer with my electric guitar. I had a difficult time getting it to work, so I called my friend Mike—who happened to be on the development team that built the device. In less than five minutes, Mike showed me absolutely everything about what the device could do and how it worked.

Because he made it.

You want to know what you're made to do? Why not ask your Creator?

You and I were made to look after the world as God's shadows and stewards. But the world is cracked, broken, and blasted. Yet God refuses to remove our responsibilities simply because we failed to execute them faithfully. So we are now called to heal the world we have broken, much like a child is required to clean up a mess that was made in the yard.

The prophets warned us about a rift between being holy and being good. Being holy means having a right relationship with God. We serve him. Being good means having a right relationship with others. We serve them too. But sometimes we tend to favor one manner of service over the other. Some of us like to do holy things while ignoring the world around us. But that's not good. Others like to ignore God while tending to more earthly matters. But that's not holy—or, if you'll forgive the pun—wholly our calling. We must love God and our neighbor, keeping both our holiness and our goodness intact as key priorities of our humanity.

Martin Luther addressed this topic in his paper "Two Kinds of Righteousness." Luther claimed the only way we could be both good and holy simultaneously was for Christ's righteousness "[to become] our righteousness and all that he has becomes ours; rather, he himself becomes us."[333] And we need Christ's power. We need Christ's righteousness. There are simply too many situations requiring too much power for us to survive on our own.

I recently performed a wedding in which one of the bridesmaids shared the story of how she came to faith. She had asked her husband to visit church because she was curious, but he refused and she went alone. That Sunday, the pastor made the statement "If you can work on your marriage, work on your marriage." It struck her as odd, but the next day she learned her husband had been hiding a severe addiction. She was devastated. But rather than call any of her friends or family members, she got into her car and drove to the church. She told me, "I knew if I called anyone they would tell me to leave my husband and end the marriage. But I heard the pastor, and I knew what he said was right." Angrily, this gal spent hours with her new pastor struggling to come to terms with what to do and how to proceed. In the end, she stood by her husband as he entered rehab, graduated, and began his new life free from addiction. Years later, they are happily married with a beautiful family.

I include this story because it illustrates that, at the deepest level, societal change requires a change in us. In our marriages. In our finances. In our homes. There will be tremendous challenges, and these challenges will often feel more elusive and insubstantial than the great injustices of our age, but that is precisely why we cannot abandon them. Relationships between neighbors are more exhausting than relationships between ideological opponents. Because you have to live next to your neighbor. Every exchange either worsens or repairs the

<hr>

[333] Luther, Martin, "Two Kinds of Righteousness," http://www.mcm. edu/~eppleyd/luther.html, accessed August 17, 2017.

relationship, and because you want to live in peace, you learn how to make it all work.

Only the Holy Spirit can teach us to do that. Only God can guide us through our private hells.

What is God calling you to repair?

(RE)CREATION

HEALING THE WORLD

> Two are better than one, because they have a good
> return for their labor: If either of them falls down,
> one can help the other up, but pity anyone who falls
> and has no one to help them up. Also, if two lie down
> together, they will keep warm, but how can one keep
> warm alone? Though one may be overpowered, two
> can defend themselves. A cord of three strands is not
> quickly broken.
> -Ecclesiastes 4.9-12, NIV

Every time we choose to help others, we heal the world.

We are called to (re)create the world. What has been broken must now be made whole. Smarty-pants people refer to this as participatory eschatology. Eschatology is the study of last things. But throughout the scriptures, the word most commonly translated "last" doesn't mean "final," but "ultimate."[334]

The "end of the world" is far better understood as God's intended climax for Creation. And God doesn't mean for us to sit back and watch the show. We are the show. He has been working in us and with us and through us for a very long time.

We are kings and priests, designed to reign with God,[335] and the manner of our rule and authority is that we perform good works God has prepared for us since the beginning.[336]

Participatory eschatology involves a twofold affirmation, best encapsulated in St. Augustine's brilliant aphorism, 'God without us will not; we without God cannot.'

> God invites us to become in the rabbinic phrase, his "partners in the work of creation." The God who created the world in love calls on us to create in love.
> - Jonathan Sacks[337]

We were made to cooperate with God in the redemption of the world. When we do that we'll experience the joy of his salvation. Our efforts to shadow God will produce profound metamorphosis, not only around us but in us as well. Looking after each other means we will flourish together. Like Jack

---

[334] 5046.*teleios, Strong's Exhaustive Concordance,* http://biblehub.com/greek/5046.htm, accessed August 17, 2017.
[335] Revelation 5.10.
[336] Ephesians 2.10.
[337] Sacks, Jonathan, *To Heal A Fractured World.*

Shepherd says, "if we can't live together we're gonna die alone."[338]

Helping others is at the root of our human operating system. That's how we've been made. When we look after one another, we emulate our Creator and in so doing we come to understand him as well.

In Genesis we're told mankind was fashioned from the dust of the earth. From the very beginning there was a connection between people and planet. In fact, the word "human" literally means "of the earth." That's part of what it means to be human—to look after the world.

We help one another because it demonstrates neither God nor his people have abandoned humanity. We're in it for the long haul. We're committed. We're the people who bring good news by being good news.

Mature discipleship is when we stop struggling to get our lives together and begin struggling with how to give our lives away.

Where is your next, best opportunity to serve others?

---

[338] "Quotes for Jack Shepherd," *IMDB,* http://www.imdb.com/character/ch0008674/quotes, accessed August 17, 2017.

Then. Now. Next.

THE FUTURE

IS GOING TO HURT

CONCLUSION

Perhaps, after reading this book, you're encouraged. I hope so. But I've saved the bad news for the last page.

The future is going to hurt.

In his letter to the church in Rome, Paul warned that we would suffer as we work for the future, yet our hardships would pale in comparison to the glories God promises to reveal.[339] It's easy to get excited about future glory, but don't be naive. The road from here to there will be steep. Arduous. Painful. And long. Nevertheless, it will be worth it. And not only for ourselves, but our noble efforts will "be a witness … to the generations that follow."[340] We will offer everything we have, making tremendous sacrifices, so that "in the future [our] descendants will not be able to say … 'You have no share in the Lord.'"[341]

We share in Christ's sufferings, so we can share in Christ's resurrection. We labor for the church today, so we can share in the church of the future. And though that may be difficult, we are resolute; because, if there's one thing Christ demonstrated beyond any reasonable doubt, it's that you can't stay dead forever.

You can live again.

---

[339] Romans 8.18.
[340] Joshua 22.27, NIV.
[341] Ibid.

SPECIAL THANKS

Pierre du Plessis, who provided some necessary non-North American perspective, thus shifting the emphasis in my writing considerably.

Melissa Evans, who understood that yes—I actually intend to do the things in this book; and double-yes—most of those ideas will require great ingenuity on her part.

Amy Gafkjen, who felt sufficiently emboldened to tell me when I was wrong about more than just grammar.

Kelly Heath, who encouraged me to write *Then.Now.Next.* in the first place.

Heath Hollensbe, whose sincere quest for better answers left me with more edits than intelligence.

Jvo, whose decade of friendship-in-ministry provided ample fodder for push back on my work, since most of what I believe about ministry was formed while he and I were working together at The Winds.

Eric Kelly, who has the most hands-on experience applying my work on happiness, and who has consistently demonstrated that gratitude brings joy.

Joe Manafo, who compared this project to a custom home that would never be mass-produced, though it would be assuredly loved by those who own it.

Rick McGarry, who told me "compliments were a waste of time."

Jacob McGarry, who told me when my ideas were dumb, and then amused himself as I struggled to fix them.

April Mueller, whose emoji-laden emails brought much-needed levity into the drudgery of editing.

Jim Mueller, whose strategic insights bolstered my theological reflections by proxy.

Joe Neill, who contributed the "culvert" imagery and has helped me cultivate generosity in my family.

Becky Veydt, who showed hilarious concern for my clunky first-draft and gently suggested I do more rewriting.

Dave Wahlstedt, who is perhaps most like me and yet was unwilling to let me get away with anything.

Amanda Zentz-Alo, who poured as much of her expertise and creativity into editing my work as she does on her own. She helped me anticipate obstacles at every turn, thereby protecting me from "jammer sadness."

And to the people of Westwinds Church, for the opportunity of a lifetime.

WORKS CITED

Alcorn, Randy. *Happiness*. Tyndale House Publishers, Inc.: Carol Stream, IL, 2015.

Anderson, Chris. *Free: How Today's Smartest Businesses Profit by Giving Something for Nothing*. Hyperion: New York, 2010.

Bauman, Zygmunt. *Community: Seeking Safety in an Insecure World*. Polity Press: Oxford, 2001.

Berry, Wendell. *What Are People For? Essays*. Counterpoint: Berkeley, CA, 2010.

Brand, Stewart, *Whole Earth Discipline: Why Dense Cities, Nuclear Power, Transgenic Crops, Restored Wildlands, and Geoengineering Are Necessary*. Penguin Group: New York, 2009.

Briggs, J.R. and Bob Hyatt. *Ministry Mantras: Language for Cultivating Kingdom Culture*. IVP Books: Downer's Grove, IL, 2016.

Brown, Stuart, M.D., with Christopher Vaughan. *Play: How it Shapes the Brain, Opens the Imagination, and Invigorates the Soul*. Penguin Group: New York, 2009.

Cain, Susan. Quiet: *The Power of Introverst in a World That Can't Stop Talking*. Broadway Books: New York, 2012.

Capra, Fritjof. *The Hidden Connections: A Science for Sustainable Living*. Anchor Books: New York, 2002.

Catmull, Ed, with Amy Wallace. *Creativity, Inc.: Overcoming the Unseen Forces That Stand in the Way of True Inspiration.* Random House: New York, 2014.

Charest, Rémy. *Robert Lepage: Connecting Flights.* New York: Theatre Communications Group, 1998.

Christensen, Clayton M. *Competing Against Luck: The Story of Innovation and Customer Choice.* HarperCollins: New York, 2016.

Cormier, Jay. *Seed Sown: Theme and Reflections on the Sunday Lectionary Reading.* Sheed & Ward: London, 1996.

Crossan, John Dominic. *The Greatest Prayer: Rediscovering the Revolutionary Message of The Lord's Prayer.* HarperCollins: New York, 2010.

Diamandis, Peter H. and Steven Kotler. *Abundance: The Future is Better Than You Think.* Free Press: New York, 2012.

Gell, Alfred. *Art and Agency: An Anthropological Theory.* Oxford University Press: Oxford, 1998.

Goff, Bob. *Love Does: Discover a Secretly Incredible Life in an Ordinary World.* Thomas Nelson: Nashville, 2012.

Kao, John. Jamming: *The Art and Discipline of Business Creativity.* HarperCollins: New York, 1996.

Krog, Antjie. *Country of My Skull.* Random House: Johannesburg, South Africa, 2002.

Kuckuk, John William. *Out of the Cocoon: Rethinking Our Selves: An Introduction to a New Future.* iUniverse: Bloomington, IN, 2012.

Lamott, Anne. *Bird by Bird: Some Instructions on Writing and Life*. Anchor Books: New York, 1994.

Lewis, C.S. *On Stories: And Other Essays on Literature*. HarperOne: New York, 1982.

Lupton, Robert D. *Toxic Charity: How Churches and Charities Hurt Those They Help (And How to Reverse It)*. HarperCollins: New York, 2011.

Maeda, John. *The Laws of Simplicity: Design, Technology, Business, Life*. Massachusetts Institute of Technology: Boston, 2006.

Maeda, John with Becky Bermont. *Redesigning Leadership*. Massachusetts Institute of Technology: Boston, 2011.

Markos, Louis. *Lewis Agonistes: How C.S. Lewis Can Train Us To Wrestle with the Modern and Post-Modern World*. Broadman & Holman Publishers: Nashville, 2003.

Mayne, Michael. *This Sunrise of Wonder: Letters for the Journey*. Fount Paperbacks: London, 1995.

McGonigal, Jane. Reality is Broken: *Why Games Make Us Better and How They Can Change the World*. Penguin Group: New York, 2011.

McLuhan, Marshall. *The Gutenburg Galaxy*. University of Toronto Press: Toronto, 1962.

McLuhan, Marshall. *Laws of Media: The New Science*. University of Toronto Press: Toronto, 1992.

Merton, Thomas. *Thoughts in Solitude*. Farrar, Straus, and Giroux: New York, 1999.

Pressfield, Steven. *The War of Art: Break Through the Blocks and Win Your Inner Creative Battles*. Black Irish Entertainment: New York, 2002.

Rowling, J.K. *Very Good Lives: The Fringe Benefits of Failure and the Importance of Imagination*. Little, Brown and Company: New York, 2008.

Sacks, Rabbi Jonathan. *To Heal a Fractured World: The Ethics of Responsibility*. Schocken Books: New York, 2005.

Schlossberg, Edwin. *Interactive Excellence: Defining and Developing New Standards for the Twenty-first Century*. The Ballantine Publishing Group: New York, 1998.

Schweid, Richard. *Octopus*. Reaktion Books Ltd.: London, 2014.

Seaver, W.L. *Prayer: Communing with God in Everything—Collected Insights from A.W. Tozer*. Moody Publishers: Chicago, 2016.

Shuman, Sandra G., Ph.D. *Source Imagery: releasing the Power of Your Creativity*. Doubleday: New York, 1977.

Tolkien, J.R.R. *Tolkien on Fairy-stories: Expanded Edition, with Commentary and Notes*. Edited by Verlyn Flieger and Douglas A. Anderson. HarperCollins: London, 2008.

Voelz, John. *Quirky Leadership: Permission Granted*. Abingdon Press: Nashville, 2013.

Wheatley, Margaret J. *Leadership and the New Science: Discovering Order in a Chaotic World*. Berrett-Koehler Publishers, Inc.: San Francisco, 1999.

Wilson-Kastner, Patricia. *Imagery for Preaching*. Augsburg Fortress: Minneapolis, 1989.

WE
SEE
A
CHURCH

WIDE-EYED *with* PROMISE *for* THE FUTURE
RATHER THAN SAD-HEARTED *about* THE
FADING GLORIES *of* THE PAST;

a **CHURCH** *that* HAS BEEN HEALED *of* HER
CYNICISM
and **MATURED** *into* A SECOND
INNOCENCE;

that **REFUSES** *to* LET HER MINISTRY BE
DEFINED *by* HER WOUNDS,
but **WILL** LOVE RECKLESSLY *and*
GIVE EFFUSIVELY *of* HERSELF.

WE
SEE
A
CHURCH

COLORED *by* **LOVE** *and* **FRIENDSHIP AT ALL LEVELS;**

a **CHURCH** *that* **RECOGNIZES** *our* **TRUE BELONGINGS ARE NOT OUR POSSESSIONS,**
but **OUR** **RELATIONSHIPS;**

a **CHURCH** *that* **DOESN'T MERELY PROMISE**
but also **EXPERIENCES**
LAUGHTER,
JOY,
HOPE,
and **STRENGTH.**

WE
SEE
A
CHURCH

FULL *of* NOBLE AMBITION *to* SHADOW GOD;

a **CHURCH** DEVELOPING NEW VOICES *to*
REFINE *and* INVIGORATE OUR FAITH;

a **CHURCH** SO COMMITTED TO THE GOOD OF
THE WORLD

that **WE** WILL TRAIN LEADERS *and*

PREACHERS *and* INNOVATORS

for the **NEXT** 10,000 YEARS

to SING *the* LORD'S SONG IN TUNE

WITH THE TIMES.

WE
SEE
A
CHURCH

that **RAISES** TECHNOLOGISTS *the* WAY
AMERICAN CHURCHES ONCE RAISED GOSPEL
SINGERS;

a **CHURCH** *that* DEVELOPS *and* IMPLEMENTS NEW
STRATEGIES
   for the **HOLISTIC** INTEGRATION *of* SCIENCE,
   TECHNOLOGY, *and* FAITH;

a **CHURCH** *that* MELDS METAPHYSICS WITH
QUANTUM PHYSICS,
   that **BELIEVES** OUR HUMANITY *is*
   REVEALED *through* OUR TREATMENT *of*
   OTHERS.

WE
SEE
A
CHURCH

that **CELEBRATES** TALENT, PASSION, *and* SKILL;

that **PERCEIVES** PERFORMANCE *as a*
CONDUIT OF FAITH,
not a **COUNTERFEIT MANIFESTATION**
of WORSHIP;

a church **COMMITTED** *to* CONTENT
CREATION *and* RESOURCE DISTRIBUTION,
where **ARTIFACTS, EVENTS,**
and **INITIATIVES** EMBODY THE
GOSPEL.

WE
SEE
A
CHURCH

that **ELEVATES** WOMEN *to the* HIGHEST OFFICES
as **EQUAL PARTNERS** *with* MEN,
SHADOWING GOD;

that **PAIRS** SURROGATE PARENTS *and*
GRANDPARENTS,
MENTORS *and* REVERSE-MENTORS,
so **EVERYONE** EXPERIENCES
HEALTHY FAMILY AMONG *the*
PEOPLE *of* GOD.

WE
SEE
A
CHURCH

that **UNDERSTANDS** WHAT YOU DO *flows* FROM WHO YOU ARE,

because **IDENTITY** *and* **VOCATION** *are* **ENTWINED.**

WE
SEE
A
CHURCH

that **INTERRUPTS** EVIL *and* SETS CROOKED
PATHS STRAIGHT;

that **INVESTS** *in* MAKING *and*
KEEPING THINGS RIGHT;

that **OPPOSES** *the* SOUR
and CULTIVATES THE SWEET
in **ANTICIPATION** *of the*
RIGHTFUL KING RESUMING
HIS THRONE.

WE
SEE
A
CHURCH

that **UNDERSTANDS** IMAGINATION *is* GODLY;
that **TRIES** NEW THINGS *and* AVOIDS
SACRALIZING CURRENT METHODOLOGIES.

WE SEE THE CHURCH *as a* PALACE
OF ENDLESS IMAGINATION,
DRAWING *the* WORLD IN
WONDER *to the* MIND OF GOD.

WE
SEE
A
CHURCH

that **POUNCES** JOYFULLY *on* NEW OPPORTUNITIES, **CONFIDENT** *in* HER ABILITY TO MAKE MID-COURSE CORRECTIONS;

a **CHURCH** *that* PROTOTYPES, ITERATES, *and* **IMPROVISES** *as we progress* IN STEP *with the* SPIRIT.

WE
SEE
A
CHURCH

where **STORY, IMAGE,** *and* **METAPHOR**
are **THE DEFAULT APOLOGETIC;**

a **CHURCH** COMFORTABLE WITH PARADOX
that **DOGGEDLY** PURSUES THE TRUTH
and **REGARDS** EASY ANSWERS
WITH SUSPICION.

WE
SEE
A
CHURCH

that **EMBRACES** *the* LONELY *and* BROKEN PEOPLE
OF OUR COMMUNITIES,
PROVIDING AID *and* COMFORT *as though*
CHRIST HIMSELF HAD SHOWN UP IN RAGS;
that **EMPLOYS** OUR UNEMPLOYED;
that **EDUCATES** OUR UNDER-SERVED;
that **ELEVATES** OUR DOWN-TRODDEN;
that **TRAINS** OUR UNSKILLED;
that **WON'T TURN A BLIND EYE**
WHEN ONE OF OUR OWN
STRUGGLES OR STARVES;
that **REFUSES** TO ALLOW
OTHERS TO GLORY IN
THEIR VICTIMIZATION.

WE
SEE
A
CHURCH

that **BURSTS** *with* THE POWER *and* PROVOCATION
OF THE SCRIPTURES,
where **GOD'S WORD** IS NOT ENDURED
but EMBODIED;

a **CHURCH** WHERE EVERYONE CAN HEAR
THE GOSPEL *in their* VERNACULAR
at **ALL** TIMES,
across **ALL** PLATFORMS,
through **ANY** MEDIUM;

that **TRANSLATES** *the* WISDOM OF
YESTERDAY *into* THE FOUNDATION FOR
TOMORROW.

WE
SEE
A
CHURCH

where **THE SIZE** OF THE GIFT *is* WEIGHED LESS *than* THE HEART *of* THE GIVER; *not* **ACTING** *as a* RESERVOIR, *but* A RIVER OF GENEROSITY, *where* **WE** ALL *give* **ALL** WE ARE *in* **SERVICE** TO OUR KING;

a **CHURCH** *through which* GOD'S PEOPLE COOPERATE IN HIS MISSION TO HEAL THE WORLD.

WE
SEE
A
CHURCH

that **DOES** A LOT *with* A LITTLE;

that **LEVERAGES** POWER *and* INFLUENCE *without* CATERING TO THE PREJUDICE *of* PRIVILEGE;

a **CHURCH** *that* SPENDS FRUGALLY *and* SACRIFICES JOYFULLY, **ANNOUNCING** GRACE IS FREE *and* GOD IS HERE.

WE
SEE
A
CHURCH

CONCERNED *with* PASTORING THE PLANET, **DRAWING TOGETHER RESOURCES** *to* BRING WISE ORDER *to our* WORLD;

a **CHURCH** *that* MAKES NO DISTINCTION BETWEEN HONORING GOD *and* HONORING GOD'S CREATION;

that **WORKS** *to* RESTORE CITIES *and* SPECIES, **LANDSCAPES** *and* ECOLOGIES, **NEIGHBORHOODS** *and* ETHNICITIES, **ECONOMIES** *and* CULTURES, *so that* **EVERYTHING** FLOURISHES IN THE PRESENCE *of* GOD.

WE SEE A CHURCH

INFUSED *with* **PLAYFULNESS, ARTISTRY** *and* **INTERACTIVITY;**

where the **LINES** **BETWEEN AUDIENCE** *and* **ATTRACTION** *are* **BLURRED;**

where the **DECISIONS, ABILITIES,** *and* **BEHAVIORS** *of the* **COMMON PEOPLE INFLUENCE** **THE FORM** *and* **FLAVOR OF WORSHIP.**

WE
SEE
A
CHURCH

that **CELEBRATES** CULTURAL EVENTS *as* TEACHABLE MOMENTS;

that **ENJOYS** THE ORIGIN *and* RITUAL OF HOLIDAYS, **PERCEIVING** GOSPEL RESONANCE *in* FESTIVAL, SEASON, *and* TRADITION.

WE
SEE
A
CHURCH

ENNOBLED *in* CREATIVITY *and* THE ARTS, *not* **EMULATING** PRESENT FASHIONS *but* SURPASSING THEM *in* STYLE, ABILITY, *and* VERVE.

WE
SEE
A
CHURCH

where **PENITENT SAINTS** and
REMORSEFUL SINNERS KNEEL
in **RECOGNITION** of THE
UNDESERVED GRACE of GOD;

that **BELIEVES** PRAYER IS LIKE OXYGEN
and that **WE** WILL NOT SURVIVE
UNLESS WE INHALE THE PRESENCE
OF CHRIST
PERSISTENTLY,
PATIENTLY
and WITH THE EXPECTATION
THAT HE RENEWS US
BOTH TOGETHER
and ALONE;

a **CHURCH** BORN AGAIN and AGAIN and AGAIN,
FINDING NEW LIFE in CHRIST
EVERY DAY;

a **CHURCH** THAT THIRSTS FOR THE HOLY
and INCORPORATES THE LONG MYSTERIES
of FAITH.

WE
SEE
A
CHURCH

DESPERATELY IN LOVE *with* JESUS,
CONSUMED *by* THE ENERGY *of* THE
SPIRIT,
and in **PERPETUAL** SUBMISSION *to*
THE FATHER.

WE SEE A CHURCH NETWORKED BEYOND
THE GHETTOS *of* DENOMINATION *and* POLITICS,
ELEVATING CHRIST *above all* COMPETING CONCERNS.

IT *is a* **CHURCH** WHERE THE MEANS *of*
EXPANDING *the* KINGDOM ALWAYS DEFER
to the **END-GOAL** *of* KNOWING,
and LOVING,
and FOLLOWING,
the KING.

Dr. David McDonald is a pastor, teacher, and lecturer in colleges and seminaries all over the world. His work with Westwinds Community Church has been featured in *The New York Times*, *Wall Street Journal*, and *Time* magazine.

David continues to integrate spiritual truth with sharp social analysis in his private work through www.doctordavidmcdonald.com.

David lives with his wife, Carmel, and their two children in Jackson, Michigan.

THE ADVENTURE OF HAPPINESS: Dr. David McDonald has researched happiness extensively--the science, sociology, psychology, and philosophy. This is where all that research has lead. We are happy because of what we do and because of who we are becoming. Happiness is available to us, increasingly, as we shift from lives of passivity to activity; from thinking to doing; and from defending to iterating (what we do). We are happy not because we don't have to change, but because we can renew our minds, govern our mouths, guard our hearts, and use our legs (who we are becoming). And in all this, we are not restrained by history, association, birth, personality, or circumstance. Want to experience greater happiness? This book can help lead you in the right direction.

THE CHURCH SURVIVAL GUIDE: Church often hinders more than it helps. We need a tool to guide us through all the painful strangeness inescapable in our churches. This book is a modern adaptation of the Benedictine Rule.

HOW TO BE WITH GOD, A PRIMER ON CHRISTIAN PRAYER: This book is designed to help you feel empowered and inspired to pray. I want you to enjoy prayer, on your own terms, without any need to justify how or when or why you pray. Because, once you begin, it's wonderful. It's easy. Like being with an old friend. Like catching up. Like getting advice from someone you admire. This isn't a book for people who already know how prayer is supposed to be. This is for everyone who wants to know if prayer can be anything other than a prison sentence, or if prayer still counts when you muff it up.

NATIVITY AND KINGDOM: There is a surprising amount of science fiction hidden within Christian tradition—a tradition that, historically, predates science and vilifies fiction. Especially concerning the Nativity.

We carry an insatiable curiosity for the lost details of Christ's life. We want to know what his father was like and how he felt about being press-ganged into marrying a teenager. We want to know about Mary's family and whether her virgin birth was the kind of scandal we've always supposed.

These legends tell us things we wish were true. We wish all our enemies were obvious and unredeemable. We wish all our problems were due to nameless servants of darkness. We wish our struggles would vanish magically as soon as we encounter Christ. We wish we could be rescued—not in the end, but here. Now.

Because of their fanciful nature, these stories allow us to see ourselves with fresh eyes. They reveal our weaknesses, our desires, and our ambitions to shadow God. They are not factual, but neither are they entirely false—they are fictions of faith, and their creators must be esteemed, even while their characters must be questioned.

Chapter 1: 3 Renewal.

24061815R00389

Printed in Poland
by Amazon Fulfillment
Poland Sp. z o.o., Wrocław